UNEASY RELATIONS
REASON IN LITERATURE AND SCIENCE
FROM
ARISTOTLE TO DARWIN AND BLAKE

UNEASY RELATIONS

*Reason in Literature & Science from
Aristotle to Darwin & Blake*

BY

JANE RUPERT

MARQUETTE
UNIVERSITY
PRESS

MARQUETTE STUDIES IN PHILOSOPHY
NO. 69
ANDREW TALLON, SERIES EDITOR

©2010 Marquette University Press
Milwaukee, Wisconsin 53201-3141
All rights reserved.
www.marquette.edu/mupress/

FOUNDED 1916

LIBRARY OF CONGRESS CATALOGING-IN-PUBLICATION DATA

Rupert, Jane, 1943-
Uneasy relations : reason in literature and science from Aristotle to Darwin and Blake / by Jane Rupert.
    p. cm. — (Marquette studies in philosophy ; no. 69)
Includes bibliographical references and index.
ISBN-13: 978-0-87462-771-8 (pbk. : alk. paper)
ISBN-10: 0-87462-771-0 (pbk. : alk. paper)
    1. Reasoning. 2. Literature and science. 3. Literature—Philosophy. 4. Science—Philosophy. I. Title.
    BC177.R77 2010
    128'.309—dc22

                                                        2010010501

♾The paper used in this publication meets the minimum requirements of the
American National Standard for Information Sciences—
Permanence of Paper for Printed Library Materials, ANSI Z39.48-1992.

Association of American
University Presses

MARQUETTE UNIVERSITY PRESS
MILWAUKEE

The Association of Jesuit University Presses

TABLE OF CONTENTS

INTRODUCTION

There is a mutuality between the kind of reasoning exercised in literature and the reasoning of science. Both empirical science and theoretical science have their origins in the same kind of reasoning exercised in literature. The human truths of literature are clarified and deepened through the kind of reason exercised in theoretical science. However, in spite of the mutuality of these two different kinds of thought, their relations have often been unacknowledged or strained because of the tendency of science to assert a hegemony over thought.

Great arbiters of method who have considered these uneasy relations have taken as a fundamental premiss that different kinds of objects are known through different pathways of the mind. Empirical induction, intuition, theoretical reasoning, and the rationality exercised in literature serve different tasks. To expect one to do the work of another is like using the sense of smell where the sense of touch is required. The method of empirical sense observation and its conclusions will be as ineffectual in the invisible realms of spirit and the secret movements of the human heart as literature's narrative wisdom applied to the practical, material purposes of modern science.

However, although all operations of the mind are important in their own domains, they may also fade or atrophy from want of exercise, just as we lose the limberness of parts of our body from lack of use. In our own era, the tyranny exercised by the method of empirical science and a philosophy of mind that dismisses the legitimacy of other modes of reasoning have led to an increasing atrophy of equally honourable modes of thought and an eclipse of the large domains where they alone shed light. The modern suspicion of both theoretical reasoning and the rationality exercised in literature has wreaked havoc in education, sewed discord in religion, and diminished our humanity in proportion to its closing of the mind. Nowhere is our intellectual one-sidedness more apparent than in the elemental failure of our systems of education which mirror the intellectual imbalance of the age.

Our problem is not new. Because there is a tendency in any age for a single method to dominate, we can understand our own intellectual

biases better through revisiting those other times when advocates
of literary reasoning pleaded its cause before the tribunals of either
theoretical or empirical science: in antiquity, in the Renaissance at the
beginning of the modern scientific age, and in the nineteenth century
as empirical inductive reasoning assumed hegemony over other modes
of thought.

In the fourth century BCE, Aristotle considered that the liberally-
educated should recognize the different tasks of the different modes
of reasoning as well as the futility, prejudice, and quackery that
result when one method usurps the tasks that can only be effected
by another. Beginning with the important premiss that there is no
possible science of the particular, Aristotle distinguished between two
equally legitimate pathways to truth: first, the mode of science that
makes connections through general abstract principles and, second,
our informed practical judgments of concrete situations based on
probabilities.

Aristotle's works on the practical intellect effectively resisted Plato's
location of the real in abstract ideas separate from the world and
deflected the constrictions that this philosophy imposed on thought.
Aristotle affirmed other pathways to knowledge that are natural to
us in the concrete matters of life: in areas like ethics or public affairs
where the luminous abstractions of theoretical science that elsewhere
serve as guideposts to thought are only of limited service. Because
there is no science of the particular, principles, axioms, laws, rules,
and premisses are only partially helpful in the ethical judgments that
inform our conduct. Similarly, Aristotle affirmed the legitimacy of
the way we reason in concrete matters that require deliberation or
interpretation such as in public affairs, court cases, or eulogies; that
is, through the reasoning of rhetoric, a species of literary thought.
According to Aristotle, rhetoric's arguments that persuade us of
truths at the heart of concrete matters are as valid a way of knowing
as the premisses of theoretical science and its conclusions in those
areas susceptible to scientific reasoning. In a similar vein, in mid-first
century BCE when rhetoric's legitimacy was again challenged by the
theoretical science of philosophy, Cicero would maintain that we
reason in all these complex, concrete matters where abstract premisses
are of little avail in the only way we can understand them: through
a combination of resemblances, differences, opposites, contradictions,

causes, consequences, or through whatever is correlative with the problem at hand.

Finally, in the *Poetics* Aristotle asserted the legitimacy of knowledge through the concrete in poetic dramas like *Oedipus* which made philosophical truth accessible to the general populace. Where Plato feared that attendance at dramatic festivals unleashed in the uneducated spectator emotions that were uncontrolled by reason, Aristotle maintained that the plays were in themselves rational structures. In them, as in the persuasive reasoning of rhetoric and unlike philosophical science, reason engages with the emotions in such a way that together they support an understanding of those recurring perennial truths about the human condition that are embedded in the concrete of the drama.

During the first quarter of the seventeenth century, Francis Bacon was also an arbiter of method. In his sweeping survey of learning in *The Advancement of Learning* (1605), he acknowledged that the theoretical and literary reason prevalent in Greece and Rome made them "two exemplar states of the world for arms, learning, moral virtue, policy, and laws."[1] He approved both of liberal learning that cultivates these modes of thought and of the use of literary tools in the interpretation of Scripture. However, as the prophet of a new era of empirical science, above all he argued passionately that the whole operation of the mind had to be completely restarted for its investigation of the laws of the material world. Both theoretical reasoning and literary thought had to make way for the new logic.

The method of inductive reasoning from sense observation of the physical world, now so familiar to us, began at the opposite pole from the verbal science of reasoning from established principles or premises that had been the glory of Greece and had dominated in Europe with the rise of the universities in the twelfth century. As well, the instrument of thought through which we understand the sequences of cause and effect in the physical world required an impartial cleared mind rather than the well-furnished mind essential to the traditional poet and to the arguments of rhetors in their engagement of both heart and mind. Because antithetical instruments of mind cannot operate at the same time and one operation of the mind excludes the

---

1 Francis Bacon, *The Advancement of Learning* (New York: Dutton, 1962) 74-5.

others, Bacon referred to the characteristics of the intellect that were an impediment to empirical science as idols or false appearances of the mind.

A little more than a decade before Bacon argued the need to restart the mind for the sake of empirical science, from a literary perspective Sir Philip Sidney already perceived a diminishment in the faculty of the imagination as it operates in poetry. This poet, diplomat, and courtier to Queen Elizabeth observed in the Puritan hostility to poetry a failure to recognize that the imagination has a different role in poetry than in any other discipline. The Puritans' perception of poetry as a corrupting influence and their plain literal use of language are both connected to a conflation of the way the imagination functions in registering the external world in the manner of science with the role of the imagination in poetry. In *The Defense of Poesy* (1592), Sidney argued that both poetry's double nature where the universal is embedded in the concrete and its capacity to be moral proceed from its unique freedom to fashion another world in the imagination.

At the beginning of the modern age, Sidney anticipated a disturbance at the very wellsprings of thought in his distinction between the task of the imagination in poetry and its task in scientific reasoning. As an arbiter of method, Bacon makes further distinctions in the relation between the imagination and reason as they function in science, morality and religion. He points out that in scientific reasoning where the imagination registers sense impressions of the external world, it is relegated to the role of messenger between sense and the reason's judgments of the sensate. In morality, the close connection between imagination and the appetite, desires, and the affections means that reason must direct the imagination to prevent reason from being captive and servile to affections and desires that know only the present. As a result, the moral function of dramatists in engaging imaginative sympathy for their characters or a rhetor's selection of persuasive concrete examples involve a different closer relation between the reason and the imagination than in science. Finally, in the domain of religious belief and in the interpretation of literary portions of Scripture, rather than being a mere servant between sense and reason as in science, the imagination may be raised above the reason. In his description of the imagination's magisterial role in religion, Bacon explains that because divine grace uses the imagination as a *locus* for illuminating the understanding, it seeks access to the mind by similitudes, types, parables, visions, and dreams.

By the latter part of the eighteenth century and throughout the nineteenth century, other voices protested that the imagination as a place for knowing the invisible world had suffered an eclipse. By then, habituation to the imagination in its sensate role both as used in the physical sciences and as affirmed by the epistemologies of empirical philosophers had led to an atrophy of the imagination as it functions in conjunction with a particular faculty of the intellect that perceives the invisible interior world. The poet, William Blake (1757-1825), spoke of the dread form of certainty in science's abstractions of laws. In contrast to the imagination's role as a messenger of the external visible world for the sake of empirical induction's abstraction of its laws and industry's material applications of them, Blake wrote of another role of the imagination, of the noetic intelligence, and of a world within the concrete and particular unknowable through the instrument of empirical induction and its analysis of cause and effect. This vast interior world is known instead through the imagination in conjunction with *nous*, the noetic faculty of mind translated variously as insight, intuition, and intelligence, a faculty that does not reason but simply knows both ultimate principles and ultimate particulars. The gates of paradise that opened on to a world resonant with spirit had been firmly shut in minds closed to the numinous through the usurpation of the intellect by the method of modern science.

Throughout the nineteenth century, John Henry Newman (1801-1889) also resisted the modern closing of the mind that would both marginalize literature and make religious belief impossible. As an arbiter of method he insisted that the various operations of the mind have different appointed tasks. We do not reason in the same way in poetry and in religious belief as in the physical sciences. To apply the method of the physical sciences to religion and poetry is as futile as expecting Aristotelian verbal reasoning to fulfil the task of sense observation and induction in the physical sciences. And to assume that there is one universal method, that only one kind of reason is applicable to all areas of truth, can only lead to error, absurdity, and intellectual bigotry.

In his observations on poetry and religious belief, Newman wrote that both operate through the same faculty; although they have different objects, both move the affections through the function of the imagination. He makes clear that the function of the imagination is simply to register impressions. The imagination itself neither makes comparisons nor draws conclusions although it is so closely connected to the intellect that it may seem one with it. Even single images like "Father" used in reference to God are understood through analogical reasoning implicit in the image.

Newman's work is especially important in its assertion that reason is indeed implicit in religious belief although the kind of reason operative in both faith and literature is not commonly recognized as reason in a scientific age. Particularly in response to those who would either reject the role of intellect in religious belief or alienate the religious imagination through scientific explanation, Newman undertook the daunting task of articulating how the reason works in conjunction with the imagination. In the impressions made on the imagination in a direct personal relation with God or, by extension, in the immediate impressions made on the imagination by a theatrical performance, we understand through an implicit, unarticulated operation of reason that grasps truth tacitly through a convergence of diverse probabilities. We can also make explicit this tacit, inchoate reasoning that is closely connected to our imaginative impressions by locating principles and making connections. But our explicit reasoning both takes its origin in tacit sources and follows the same pattern of reasoning through a persuasive convergence of various probabilities, the only possible way we can know the truth at the heart of particular or concrete matters. In reflecting explicitly on religious belief or on a play that we have attended we know through the same operation of the mind described by Cicero as characteristic of the suasory reasoning of rhetoric: through what is correlative with the problem at hand in opposites, differences, resemblances contradictions, consequences, causes.

The large genus of reasoning through diverse, converging probabilities is as broad and varied as human deliberation itself as it considers concrete or particular questions. Literature is one species of this larger genus of congruent reasoning that understands through opposites, resemblances, differences. In Shakespeare's poetic drama, *King Lear*, we understand in the concrete the awful simplicity of the commandment to honour our parents through the juxtaposition of Cordelia's integrity and her sisters' unbounded treachery; through the parallel interwoven story of the fidelity and duplicity of Gloucester's two sons; through the variations on a theme in the court-jester's anguished jibes about the king's foolishness and his courtier's advice and dogged fidelity.

This course of reasoning through personally perceived connections is the rationality not only of poetry, of rhetoric's literary reasoning, and of individual reflection on religious belief. It is also the pattern of thought followed by pioneers in the physical sciences in their quest for hypotheses. Cicero, Charles Darwin, and John Henry Newman as preacher at Oxford all reasoned through the juxtapositions, contrasts, collateral references, and associations characteristic of this mode of thought in its grasp of truth.

In a long tradition of liberal learning, this reasoning through diverse congruent probabilities was cultivated through the study of Letters or literature. When Aristotle was court tutor for the future great military strategist and conqueror, Alexander the Great, he inspired his pupil through the poetry of Homer. In Rome when Cicero pleaded the cause of the higher learning of rhetoric, he extolled the value of this non-scientific reasoning in statecraft and forensic arguments. In the nineteenth century, in *The Idea of a University* John Henry Newman renewed the cause of liberal education in defending its study not only of theoretical reasoning but also of literature for the sake of their cultivation of two different parts of the intellect.

My own cause is like Newman's, like Cicero's in his defense of rhetoric, and like Aristotle's: that is, to validate the mode of reasoning of literature challenged by contemporary assumptions regarding the nature of mind, particularly in the field of education. Our largely unconscious assumptions stand in contrast to the great philosophers of method who recognized the absurdity of a universal method, the importance of understanding that various methods have different tasks, that each way of knowing is only one part of a whole.

In our universities the dominance of the sciences has meant the marginalization of the humanities. Our elementary and secondary schools are driven by a philosophy of education and an epistemology which assume that we know in one way only: through sense observation and personal experience. As a result, in elementary and secondary schools literature and its important mode of reasoning are diminished; languages are taught not only without connection to literature but are forced into a methodology based on sense observation and personal experience which in itself largely eliminates the literary use of language. This insistence on a universal method has not only disabled students from learning languages; it has run aground mathematics and has even failed the sciences by locating its ultimate goal in Rousseau's ideal of self-esteem rather than in knowledge. The real hardship and suffering caused by a philosophy of education based on a single method was the original impetus for this work.

I have undertaken the cause of investigating method and our intellectual integrity by examining both the recurring uneasy relations between science and literature and the need to distinguish between them. Throughout this exploration, I have used literature's mode: of parallels, resemblances, contrasts, contradictions, and the juxtaposition of opposites where truth speaks through the details. The sensate limitations on reason of Thomas Hobbes are juxtaposed both with Newman's exposition of literary rationality and with the literary sensibilities in Scriptural interpretations by the Greek Church Fathers. The Renaissance defender of poetry, Sir Philip Sidney, stands in contrast to seventeenth-century educational reformers who in their messianic hope for the baconian method resolutely excluded literature, the function of the imagination as exercised in literature, and literature's mode of reasoning. Charles Darwin is placed beside the poet, William Blake, who championed the world of spirit excluded by the material investigations of the physical sciences. And throughout this inquiry, in the mode of literature I have attempted to let the personal voices of these diverse witnesses emerge.

I

PRELUDE

EDUCATION AND THE BATTLE OF METHODS

The crisis in modern education is a crisis of the intellect. In our pedagogy, an empirical, inductive epistemology or theory of mind has so restricted the range of reason that it marginalizes the other primary ways of knowing: the converging rationality associated with literature and deductive reasoning from received principles or rules. Both the rationality of literature and deductive reasoning, the twin pillars traditional to studies in the humanities, have become victims of a modern hegemony of method that has dislodged them from their proper spheres. Because this crisis in education is fundamentally a quarrel between different methods of reasoning, the injunction from antiquity to "know thyself," or to understand the constitution of the human mind, has again become a modern imperative. There is a radical need to reconsider the various operations of the intellect in their own constituencies: to stand outside the epistemological assumptions that hobble our educational practices and to re-examine the reflections of great arbiters of method from the past, such as Aristotle in antiquity and Francis Bacon at the beginning of the modern era.

It is in partial answer to the immense, imperial pressure exerted on contemporary education by a dominant inductive epistemology that I have set as my task to elucidate the nature of literary rationality as one of the primary modes of reasoning cultivated in a long tradition of liberal education. If literary reasoning is to be recognized as a legitimate operation of the intellect, it must be justified before the tribunal of the regnant epistemology through describing how this rationality functions, its domain, the human need it fulfils, how it differs from the other modes of reasoning, and where encroachments have occurred against it. In the long history of the jostling for position by the various modes of thought, representative figures like Cicero, Shakespeare, and Erasmus have given voice to the mode of literature; Francis Bacon and seventeenth-century Baconian educational theorists speak to the modern quarrel between induction, deduction, and literary thought.

The rise of the inductive method of modern science and the decline of both deductive and literary reasoning began in earnest in the seventeenth century. As an arbiter of method, in the first part of this century Francis Bacon surveyed the various paths to knowledge which connect particulars to intelligible principles: deduction and induction, the two scientific modes of reasoning, and the literary mode of reasoning described by Aristotle as reasoning in orb or circle. Bacon recognized the service rendered to both human and divine knowledge up to his period through the instruments of deduction and literary reasoning. However, since his own mission was to reorient learning towards the domain of the physical world for the sake of the common good in the material betterment of humankind, he promoted passionately empirical inductive thought as the *novum organon* or new logical instrument of modern science. This method, heralded by Bacon and now so familiar to us, is the instrument proper to the study of the material world because it begins with the sense observation of particulars in order to discover the general axioms or laws that govern them. Although because of their starting-point in particulars, these axioms must always remain provisional pending further investigations, general laws afford mastery of a field and open the way to new material applications. In his day, in order to promote inductive reasoning for the sake of the brave new departure of modern physical science, Bacon had to dislodge deductive reasoning exercised in Aristotelian or scholastic speculative thought from its exclusive stronghold in the field of scientific reasoning.

A relentless battle was to be waged against deductive thought in the ensuing centuries. Accusations were leveled against speculative reasoning: against its inutility, its fractious quibbling, its quarreling about matters that for the sensate observer simply do not exist. In the wake of the victory of empirical induction, in our own period the assumptions of inductive reasoning and its biases are taken for granted. From the beginning of the conflict, deductive science was an affront to induction both in its aims and in its process of reasoning. Deduction begins at the opposite pole of thought; it reasons not from particular physical observations for the sake of new discoveries but from abstract principles or starting-points that have been assumed or previously attained. Unlike Baconian induction, deductive reasoning is concerned not with material applications but with understanding the perennial nature of things, with their beginnings and ends through first and final causes, or with ideas and their particular consequences. Its distillations abstracted originally from particulars are found in the wisdom that provides the luminous guideposts to our thought in the human domain: in the speculative truths of ethics and politics; in the laws of jurisprudence and the principles behind these laws; in the popular wisdom of maxims and proverbs; in the axioms of geometry; in all logic that begins with accepted propositions; in the rules of language in grammar and the thought reflected in these rules; in the rules of games like chess. In other words, deductive science proceeds from *a priori* principles or rules. In its starting-point, deduction is antithetical to the *tabula rasa*, the cleared mind Bacon understood to be required at the beginning of the process of inductive science in order to attend to the careful observation of particulars in the physical domain, to trace the sequence of cause and effect, to examine, as he said, secondary causes.

Although exclusive habituation to either deduction or induction makes the contrary process of thought seem irksomely inadequate, yet as sciences both share common ground. Both can only analyze and divide; both must deal with only one fixed aspect of things at a time. For this reason, their use of language is similar; although the intelligible principles of induction and deduction are located at opposite ends in their reasoning processes, both express these principles in the impersonal, univocal language of science.

It is otherwise with literary reasoning which functions in a different way from these scientific instruments of thought. In its scope, literary reasoning does not draw on a single department of knowledge, like science, but on the whole interconnected domain of the human and the divine. Literary rationality begins neither with a *tabula rasa*, as supposed in Baconian induction, nor from an impersonal single idea, like deductive reasoning. Rather it seeks out the truths embedded in the real or concrete by engaging heart and mind and what is unique to the individual person. It also uses language differently, expressing thought in a way that is inseparable from words. Words used in a literary way are not univocal but have a multivalent, personal resonance that mirrors the associations, nuances of thought, and the feelings of the literary reasoner. In the aim and field of operation of literature, neither inductive reasoning within a single department of knowledge nor the theoretical principles that guide deductive reasoning are competent to its task.

The realm of literature is the human drama. As its mirror, literature expresses life experienced in its several dimensions rather than on a single plane. Literature reflects life in the concrete where deliberation and choice must be effected in matters with multiple implications and considerations. It takes as its domain the whole of the human condition including the inner invisible world of ethical judgments, the motives that animate decisions and actions, and moral responses like guilt or remorse. The human drama reflected in literature is a mutual, relational world where the emotional register of protagonists resonates in response to others. It is a world marked by the repercussions that the actions and choices of one person have on those around them: on their families, or on the *polis*, or on their own relation to the transcendent. Unlike the static categories of science, literature's mirror reflects movement and change: subtle shifts or the unexpected arrival of good and bad fortune that is beyond scientific control. Ever-renewed truths about the human condition are embedded in the concrete in such a way that particular contexts and enduring truths are inseparable from each other. For this reason, good literature is philosophical without philosophizing, it is moral without being didactic, it presents rather than explains. And in all of this, parts are understood as belonging to a larger whole where both good and evil reside, where past and present and future possibility meet, where irreconcilable opposites are held in tensile unity.

Within this broad, multifaceted realm of the human and divine, of life lived in relation to others, of contradictory stances, and parts understood in relation to a whole, literature has its own rationality no less than induction or deduction in their connection of intelligible principles to particulars. With regard to the reasoning implicit in plots of Greek poetic drama, Aristotle wrote of the logical connection effected through the sequence of concrete events and through responses which from beginning to end seem plausibly or even inevitably connected.

However, the nature of literary rationality as a personal instrument of thought comes to light in considering not the plots but the thinking authors and their receptive readers. The truths embedded in the drama of life expressed in literature are conveyed by authors and understood by their readers through the instrumentality of a distinctive literary kind of reasoning that considers a matter from several sides and from different facets: through opposites, concrete juxtapositions, reiterations through variation, through parallels, and nuances. Of equal importance in this literary rationality is the personal way in which both authors and readers grasp the underlying realities in what is concretely expressed. In literary reasoning, apprehension of truths about the human condition takes in the whole range of a person's accumulated knowledge and experience of life; it draws on all that is connected to the matter at hand along with those feelings associated with personal experience and knowledge. Finally, this response of heart and mind is quickened by the indelible impression made on the imagination and the affections during the immediate pre-reflective effect on us of literature's concrete drama. In both the moment of this initial imaginative impression that harbours implicit thought and in the drama's further working on our sensibilities we know feelingly.

In this logic characteristic of literature, human and moral truths are known not through the abstractions of science but in the stuff of life. For example, in Shakespeare's poetic drama, *King Lear*, the causal or logical sequence of the actions in the play is set in motion by Lear's initial rash act of giving control of his kingdom to his daughters, inverting the relation of parent and children. From this moment, the awful simplicity of the commandment to honour and love parents is known through a whole complex fabric of concrete contrasts, parallels, juxtapositions, and variations: through the actions and words that demonstrate Cordelia's integrity and her sisters' unbounded treachery and greed; through the parallel interwoven story of the fidelity and duplicity of Gloucester's two sons; through Lear's decline from regal strength into madness and destitution on the bleak, storm-swept heath; through his court-jester's anguished jibes about the king's foolishness and through his courtier's advice and dogged fidelity. In the web of circumstance, the action of one person not only recoils upon himself but also impinges on others and reverberates through families and the *polis*.

In contrast to scientific reasoning, through the literary rationality of the play the theme of filial ingratitude and other related themes are known through the unlike as well as the like; they are walked around from many sides to capture life in the concrete. And members of the audience grasp the fundamental realities of our flawed humanity that the play represents through their own personal frame of reference and unique composite background: through their experience of families, their awareness of topsy-turvy relations, of innocence abused, of injudicious figures in authority, of ingratitude, of disloyalty, of integrity, as well as through a wider reading, a sensibility to language, or a scholarly knowledge of Shakespearian allusions.

The rationality exercised in literature's reflection of life is exactly the same kind of reasoning we exercise in all areas of life that require deliberation and personal judgment; that is, in the large terrain of specific probable matters. Reasoning through a convergence of probabilities is the instrument used by judges in courts of law to arrive at their decisions by weighing evidence from various quarters. It is the rationality engaged in religion by those who seek a personal intellectual understanding of particular matters in their faith. The same kind of reasoning through juxtapositions from various areas is used in the pioneering phases of modern science to reach hypotheses that later may be proven scientifically. All of us exercise this kind of unscientific congruent reasoning when there is a need for a personal grasp of specific concrete situations: where answers are not straightforward or obvious, where we must rely severally on tacit comparisons, parallel experiences, and considered hunches until we reach a moment of recognition like the protagonist in a drama.

In a long tradition in education dating from antiquity, this kind of interpretive, deliberative reasoning was practised especially in two of the language disciplines that were to constitute the medieval *trivium* of grammar, dialectics, and rhetoric. Literary reasoning was cultivated first in grammar, which meant the study of language in conjunction with literature until their separation in the modern age. Then it was refined through the study of rhetoric, a field eclipsed in our own period and now viewed with suspicion as hollow verbiage, as futilely repetitive, and deceptively manipulative. To understand the nature of literary reasoning as exercised in rhetoric, we do well to inquire instead from one of its own greatest practitioners: from Cicero, a Roman who emulated Greek practice, whose eloquent reflections on oratory were studied in the sixteenth century by Shakespeare and his grammar school contemporaries, as by students in the nineteenth century wherever the classics were still cherished.

In mid-first century BCE, Cicero provides a lucid theoretical description of literary rationality[1] used then, as now, especially in statecraft and forensic pleading: in upholding civil rights, as he says, or in the safety of the state; or again in challenging the wicked and seeking revenge; in subduing lawless desires; in providing healing in suffering or help in trouble. He describes the literary reasoning of rhetoric as predating the scientific reasoning of Greek philosophy and the problematic splitting of knowledge into super-refined specialized departments.[2] As an instrument of thought, literary rationality includes a knowledge of the general recurring questions of humanity, but its approach takes in the web of human affairs as particular, complex, interconnected, and multifaceted in the only way that we can understand them as such: that is, through what is correlative with the problem at hand such as a combination of resemblances, differences, opposites, contradictions, causes, and consequences.

With regard to its essential principles, Cicero wrote that the domain of the literary reasoning of rhetoric is the life of humankind; it comprehends all matters human and divine; and it is grounded in a cosmological view that assumes the unity of all things. Contrary to the empirical enlightenment's idea of the mind as a cleared slate, a *tabula rasa*, the literary rationality of rhetoric as described by Cicero requires a well-furnished mind: educated in the nature and principles of things, free-ranging as the poet's, aware of opposing viewpoints but in a wider way than in debate. This reasoning is uniquely personal both in how it grasps particular problems and in its expression. Differences between persons and their frames of reference make both literary authors' and rhetors' styles unmistakably their own even when they draw on the same supply of ideas and impressions; for example, in the distinctiveness of the various Greek dramatists in their interpretations of the same legends and myths. Finally, not only through what is said, but through cadences and rhythms, through choice of words and

---

1　Cicero, *De Oratore*, vol. 1, 2, introd. H. Rackham (London: William Heinemann, 1942).

2　Cicero refers to Greek military men, playwrights, statesmen, and physicians who had been educated as men of general culture: Alexander the Great, Aristotle's pupil; Pericles, the great Greek statesman, who had been educated by Anaxagoras; Aristophanes, the dramatist who had embraced culture as a whole; and Hippocrates, the physician of Cos, before he specialized in surgery, opthalmics, etc. (Bk. iii, 103-7).

phrasing, both the mind and heart are reached, a place where more is decided, Cicero says, than through statute, judgment, or authority.

Literary reasoning with its personal resonances differs from scientific thought, then, in its operations, in its interconnected unified domains, and in relation to words. Cicero describes different facets of the distinctive character of literary reasoning where wisdom begets eloquence, where thought begets words and is inseparable from them. From his vantage point as a literary reasoner, Cicero observes the tension between literary and scientific reasoning that exists in any age when scientific reasoning dominates. He complains that not only has the unity of knowledge been shattered by half-educated minds, but equally disastrously, words have been separated from thought. He laments that philosophical science has driven out the literary reasoning of rhetoric from its own estate in representing both sides in general questions, and that rhetoricians who are defenders of other people have been unable to hold and to safeguard the domain of rhetoric, their own possession. Finally, in advice that was to reverberate in education in succeeding millennia wherever rhetoric was studied, this great master of literary rationality writes that training in literary reasoning requires a natural talent that can be aided through the broad culture of a liberal education, through studying and imitating the best literature, and through much practice in exercising its principles.

Like Cicero in ancient Rome, in sixteenth-century Europe Erasmus was another advocate of literary reasoning. As a movement, the Renaissance represented in figures like Erasmus restored to prominence a literary mode of reasoning whose vitality was a needed counterbalance to the deductive speculative science that had assumed dominance with the rise of the universities in the twelfth century and risked decadent sterility without the instrument of literature's reasoning. While Cicero championed rhetoric, the final refinement and mature phase of the language disciplines, Erasmus promoted the foundational level of language study in the Renaissance grammar schools. In these schools, grammar meant the study of the Latin language first in conjunction with its poetry, plays, history, letters, and later with the forensic, deliberative, and panegyric speeches of its rhetorical tradition. Grammar included whatever was necessary for the understanding of this literature in all its resonances. As the science of language, it had been studied similarly in Greece for the interpretation of Homer; so too, in the early Church grammar had been the instrument for interpreting Scripture where literary polyvalence allowed its historical accounts to be understood simultaneously in their transcendent divine significance and their individual or collective moral sense rather than just in the literal sense of the univocal language of science. For schoolboys in sixteenth-century England, the study of grammar meant knowledge of the literary, polysemous use of Latin words: their roots and the history of their transmission, their relation to other words, and the nuances of their authoritative use by different authors in particular contexts. It meant the correct understanding of the structure of the language both for reading texts and in the students' own literary use of Latin. As they advanced in their studies, grammar required all the erudition necessary for the full understanding of the literature that they read.

Erasmus' enormous collection of maxims or adages which were used as texts in sixteenth-century European schools illustrates how literary reasoning was cultivated through grammar, the earliest phase of the *trivium*, in the kind of education in Latin language and literature that Shakespeare would have experienced. Indeed, the moral or practical wisdom of such pithy sayings as "Time reveals all" (*Tempus omnia revelat*) or "The mountain in labour brings forth a mouse" (*Parturiunt montes, nascetur ridiculus mus*) informs not only Shakespeare's plays but works as diverse as Francis Bacon's and the fables of LaFontaine. The primary educational function of the adages was the same as Erasmus' original purpose for beginning his vast collection; that is, as a way to master Latin language and style through literature where thought, word, and image are inseparable. When used in later studies as a text for students' exercises in writing, they provided a kernel of perennial wisdom for topical development through the converging reasoning of literature.

Like Cicero's reflections on rhetoric, Erasmus' own erudite and engagingly personal meditations on the adages reflect the general culture of literary reasoning which assumes the interconnected unity of knowledge. In his meditations, he draws on the whole range of his experience of life, on his reflections on what he had read, on facts, on philosophical ideas, and on his opinions, all in their connection to the single idea represented in the highly polished, succinct language of the adages. As he delves into the adages' literal and figurative meaning, explores their geographical and historical context, and considers their sources in custom and legend, he simultaneously underlines the continuity of human wisdom from the classical to the Christian era and makes readers feel they walk in Rome.

We find the circling reasoning of literature, for example, in his reflections on the riddle-like proverb, *Festina lente* (Make haste slowly).[3] As Erasmus examines its origin in antiquity, this proverb, both old and ever new, applicable to the sixteenth-century prince as to the Roman emperor, is traced in his meditation to Homer, Virgil, and to an ancient coin he saw in Italy. On one side was inscribed the effigy of the Roman emperor, Titus Vespasianus, and on the other the image of an anchor with a dolphin wound around the middle. Erasmus explains that to interpret delightful hieroglyphics or emblems like this, one has to look deeply into the quality of the things themselves; the dolphin shooting out of the water is like the dauntless activity of the mind and the anchor represents the need for slowness and delay. As his thought converges around the proverb, Erasmus ranges freely. He comments on the profundity of Aristotle's insight in the *Physics* into the analogy and similarity between space, time, and movement. He expresses irritation with sloppy current editions of books and with the swarm of new books, indiscriminate rubbish of minor importance in comparison to those who looked over whole fields: for example, Aristotle; Chrysostom (ca. 345-407), the eloquent Church Father; or Jerome (ca. 340-420), translator of the Scriptures into Latin, and author of a classic work on the lives of famous men. Throughout Erasmus' meditation we have a demonstration of literary reasoning: juxtapositions subsumed as parts of a whole; reflections that are at once drawn from a personal frame of reference and linked to the perennial truth of the proverb; language inseparable from the nuance of both thought and feeling.

In education in subsequent centuries, the literary reasoning which had been fostered since antiquity in liberal education and was the glory of the Renaissance yielded increasingly to the method of the physical sciences and to an exclusionary epistemology derived from this method. In the modern era, philosophy, too, has felt the sterility resulting from the eclipse of literary reasoning and has been hampered by a similar narrow epistemology. Limited by the instrument meant for its own kind of scientific reasoning and under the constraint of its

---

3   Erasmus, *The "Adages" of Erasmus*, introd. and trans., Margaret Mann Phillips (Cambridge U.P., 1964).

univocal use of language, philosophy has yearned for what only literary reasoning can provide; that is, a personal engagement of heart and mind that grasps truth in its multiple dimensions and in all its vitality embedded in the concrete. In the nineteenth century, for example, John Stuart Mill found in the poetry of Wordsworth emotional and imaginative release from the positivist utilitarian philosophy in which he had been raised which shuts out the imagination and reason as they function in literature. Neitzsche discussed the modern separation of passion and intellect in contrast to the mode of Greek tragedy where both passion and intellect prevail; he hoped that the saving power of art might restore a synthetic force and recover the lost vivifying power of traditional religion. This same project of revitalization through myth was embraced by Wagner in his operas and by the twentieth-century American poet, Hart Crane. The quasi-religious expectation of poetry is found in Matthew Arnold in the nineteenth century and in Reiner Maria Rilke (1875-1926) who looked on the poet as priest attuned to the being of things. In the twentieth century, Heidegger, too, turned his philosophic attention towards the end of his career to poetry and, with a sense of its loss to modern philosophy, Hans Georg Gadamer spoke of the rationality of aesthetics and of the close connection between thought and language as found in rhetoric and practical philosophy.

Our modern philosophy of education is beset by constraints similar to those felt by these philosophers. From classical antiquity to the Renaissance, education had focused on the study of the human and the divine through both the deductive and literary modes of reasoning of liberal learning. However, in a continuous history of deep antagonism between methods both deductive thought and literary rationality have been forced to yield their terrain to the dual influences of modern inductive science and a materialist empirical epistemology. Since this epistemology insists that we know only by drawing our own conclusions from our sense impressions and from our own experience, the methodology for teaching all disciplines, including languages, had to conform to a method meant for the study of the material world.

Because the traditional methodology for language teaching associated with the Greek and Latin classics was adapted to literature, to its mode of thought, and to its use of language, this pedagogy had in itself transmitted the rationality of literature, just as the method of sense observation in the physical sciences transmits an empirical mode of thought. For millennia, literature's evocative use of language expressing the inner realm, the shadings of our motives or the emotions that colour our thoughts and actions, was honed through a study of words: the accurate, precise meaning of words; families of words, the roots of words, and their etymological development; the wealth of words in a *copia verborum*. Literary reasoning that knows through opposites, parallels, and variations was transmitted through a study of antonyms, synonyms, and the comparisons of the various contextual use of words by authors whose genius helped shaped a language. Learning by heart Aesop's fables or adages, like those collected by Erasmus, not only internalized the words of a language, its rhythms, and its structures but also conveyed the concrete mode of literature's thought. As in other arts which begin with imitation, pupils were exercised in writing by imitating good models, then by making minor variations on the models, and later by writing more freely. Their own amplification of maxims and mature suasory writing in the rhetorical mode put in practice literature's mode of reasoning around a central organizing principle. From the beginning of their studies, language was made intelligible through the study of grammar which had mapped out the structures of language expressing the human world of thought; such as our sense of time in verb tenses or relations of causality and condition in clauses beginning with words like "because" and "if." Through this study of grammar language was made intelligible like the laws of the physical world for the student of physical science. Finally, translation, another important teaching technique, refined both the student's own language and the Greek or Latin that he studied. Shakespeare studied not English but Latin at his grammar school through the poetry of Ovid and Virgil or the dramas of Terence; yet the refined sense of both English and Latin that comes from double translation honed his unparalleled sensibility to English.

However, as a consequence of the unilateral cultivation of inductive reasoning from sense observation, in the modern period for the first time in the long history of western education the teaching of language has become separated from literature and from its methodology in the deductive reasoning of grammar with its scientific analysis of the human realm of thought. Shortly after the death of Francis Bacon, full of messianic hopes and dazzled by the promises of empirical science, Puritan educational reformers in England developed a curriculum that excluded literature, focused exclusively on scientific utility, and was based entirely on the method of induction advocated by Bacon for the advancement of the physical or material sciences. As their theory of child development also adhered to the Baconian method, they declared that all learning must conform to the natural development of the child by beginning with the sense observation of concrete things. As a result, because at that time Latin texts on subjects like natural science were still useful, educational reformers developed ways of teaching Latin through the visual observation of things or through techniques that avoided the abstractions of grammar rules. For example, in the influential school texts of the Czech reformer, Comenius, sentences in both Latin and the vernacular were connected to labeled pictures representing things and common useful occupations. Other reformers devised "ready and easy ways" to learn Latin through interlinear translation without using the deductive reasoning from rules of grammar.

In the periods that followed, the dismissal of grammar and the divorce between language and literature were continued in the work of other educational theorists. By the end of the seventeenth century, the importance of a second language for John Locke lay in its usefulness to business communication. He suggests that enough French could be learned for this purpose by just prattling in French with a French speaker in the same way as ladies of breeding. By mid-eighteenth century, Rousseau considered it futile for a child to learn other languages and maintained that the techniques recommended by Locke for learning to read were unnecessary. The desire of a pupil to read would in itself suffice for him to learn.

In mid-nineteenth century, the fledgling English system of popular education was largely controlled by the empirical theory of mind of seventeenth-century reformers like Comenius and by Rousseau's empirical educational philosophy transmitted through the nineteenth-century Swiss model of his disciple, Pestalozzi (1746-1827). The invocation of the word "science" or "scientific" was itself sufficient to justify an educational philosophy that dictated beginning with sense observation. In the name of the scientific or concrete pedagogy of the period, the methodology traditional to the study of language and literature was aggressively attacked: the memorization of poetry, for example, or deductive reasoning from abstract rules in grammar.

Matthew Arnold, classically educated and both poet and school inspector, found his literary sensibilities baffled by the methodology in the English elementary schools that he visited for over thirty years. Arnold recognized the sources of the bias against literature and literary reasoning in the theory of child development that redefined the mind and limited its early operations to the empirical inductive observation of things. In a school report for 1878, Arnold remarked that the scientific teachers of pedagogy recommend the disuse of rule-teaching in favour of teaching things "'in the concrete instead of in the abstract,'" following Pestalozzi's ideas of the "'natural process of mental evolution.'"[4]

In language teaching, the campaign against rule-teaching or the logic of deductive reasoning from abstract starting-points meant the banishment of grammar, a subject Arnold believed to be a better instrument for training in logic than mathematics. In the school system's emphasis on the sense observation of things, Arnold also felt acutely the marginalization of the literary imagination and the literary use of language where words themselves are portals to thought. He remarked on the paucity of children's vocabulary in the schools he visited and maintained that an increased vocabulary is an increase in a pupil's circle of ideas. The literary way of using language was also neglected in the choice of reading selections where language was taught in its univocal scientific mode: for example, in utilitarian, positivist descriptions of gas lighting in the streets. In the dreariness of such reading, Arnold believed that children were deprived of the beauty and delight offered in literature and poetry through the engagement of the literary imagination and the affections.

Finally, there was a potential for ineffectual lessons in science as well as in literature through the application of a universal method emphasizing utility and based on the passive impressions made by sense observation on the imagination and memory. In science, Arnold gives the example of a feeble lesson in which a teacher holds up an apple in a gallery to a group of little children for their observation, saying: "An apple has a stalk, peel, pulp, core, pips, and juice; it is odorous and opaque, and is used for making a pleasant drink called cider." By contrast, he praises a lesson in which the pupil is not merely a

---

4   Matthew Arnold, *Reports on Elementary Schools 1852-1882* (London: Eyre and Spottiswoode, 1910) 189.

passive observer, where the subject matter is "not *talked about*, as in too many of our elementary schools, but *learnt*."[5] As for the methodology traditional to language and literature, he recognized that it simply stood outside the epistemological borders of the concrete, scientific method which did not admit of either the literary imagination's freedom to range beyond the actual and sensate or the close connection between language and thought in literature that makes memorization one of its instruments. Arnold complains: "Learning by heart is often called, disparagingly, learning by *rote*, and is treated as an old-fashioned, unintelligent exercise, and a waste of time."[6] He defends learning by heart in spite of the opposition to this "old rhetorical practice" and praises the recitation of poetry as having a "formative power."[7]

Since the latter part of the twentieth century, the same epistemological narrowness experienced by Matthew Arnold in the concrete or scientific pedagogy of his period has prevailed in what is called the discovery method. Because the teaching of language in connection to literature had been based traditionally on both deductive and literary reasoning, its methodology once again became a battleground for the war between methods. In particular, grammar with its rule-teaching was a foe to be vanquished.

Modern pedagogy sought to overthrow the methodology for learning languages through the elements that are constitutive of language and make it teachable. Since ancient Greece, in the initial stages of grammar (Greek *gramma*: letter) children became literate through first associating sounds with letters, then with pairs of letters, syllables, and finally with multisyllabic words. When syllables and words were mastered thoroughly, children were then allowed to read passages of continuous prose. In this way, for nearly two millenia children learned not only to read with facility and to spell through having the keys to sounds and letters, but they were also impressed from the first with an inherent discipline and coherence in this beginning of deductive science, of mastering first one thing and its application and then another in a progressive, cumulative manner. By contrast, in the latter part of the twentieth century literacy was to be achieved through sense observation in accordance with the prevailing empirical epistemology:

---

5   Ibid., 88. Arnold's italics.

6   Ibid., 186. Arnold's italics.

7   Ibid.,188.

in the visual observation of words or in practices like reading for general meaning; that is, by using visual clues in pictures to guess the meaning of words in the printed text.

In other words, this methodology traditional to the study of language as associated with literature is exactly what the epistemology of the discovery method will not under any circumstances allow. The direct teaching of rules of grammar, memorization, imitation, and translation which were the staple methodology of the language disciplines since antiquity are anathema. Because the discovery method emphasizes a child's own discoveries through sense observation and personal experience, young children are asked not to be imitators but to be creative in their writing; writing topics for older students tend to refer to personal experience rather than to perennial wisdom as in Erasmus' adages. Since learning is to occur through their own inductive observations, writing is taught through a process that requires the teacher to elicit from students how they might improve what they have written. Rules of grammar can only be mentioned incidentally and, as it is the discovery method itself that is important, marks are allotted proportionately not just for results but for the process of writing and re-writing.

The discovery method which touches other areas of children's schooling in the methodology of projects and case studies in fact disables children in learning to read, to spell, to write, or to learn a second language. It tyrannizes those teachers of literature and language who recognize that the very nature of their disciplines is distorted by its methodology. To understand how a single method has wreaked havoc in education through its usurpation of the other modes of reasoning, we must turn to two historical sources.

As we have seen, in the period immediately following the age of Shakespeare and Francis Bacon, Baconian educational theorists pursued a wisdom different in kind from that associated with liberal education: that is, the perennial truths of the divine and human domains known both through the converging probabilities of literary reasoning and through deductive reasoning from principles. Wisdom was relocated instead in the House of Solomon of Bacon's *New Atlantis* where through the instrument of inductive reasoning principles might be discovered in data collected from the material world and then newly applied for the relief of suffering and the common good. With a supreme confidence in the Baconian method as the criterion of all truth, the inductive observation of material things became the sole focus in the program of Baconian educational theorists. Classical languages were important only to the extent that authors from antiquity, such as Pliny's work on natural history, were useful to the cause of physical science. In this incipient hegemony of method, the literary and deductive modes of reasoning traditional in education up to that time were now considered impediments; that is, both the well-furnished mind of converging literary reasoning and deductive reasoning from rules and principles were obstacles to the new program of useful knowledge to be achieved through training in sense observation and inductive reasoning.

However, it is in the eighteenth century in Rousseau's works on education that the most irradicable and deep-seated difficulties of our own period began. With Rousseau, the inductive method was transmuted into an epistemology, a theory of mind that recognized only one way of knowing: through the comparison of one's own sensations derived from the physical observation of things or from one's own experiences. Not only were the two other primary modes of reasoning excluded but empirical scientific reasoning was itself impaired. In Rousseau's philosophy of education, the cultivation of the empirical method took on a radical new twist as it was diverted from its end in the common good to a *telos* located at the opposite pole; that is, in the individual. Rousseau's philosophy of education does not promote the advancement of science; rather, the physical sciences are entirely subordinate to his individualist, materialist philosophy. This materialist philosophy and its narrow epistemology also dismiss as prejudice and pre-judgment the luminous starting-points of principles and ideas that are the signposts and guides for deductive reasoning; in pedagogical method reasoning from rules is forbidden. Similarly, the rich and vast world of personal reasoning that grasps truth in the concrete as exercised by Cicero and Erasmus was eclipsed.

Rousseau's thought is crucially important because it has been profoundly formative both in elementary education from the beginnings of popular education in Europe in the nineteenth century and again in its reincarnation in the culture of the discovery method in our own era since the 1960's. To appreciate its peculiar limitations, his educational thought must be understood within its sources in the neo-epicureanism introduced into the modern enlightenment tradition by

Pierre Gassendi (1592-1649).[8] The name and seminal influence of this French philosopher, as celebrated as Descartes during the seventeenth century, have receded behind the prominent philosophers who succeeded him. Yet these philosophers are indebted to Gassendi who found in the Greek philosophical school of Epicurus a neutral view of the material world shared by modern physical science and a concept of mind compatible with its empirical observations and experimental method. In Gassendi's seventeenth-century revival of epicureanism we find the roots of schools of modern empirical philosophy in the enlightenment tradition including educational philosophy in our own day. Hobbes knew Gassendi personally; Locke derives his epistemology from the epicureanism he described; Condillac's sensate philosophy and Diderot's materialism and atheism proceed from it; the utilitarian philosophy of Jeremy Bentham and liberalism in its nineteenth-century form have epicurean roots. Although Rousseau is linked with various philosophical influences, his educational philosophy bears the firm imprint of neo-epicurean philosophy.

For Epicurus (341-270 BCE), the goal of life was to maintain personal serenity or tranquility through both an economic and inner self-sufficiency or freedom (*eleuthera*), a life within the garden walls. This state of *ataraxia*, of bodily health and freedom from psychological distress and turmoil, was to be attained through the avoidance of pain and the pursuit of pleasure and through knowledge of the natural limits of both. For Epicurus, the perturbation of personal serenity through the two great fears, fear of the gods and fear of death, was eliminated through the atomist theory of Leucipus and Democritus.

---

8   Like Francis Bacon (1561-1626), Pierre Gassendi (1592-1649), Proven-
çal abbot, philosopher and teacher of mathematics, was repulsed by the
method of Aristotelian verbal logic and its domain of speculative truth
which was counter to the new bent of the age represented by astronomers
like Galileo, and to the kind of logic or method needed for empirical observation in the physical sciences. In *On the Aristotelian Logic* (1624), Gassendi wrote typically of the lack of utility of verbal method in arriving at
truth, or that dialectic has no necessity or utility; that definition or division
in artificial language is useless in distinguishing the true from the false.
In 1626 Gassendi began his work on Epicurus in whose ideas he found
a philosophy more suited to the empirical tendency of his age. His work
culminated in the *Syntagma philosophiae Epicuri* (*Treatise on Epicurean Philosophy*), a commentary on the work of the third-century biography of Epicurus by Diogenes Laërtius which was published posthumously in 1659.

According to their prescient theory of physics, everything was begotten and dissolved by the motion of an infinite number of atoms, travelling through the void with great swiftness, combining and colliding. As a result, in the words of the Roman epicurean poet, Lucretius (c. 95-55 BCE), "nature is seen to be free at once and rid of proud masters, herself doing all by herself of her own accord, and having no part or lot in the gods"[9]; for their part, the gods live immortally and remotely in tranquil serene peace removed from the tribulations of the world in a state similar to the ideal state of the adherents of epicurean philosophy.

In this epicurean cosmos, not only is nature its own pilot but death is not to be feared. Mind and spirit born in living creatures, like the body, are mortal. Death is more peaceful than sleep, a release of matter that coming generations may grow rather than a horrible and gloomy deliverance into the pit or black Tartarus (*De Rerum natura* 237). In this purely material cosmos removed from the gods and where personal tranquility is the ultimate good, morality or the sense of what is right and wrong is newly redefined. Virtue is what is useful to individual tranquility or happiness through avoidance of pain and the pursuit of pleasure. In other words, this redefinition of virtue removed it from the register of right and wrong, from religious sources of morality, as well as from universal or perennial ideas and definitions. In the epicurean perspective on virtue and vice, justice is utilitarian, based on mutual advantage. Laws are pragmatic and relative, human constructs subject to change in accordance with evident advantage. They are meant to provide security to those within the garden walls from attacks by others. Friendship is an egotistical pleasure.

Rousseau iterates this epicurean *telos* and its tenets in the conclusion of his first work on education, his *Discourse on the Sciences and Arts* (1750). True philosophy, he says, lies in knowing how to be content with ourselves and, with passions silenced, to enter into ourselves to listen to the voice of conscience; here the experience of conscience is Rousseau's particular adaptation of epicureanism to natural religion. Couched carefully in the terms of disapproval made necessary by eighteenth-century censorship, he writes of a philosophy that claims

---

9   Lucretius, *De Rerum natura* (London: William Heinemann, 1924) 7.

that only matter exists, that there is no God but this world, that neither vices nor virtues exist, and that good and evil are dreams.[10]

Rousseau's pedagogical method in *Emile* is a perfect development of this epicurean materialist philosophy and its epistemology illustrated through the framework of child-rearing and education, a model provided in Plato's *Republic* which Rousseau admired. His pedagogy is entirely in accordance with the path to wisdom announced in the projected title for his work on education; that is, "Le Matérialism du Sage" or "The Materialism of the Sage." It is also entirely consistent with the materialist philosophical platform outlined in his *Discourse on the Sciences and Arts* with its repudiation of the Renaissance and the fine arts and its disparagement of the liberal tradition in literature and philosophy. In this earlier work, to forward neo-epicurean philosophy and its materialist method Rousseau first associates the arts and sciences with luxury, idleness, and the corruption of wealth; he praises the virtuous simplicity of life before the advent of the arts and sciences in primitive and rustic peoples; and, claiming that Bacon is perhaps the greatest philosopher, he ridicules philosophical tradition and recommends in its stead the new model provided by the Bacons, the Descartes, and the Newtons.

---

10   If all of these philosophical references are couched in terms of disapproval, Rousseau had good reason to present his case in this way in light
of eighteenth-century censorship. When he undertook the writing of his
Discourse, his friend Diderot, was in prison for his daring exposition of
the doctrine of materialistic atheism emphasizing human dependence on
sense impression as found in his *Lettres sur les aveugles* (1749), or *Essay
on Blindness*. The other ancient philosophers that Rousseau mentions in
the *Discourse* are also connected to epicureanism, materialism, and atheism and are again presented under the guise of disapproval. He refers to
the unwelcome influence on Rome of Epicurus, Arcesilas, the sceptic, and
Zeno, perhaps Zeno of Sidon, a first century BCE disciple of Epicurus
whom Cicero heard in Athens in 79 BCE. He also mentions the ancient
philosophers associated with the atomist physics of Epicurus: Leucippus
and Diagoras, referred to as the atheist and thought to have been a student
of Democritus. Rousseau refers, too, to Spinoza, frequently used in the
eighteenth century as a cover for atheism, and to Hobbes whose asocial,
apolitical individual acting from self-interest and self-preservation was
strongly influenced in the previous century by the revived epicureanism
of Gassendi.

In *Emile*, Rousseau's concept of mind and its attendant method, the starting point of his educational theory, are derived from the epicurean assumption that only matter exists. Accordingly, in Rousseau's epistemology ideas originate only from a comparison of sensations or experiences; no other way of knowing exists. To explain the relation between judgment and sensations, Rousseau uses examples similar to those used by Lucretius in *De Rerum natura* for his criterion of truth (*kriterion*: instrument of judgment) based on epicurean physics. Rousseau's explanation of this epistemology through the example of a stick partially submerged in water[11] is at the same time an illustration of the empirical discovery method, the only pedagogical method that his epistemology will allow.

To illustrate the first premise that the judgment is passive in simple sensations and simply affirms that one feels what one feels, Rousseau states that when Emile sees a partially submerged stick in the water, his sensation that the stick is broken is certainly true. However, because Emile has been trained to reserve his judgment until it can be ascertained by inspection or observation, he will arrive at an accurate idea through compared sensations. This idea will become apparent through the instrument of the judgment which is active in bringing together, comparing, and determining relations. As Emile and his teacher walk around the stick they notice that the break in the stick turns as they do; looked at from straight above, the stick is

---

11   In *De Rerum natura*, Lucretius' description from epicurean physics of how we perceive through our senses the images of things comprised of minute atoms was an affirmation of the validity of sense observation, also emphasized by Bacon as important to empirical modern science. Lucretius states as a criterion of truth that our senses are not deceived but rather our mind's judgment of sense impressions. He cites multiple instances to prove his point; for example, when we are on a ship, we are not aware of its motion and have the impression that a stationary boat is moving; at night when winds scatter clouds across the sky, the shining stars seem to glide against the clouds; on boats in harbour the part of the oar that is above water seems straight, the part that is submerged seems "to be all broken back and wrenched and turned flat upwards." Rousseau uses similar examples: through a hasty induction a poorly trained pupil will believe as he looks at clouds in the night sky that the clouds are stationary and the moon is moving or that the shore is moving when he drifts in a boat. Rousseau then uses the example of a stick in water that appears broken to illustrate the origin of ideas.

no longer curved; when they stir the water's surface, the stick follows the undulations of the water; and when the water flows out, the stick straightens out as the water goes down. Guided by his teacher, Emile will discover for himself the idea of refraction without actually articulating it in words.

In the epicurean materialist world, then, one method monopolizes all learning in accordance with this philosophy's epistemology. Emile's education will be conducted entirely through the lessons taught him by things as experienced through sensations and then compared by the judgment. There are several serious consequences for education. First, the three primary modes of reasoning are either eclipsed entirely or impaired. Literature and literary rationality are simply excluded, eliminating the personal mode of thought that is the bridge to perennial truth embedded in the concrete as well as the polyvalent use of language that is its instrument. The abstract principles or concepts integral both to deductive and inductive science are also eschewed because they are separate from things. Since ideas are compared sensations, sensations take the place of propositions. Rousseau says that Emile "sees common qualities in certain bodies without reasoning about these qualities in themselves." Indeed, he boasts that at the end of the training of his judgment through the comparison of sensations Emile will hardly know "how to generalize ideas and hardly how to make abstractions."[12] In an education that is not oriented towards the verbal world of literature, a rejection of the verbal is not surprising. However, Rousseau ridicules verbal learning even in connection to things. He writes: "I do not like explanation in speeches. Young people pay little attention to them and hardly retain them. Things, things! I shall never repeat enough that we attribute too much power to words. With our babbling education we produce only babblers" (*Émile*, 180).

Secondly, the relation between teachers and students is altered in a pedagogical method that is focused on learning through material things. No direct teaching is to take place. Instead, the role of the teacher is limited to contriving situations that facilitate the students' observation of things in which alone authority rests and from which they are to draw their own conclusions using their own reason. In

---

12   Jean-Jacques Rousseau, *Emile or On Education*, introd., trans., notes by Allan Bloom (New York: Basic Books, 1979) 207. Remaining citations are from this edition.

accordance with the epicurean concern for the self, the students' own desire to learn will be their motivation; when needed, the teacher is to arouse this desire by interesting them in materials which should be of immediate practical utility or relevance to them. In adhering only to the morally neutral, necessary laws of the material world of things, epicurean self-sufficiency is thus assured in students' relations to their teacher by freeing them from either dominating or being dominated; as well, their virtue or happiness is achieved since the necessary laws of things keep their own passions and desires within bounds.

In Rousseau's terms, through obedience only to things Emile will be spared "amour-propre," the self-conceit or self-will that results both from tyranny in relations with others and from the imagination in one's own fantasies and caprices.[13] Rather he will acquire the ultimate virtue of happiness through self-sufficiency, what Rousseau calls "amour de soi" or self-esteem. Rousseau admonishes: "Keep the child in dependence only on things"; he explains that since this dependence on things has no morality, it is in no way detrimental to freedom and engenders no vices. Conversely, dependence on men "engenders all the vices, and by it, master and slave are mutually corrupted" (*Émile*, 85). Finally, although the goal is not to build cumulatively, to proceed logically from one step to the next, or to master material through concepts or abstract principles, nonetheless, in order to direct and guide their students teachers themselves must have been trained later to be aware of principles, such as the principle of refraction grasped concretely by Emile.

The rearing of Emile and his education provide abundant examples of this methodology based on Rousseau's materialist philosophy

---

13   Rousseau illustrates all this through what appears to be an engaging tip to parents concerning the early stages of child-rearing. We are advised that if a child who is as yet unable to talk complains and screams when trying to get an object beyond his reach, we should walk slowly with the child to the object rather than bring the object to him. In this way, he will be made to understand that objects are not subject to his passions and will not come to him. Not only will the child be taught that he does not command things but also that he is not to command others in matters beyond his dependent needs in accordance with the epicurean idea of a simple life of pleasure in which utilitarian relations are based on these needs. If it is apparent that the child both exceeds his real needs and intends to manipulate and domi-nate his parents, his cries are to be ignored to prevent him from becoming tyrannical, difficult, wicked, and unmanageable.

and its concomitant epistemology. For instance, to teach a lesson in astronomy of immediate use to Emile, his teacher pretended that they were lost in a neighbour's woods. After examining the lie of shadows cast by trees in order to reorient himself, Emile learned an empirical lesson facilitated by his teacher which was of immediate practical utility to him and had no reference to abstract principles. In this lesson, the concern for the self that is also central to motivation in Rousseau was supplied by Emile's hunger and his desire to be home in time for lunch. Or again, rather than teaching world geography through maps, Emile will learn geography through his own observations by making a map of the area between the city where he lives and his father's country house. Rousseau exults: "See the difference there already is between your pupils' knowledge and mine's ignorance! They know maps, and he makes them" (*Émile*, 171). As for history, because words are known only in relation to things, Emile will not even know the word.

However, the single most serious consequence for education of Rousseau's philosophy is the assumption that there is a universal method, a kind of new philosopher's stone that provides a key to all that is needed and exercises absolute control over knowledge. Rousseau admits that Emile is largely ignorant but contends that he "has a mind that is universal not by its learning but by its faculty to acquire learning." That this theoretical dismissal of the other primary modes of thought is in practice impossible is evident even in Rousseau's *Emile*. Not only does Rousseau dogmatize throughout the work in a way forbidden by his pedagogy, but the vivid impression made by his elaboration of epicurean philosophy through the story of the education of a fictitious character is a brilliant exercise of literary rationality. The solicitude of the tutor for Emile, his righteous indignation at methods contrary to his own, the philosophy embedded in the compelling details of the life of Emile win over readers and draw them into the cosmos created by the author. The seductive power of Rousseau lies in the genius of his literary mind.

In a school controlled by the neo-epicurean method, students will miss everything that can be apprehended only through the other operations of the mind. They will be unaware of about nine tenths of what they might know, as Virginia Woolf says of the utilitarian Robinson Crusoe, hero of the only book allowed Emile because

Rousseau found in it a pattern for his philosophy.[14] They will not enter into the human and divine wisdom discerned through the modes of thought and the verbal reasoning of the liberal arts and sciences: on the one hand, through the well-furnished mind, sensibility to language, and convergent reasoning of Erasmus' students or of Cicero; and, on the other hand, through deductive reasoning from received abstract principles, from inherited ideas, and from rules of mathematics or grammar.

Indeed, not only modes of reasoning but important functions of the mind will be denied their legitimate use. The imagination will be associated with caprice and fantasy, with the undesirable passion of amour-propre; it will be suppressed as a distraction from the world of present utility. The imagination's magisterial role in the apprehension of invisible realities in the concrete both in literature and in religion will go unnoticed. In a similar reductionist approach, memory will be denied its important function in literary reasoning with its dependence on a well-furnished mind and its dictum that to retain words is to retain thought. Instead, the polyvalent literary use of language where thought and word are inseparable will be considered a dispensable, frivolous ornament, an impediment to the univocal use of words in connection to things. Education in such a school will resemble Emile's where the study of other languages is considered a waste of time, learning to read through traditional methods is considered foolish, and books have little relevance.

Incredible as it may seem that a theory rejecting most of the faculties and operations of the mind might dominate whole systems of education, yet such in fact is presently the case. Even papers written at institutes for research in education and government policy documents on education find their model in the empirical method as they take surveys and collect data but omit theoretical frameworks, principles, and logical argument. And in our classrooms Rousseau's spirit and empirical inductive method hold sway. The sciences and mathematics are estranged; languages, literature, and the arts are alienated from

---

14   Woolf says that in the utilitarian world of Crusoe, death does not exist, God does not exist, and nature exists only insomuch as it is useful or hostile to the protagonist. "He is so busy and has such an eye to the main chance that he notices only a tenth part of what is going on round him." Virginia Woolf, *The Second Common Reader* (New York: Harcourt Brace, 1986) 56.

their own principles. In the teaching of language where the usurpation by inductive reason has caused real hardship, its sovereign hold requires that language instruction forgoe its own self-understanding and its own methodology which include deductive reasoning from the rules established by the science of language; that is, grammar. It is on the field of grammar that the most hard-fought battles of method have been waged between antithetical modes of reasoning.

Papers from a conference for second language teachers in Britain in 1993 represent this stand-off as they evaluate the communicative method, a present-day application of Locke's idea of teaching language for communication. The papers illustrate how the resolute insistence on using only induction, a method associated with the physical sciences, affects the teaching of languages and forces the grammatical science of language to conform to its mode. One speaker at the conference reviewed two historical sources for the inductive teaching of languages: first, in seventeenth-century educational reform represented by Comenius' dogmatic slogan that percept must come before precept; and, secondly, in the Great Reform in Britain from 1880-1914. Although this twentieth-century proponent of the communicative method identified its sources only in the scientific method of the seventeenth-century reformers and their nineteenth-century counterparts, nonetheless its methodology is also permeated with the assumptions of Rousseau transmitted to nineteenth-century Europe especially through the Swiss model of Pestalozzi, the source noted by Matthew Arnold. Finally, the same speaker referred to the period following the 1960's and 1970's when the inductive method was again applied to languages after its interruption in Britain by the Leathes Report of 1918. This report, written by a Cambridge history don, faulted the inductive teaching of language as concentrating too much on the spoken language and on the teacher's rather than the student's contribution; he suggested that students' knowledge was superficial and inaccurate, and that, instead, the highest accuracy and scholarship should be cultivated to give modern languages their due estimation.

Several of the conference reports on classroom lessons illustrate what happens when verbal arts are taught solely through an inductive materialist epistemology. As in *Emile*, instruction is effected through physical things and the goal is in immediate practical utility. The functional aim of the communicative method is a kind of tourist-speak connected to popular, topical matter. In this instruction, the deductive reasoning of grammar is resolutely excluded as well as translation, a purely verbal exercise removed from things. Following the method of Rousseau's epistemology, teachers begin their lessons typically with physical things, resourcefully avoiding both translation and any initial reference to the rules of grammar. To teach the partitive articles, "du, de la, and des" (English: "some"), a French teacher began the class by distributing groceries that had been colour-coded to indicate gender. To teach the past tense, another teacher brought to the classroom a selection of objects from the nineteenth and from the twentieth centuries such as an old iron and an electric steam iron, a carpet beater and a miniature vacuum cleaner. Yet another teacher provided a dozen exercises in which words themselves were moved around physically like things: cut-out words which could be pegged on a clothesline to complete sentences, and words of sentences that the teacher had cut into jig-saw shapes which fit together only with adjectives in the right word order.

In this inductive teaching of language through things, memory is not connected to the literary use of language where words are inseparable from thought, where to learn a word is to acquire an idea, nor is memory connected to the imagination as it functions in literature. Since in the epistemology of this pedagogy memory is connected only to direct sense impressions, students learn especially through the aural sense rather than through written texts; their retention of the second language is based on varied multiple classroom repetitions of patterns of speech. Like Emile's teacher, the role of the modern teacher-facilitator is to contrive contexts that will lead students to discover for themselves through induction the idea or pattern that is to be learned. For example, through the fictional character of Béatrice, represented by a photo of a nineteenth-century woman, the past tense, "elle avait" ("she had"), is taught by associating her with the nineteenth-century objects distributed to students and this past tense is contrasted with the present tense, "nous avons" ("we have"), connected to the twentieth-century objects. Finally, using the only method of reasoning that is recognized, students were invited to draw a conclusion inductively regarding verb tenses and endings.

Because the discovery method through sense impressions associated with Baconian science determines entirely how language is to be taught, the lesson on the past tense not only follows the pattern of classification associated with science but is connected to Baconian utility. Students are asked to classify nineteenth and twentieth-century objects as "ancien" or "moderne"; they identify the utility of the items such as "faire le repassage" (to iron). Similarly, following the model of scientific investigation, their initial analyses of rules of grammar are to be considered provisional and to be followed by a further investigation of examples before more definite rules are reached. Even terms used to describe teaching methodology are related to utilitarian functionality: speaking and writing are referred to as production or producing language.

But, more gravely, as in Emile's discovery of the idea of refraction, the discovery of rules of language tends to remain immersed in the particular contexts of lessons without rising to the level of abstract understanding applicable to many other contexts. The structural nature of language, its rules and principles that are the luminous footfalls of thought and the keys to its use remain at best partially known. In the lesson on the past tense, students learn through repetition to use the phrase "elle avait" in the particular context of Béatrice and nineteenth-century objects but they are not taught the intelligible principles of the language: neither the name of the tense they are using nor its nature which distinguishes the imperfect tense from all other past tenses. The constraints of the context determine that "elle avait" is taught in isolation from all the other persons (je, tu, il, on, etc.) that comprise the paradigm of the imperfect tense of "avoir," illustrate clearly its pattern, and engender a mastery of it.

The strange premiss that language is to be learned only through one operation of the intellect, through discovery from sense impression, prevents any initial explicit explanation of the rules of language which are eschewed as abstractions removed from sense and as belonging to the enemy camp of deductive reasoning. Without a clear understanding of rules and principles, learning is protracted; students cannot transfer what they have learned in one context to another; they are deprived of the keys to language that lead to its accurate mastery through moving back and forth, first deductively from rule to context and then inductively from context to rule until rules are absorbed into the practice itself. The insistence on teaching languages through things rather than from rules and the conformity to the seventeenth-century slogan that percept must come before precept not only reduces language to what is merely physical, not only bars the translation that ensures understanding; it obstructs the sequential, cumulative instruction of language through grammar which leads to progressive mastery and makes of it a logical science or system. The severance of language instruction from literature is also a diminishment of the intellect. This separation means the complete neglect of the polyvalent literary use of words conveying literary reasoning with the interplay between opposites, synonyms, and cognates traditional to the methodology of language teaching. Both the free-ranging imagination engaged in literature's reasoning and the exactness required for an accurate reading of it are suppressed. Finally, as Arnold noted in the nineteenth century, the literary imagination is also excluded with its connection to the affections which delight and give us a glimpse in the concrete of the invisible interior world of humanity.

With the mind hobbled by a method meant for the empirical sciences, with the keys to understanding withheld by its exclusion of the explicit direct teaching of grammar, and operating in a distrust of the whole realm of language removed from physical things, language teaching can only fail. Although the key-note speaker at the British language conference referred to the "muddled failure to accept that grammar is central to language learning,"[15] nonetheless, the epistemological assumptions of the communicative method mean that any proposed changes have to remain within the same empirical paradigm. For example, like Rousseau's Emile whose learning was to be motivated by his own desire, the suggestion is made that teacher-training include techniques for negotiating with learners and regularly asking them "to set the pace and the direction of the grammar syllabus, making the approach far more 'learner driven'"(*Grammar*, 123). Or again, while recognizing both the need for future teachers to know grammar and the frustrations of good language students who want to know the principles of language, recommendations to remedy the situation all fall within the same disabling methodology of Emile's discovery method. Suggestions include: students' self-study of grammar; or their keeping of their own log in a journal of the "structures and contexts that they encounter, analyze, understand, and re-use" (*Grammar*, 83); or again, that the too-often neglected

---

15 *Grammar! A Conference Report*, ed. Lid King & Peter Boaks (London: Centre for Language Teaching and Research, 1994) 121. The remaining citations are from this report.

more able learners who may become future language teachers might explore patterns and principles as a treasure hunt which challenges pupils to collect examples and classify them. Like seventeenth-century reformers who promised that without grammar language would be learned quickly and easily, their twentieth-century counterparts connect learning language with fun. Independent learning is suggested for students through text-manipulation computer programs such as *Fun With Texts* which they could then adapt as exercises for use with their peers. Finally, as with other departments of learning where the discovery method has foundered, enormous compromises are made to accommodate its failure. For example, the suggestion is made that a distinction might be made between comprehension and production, that with less-able students teachers might use the second language and students their own. And overwhelmed teachers look elsewhere for help such as the proposal for grammar consciousness-raising in all classes across the curriculum.

The late twentieth-century conference of second language teachers shows the debilitating effect in elementary and secondary schools of their alignment with Baconian induction and Rousseauian philosophy. Nineteenth-century Oxford offers fertile ground for examining at the level of the university the effect of the increasingly exclusive dominance of Baconian induction in that period. In the course of the nineteenth century, heated debates raged on matters ranging from religious belief to teaching methodology: for example, on the advisability of lectures in the manner of German universities in contrast to the more personal Oxford tutorials associated with the humanities. Underlying the fiercely-fought battles on such subjects were fundamental differences regarding concepts of mind: for instance, between those who insisted on the sole validity of inductive reasoning and those like John Henry Newman and members of the Oxford Movement who insisted on the equal validity of personal convergent reasoning: the mode of literature, of religious reflection, and of all reasoning in concrete matters.

Mark Pattison, student at Oriel College during the 1830's, classics scholar, and Master of Lincoln College for thirty years, illustrates the effects of adherence to an inductive habit of mind as it took him on the path towards nineteenth-century philosophical liberalism. Like nineteenth-century utilitarianism, nineteenth-century liberalism aligned itself with science and progress and had inherited the empirical enlightenment's assumption that induction alone provided the criterion of truth. In the manner of Jeremy Bentham who considered that he applied to the moral world the experimental method applied by Bacon to the physical world,[16] Pattison believed philosophically that induction was the only mode of reasoning and he came to apply the same criterion of judgment to religious belief. However, in contrast to induction's discovery of impersonal necessary laws in the physical realm, in the indemonstrable area of religion induction led not to necessary laws but to private, individual conclusions and personal opinion. In accordance with the principle that all must draw their own conclusions, like other inductive reasoners in religion Pattison eventually reached a position of universal tolerance. And like other inductive reasoners, although tolerant of all religions the one thing he could not tolerate was any other way of knowing which effectively exluded points of view quite different from his own. The liberal or utilitarian reasoner could tolerate neither the *a priori* premises of deductive reasoning, nor the magisterial role of the imagination in religious belief, nor the exercise of convergent reasoning on this belief.

In his *Memoirs*, Pattison describes how during his formative years at Oriel his reading and re-reading of the *Elements* by Dugald Stewart of the Scottish common sense school of philosophy grounded him "in the principle of strictly applying the Baconian induction in psychology." Because this inductive reasoning is antithetical to deductive speculative thought with its assumed starting-points, he relates how in philosophy the strict application of Baconian induction as a principle saved him from "being led away by the gratuitous hypotheses and *a priori* constructions of Kant and the other German schools."[17] From Pattison's inductive perspective, adherence to the starting-points of deductive reasoning resting on received authority was slavish. Similarly, in regard to religion he refers to the heyday of the Oxford Movement with its "abject deference fostered by theological discussions for authority, whether of the Fathers, or the Church, or the Primitive Ages." In contrast to the inductive method associated with modern science and progress, he explains that this deference to authority is "incompatible with the free play of intellect which enlarges

---

16   Fredrick Rosen, *Classical Utilitarianism from Hume to Mill* (London & New York: Routledge, 2003) 177.

17   Mark Pattison, *Memoirs* (London: Macmillan, 1885) 129.

knowledge, creates science, and makes progress possible" (*Memoirs*, 238).

In the course of his lifetime, as Pattison rejected religious tradition and applied instead the empirical inductive criterion of judgment with its basis in personal experience, his religious opinions changed. In the eyes of his friends, he had moved from "High Anglicanism to Latitudinarianism [characterized by latitude in religious matters or tolerating free thought in religious questions], or Rationalism, or Unbelief." Pattison himself describes his religious opinions as an expansion towards "that highest development when all religions appear in their historical light, as efforts of the human spirit to come to an understanding of that Unseen Power whose pressure it feels, but whose motives are a riddle" (*Memoirs*, 327-8). In this accommodation of religion to inductive reasoning where belief is based on the criterion of one's own experience, the emphasis is on feeling rather than on knowledge of the Object of this feeling. In Pattison's conclusion, the pre-Christian approximates the post-Christian. He considered, for example, that the application of the study of Greek to reading the Greek Testament and the Greek Fathers, as Newman had done, was to side with the "enemies of humanism," with a church organization that had triumphed "over the wisdom and philosophy of the Hellenic world" (*Memoirs*, 96).

Similarly, the type of book approved for reading at the University was redefined according to the same criterion which considered texts on the subject of religion irrelevant to the progress of a scientific age and contrary to its *organon* or method. Pattison relates that he was a member of a liberal board of examiners that succeeded in removing from a list of texts Bishop Joseph Butler's previously influential book, the *Analogy of Religion to the Constitution and Course of Nature* (1736). Although he admired the logic of its analogical reasoning, he explains that the *Analogy* diverted the mind from the great outlines of scientific and philosophical thought, and fastened it "upon petty considerations, being, in this respect, the converse of Bacon's *Novum Organum*."[18]

Finally, Pattison characterizes rightly the modern difficulty of accommodating inductive reasoning not only with deductive thought

---

18   *Memoirs*, 135. Pattison also refers to the "heavy controversies" with his tutor in 1835 over sermons on the religious doctrine of conscience which his Dugald Stewart training would by no means allow him to accept.

but also with the personal mode of convergent reasoning through which we apprehend truth in the concrete or the real. He wrote that although he was reared on the strict line of the inductive philosophy and as a disciple of Bacon, Locke, and Dugald Stewart, nonetheless around 1837 for a while he fell under the influence of the realistic philosophy of Coleridge. He says that he had either been seduced from his principles, "or from want of clear-headedness, had endeavoured to accommodate them to ideas with which they really could not amalgamate." As Pattison indicates, this battle between methods and their tendency towards mutual exclusion meant that at Oxford since 1830 there "has been among us an ebb and flow" of nominalistic logic, represented typically in Mill's work on induction, and of *a priori* logic which Pattison links with sacerdotalism. He observes that in turn one or another type of logic prevailed or asserted itself over the opposite system "which it denounces as false" (*Memoirs*, 164-5). The partisan feeling engendered by habituation to a particular logic or mode of thought is registered in this liberal humanist's description of the end of the Oxford Movement with its religious concerns and Newman's departure from Oxford in 1845 as a dissipation of the darkness and an instant letting in of the light.

Mark Pattison's autobiographical account illustrates the danger of a seduction of mind through immersion in a single vein of philosophy in one's formative years without the counterbalance of other schools of philosophy. Like Rousseau, Pattison's school conflates philosophy with a method, thereby excluding all other methods with their own antithetical or different starting-points. Finally, as Pattison indicates, like any other dominant philosophy this philosophy with its inductive logic had the power to determine the ethos and direction of an educational institution.

For his part, Newman recognized quite simply that methods themselves are starting-points and that each has its own specific task. All are legitimate within their own proper spheres but are ineffectual or damaging when they encroach on the realm of other methods where a different instrument of thought is required. Because Newman was acutely aware of the imperial pressures and factious feuds described by Pattison, he became an arbiter of method in his own period, defending the modes of reason whose credibility was undermined by inductive reasoning's monopoly on thought. In *The Idea of a University* he championed liberal learning for its cultivation of the mind both through literature and through theoretical deductive reasoning. He spent his life articulating how in fact the mind operates in its apprehension of religious belief, a domain where empirical induction can only be ineffectual.

In his own day, Newman was a spokesperson for reason under siege; he remains so in our own time when we are similarly besieged.

2

ARISTOTLE'S *POETICS* AND
THE NATURE OF LITERARY
RATIONALITY

In his seventeenth-century survey of learning, Francis Bacon commented that playacting, which can influence audiences towards either discipline or corruption, had in modern times come to be considered largely a toy; by contrast, in antiquity communal performances of the poetic dramas had educated men's minds to virtue. The influence and power of poetry in ancient Greece is attested by its place both in education and at festivals. In Greece, at the fountainhead of western liberal learning, the education of youth had been at first through epic poetry. Homer's *Iliad* and *Odyssey* had formed young minds, inspiring them to chivalry and courageous deeds; at the same time, through their immersion in poetry Greek youths were exercised in the mode of reasoning of literature. Then, in the fifth century as the poetic drama evolved, the great Greek tragedians educated the audiences gathered in amphitheatres for festivals. Their plays spoke not only to justice, fortitude, piety, and courage, but also about the irresolvable, irreconcilable complexities of life, about single-minded stances that recoil on the individual, and of the connection between communal and individual suffering. At the same time, like the epic poetry of Homer the incomparable plays of Aeschylus, Sophocles, and Euripides exercised audiences in the instrument of literary reasoning, the kind of reasoning we most commonly use in the contingent realities and practical decisions of our own daily lives.

The first great age of tragedy in the fifth century BCE, like its second flourishing in the Shakespearian moment in Renaissance England, was at the threshold of a great new age of scientific reasoning. The tragic moment in Greece developed just at that point when scientific reasoning dealing logically and explicitly with abstract universals was emerging from religious and literary thought where universals are embedded in the concrete.[1] In the pre-scientific era when education was through poetry, the habit of mind of poetry and the habit of mind of religion had coincided in a union of the human and divine, the province of literary reasoning as described by Cicero. In Homer's works, human action and motive were not dissociated from the divine; help came for the hero from protective presiding deities. Similarly, in the tensions of poetic tragedy mythical truth is inextricably connected to the conflicting claims and partial human knowledge that plague the characters. The religious inclusiveness of mythical thought balances "forces of a natural and at the same time numinous order, which conflict mutually, and from whose incessant conflict life continually emerges."[2] Contradictory and numinous life forces like Aphrodite, as the nature-force of love, and Hera, as the social force of family order, were both right, and their conflict was also right in an order where all is divine and life "persists as a supra-intelligible whole." In this mythical mode, people lived their lives in attentive reference to figures and legends handed down by religious tradition and perceived as working, not only in the constellations, in the rhythms of growth, but also in mankind's own being, in the instinctive life, and in the passions of the mind; the order of family and community life "results from their operation and at the same time affords a protection against their tyranny."[3]

The abstract speculative mode of scientific reasoning had been emerging gradually from this religious and literary mode of thought. During a period of equipoise between scientific and literary rationality,

---

1 Jean-Pierre Vernant refers the tragic moment to the development of law and its categories for the legal responsibility of the individual. In this new direction emerging from a religious and collective ethos, he maintains that tragedy is a particular stage in the development of the categories of agent and action and of the modern sense of self and will. Tragic man lives on both planes simultaneously. Jean-Pierre Vernant and Pierre Vidal-Naguet, *Tragedy and Myth in Ancient Greece* (Sussex: Harvester P., 1981) 39-47. This book was originally published as *Mythe et Tragédie en Grèce Ancienne* (Paris: Editions Maspero, 1972).

2 Romano Guardini, *The Death of Socrates* (Cleveland: Meridian Books, 1962) 10.

3 Ibid.,11, 10-15.

the practitioners of the new mode of reasoning drew on the wisdom of religious and literary tradition, and, unlike the modern progressive view of science, considered that the ground and origin of truth lay in the most ancient depths of traditions known only to poet and priest. As a complement to religious and literary tradition, their investigations of moral conduct sought norms and guarantees for life through contemplating phenomena in order to define their nature explicitly and give them their proper due.

We find an emblem of this era of scientific reasoning rooted in religion and poetry in the figure of Socrates (469-399 B.C.E.) whose dialectical quest for abstract universal principles concerning right conduct was prompted by a pronouncement made by the oracle of Apollo at Delphi.[4] The large questions about the human condition such as "what is piety? what is justice? what is courage?" were asked in a concrete, literary way in the tragedies; Socrates' efforts were directed to locating answers to these moral questions through universals or definitions. It is at this moment of balance between speculative scientific reasoning with concrete literary and religious thought that the classical tragedies flourished: of Aeschylus (525-456 B.C.E.), Sophocles (ca. 496-406 B.C.E.), and Euripides (ca. 480-407 B.C.E.). This temporary equipoise in the very foundations of reasoning underlies the powerful tragic tension where human initiative is weighed in the balance of overarching divinity and of time that reveals all.

By the end of this unparalleled era of poetic tragedy, a division had already begun to open between scientific reasoning and literary rationality. The great dynasty of philosophy that began with Socrates had continued in Plato (b 427 BCE) whose mistrust of poetry led his pupil, Aristotle, to analyze and vindicate it. Aristotle (384-322 BCE) was the most completely rounded of the philosophers; he was not only a philosopher and man of Letters but, as a biologist, was also

---

4   The oracle had informed an Athenian named Chaerephon that "no man is wiser than Socrates." Because Socrates knew both that Apollo could not lie and that he himself possessed no wisdom, he set out to find a wiser man. However, after questioning many from all classes of society about piety and justice and other virtues of right conduct, after hearing a mass of contradictory opinions, feeble examples, and convenient shreds of myth, he came to the conclusion that he was indeed the wisest of men, because, unlike others, he admitted his ignorance. *The Reader's Companion to World Literature* (Toronto: Mentor Books, 1962) 416-18.

an empirical scientist. His extant treatises range through subjects that include the divine, the human, and the physical world: for example, the history of animals and their classifications; rhetoric and poetry; politics, ethics, and our various modes of reasoning. The legacy in thought bequeathed by Aristotle to posterity has prompted tributes diversely from those eminent in empirical science, theology and philosophy, and poetry. In the nineteenth century, Darwin remarked that modern biologists like Linneus and Cuvier had been his gods but were only like children in comparison to old Aristotle. In the great medieval era of speculative theology, the Moslem, Averroës, the Jew, Maimonides, and the Christian, St. Thomas Aquinas, all found through Aristotle's philosophy a means of giving coherent expression to their faith. And the great Italian poet, Dante Alighieri (1265-1321), followed Aristotle's cosmology in his *Divine Comedy* and paid tribute to him as master of those who know.

This master of those who know took as his domain knowledge from all its broad areas according to the methods of reasoning proper to them. In the twenty years that Aristotle spent at Plato's Academy (367-348 BCE), he absorbed and later came to modify the luminous speculative thought of his master with its grounding in intelligible ideas. Then after Plato's death he left Athens for about twelve years, spending much of his time in biological observations on the island of Lesbos. When at nearly fifty years of age he returned to Athens in 335 BCE to open the Lyceum as his own school of philosophy, his teaching and research included simultaneously investigations into biology, speculative reasoning, and literature.

This inclusiveness of Aristotle, the breadth and depth of his philosophy, and his religious belief equipped him for his critical work on the Greek poetic dramas with their tensions between the divine and human and their specifically literary mode of reasoning. In the newly developing quarrel between modes of reasoning, Aristotle was an arbiter of methods. He understood from his own broad first-hand experience that different areas of inquiry require different intellectual instruments simply because these instruments perform different tasks. For example, he recognized the folly of expecting the method of the exact sciences to operate in the deliberative suasory matters of government where complex issues are understood instead through the kind of literary rationality exercised by Cicero. In this beginning of what was to be an almost continuous quarrel between modes of reasoning, Aristotle deemed that a liberal education should prepare a person not only to understand the principles of things but, equally importantly, to recognize such inappropriate applications of methods to domains where they are simply ineffectual.

As an arbiter between quarrelling methods, none could have been better prepared than Aristotle. His breadth rested on inclusive philosophical foundations that recognized not only the material world but intelligibility in matter. Like our own era, Aristotle's knew well the pull of materialist philosophy. In his survey of previous philosophers, Aristotle reviewed thinkers who for two hundred years before him had wrestled with problems of material or physical change, maturing around 420 BCE in the atomist system of Democritus. Although Epicurus (341-270 BCE) in the generation that followed Aristotle embraced Democritus' materialist assumptions, Aristotle believed that civilization had advanced through a shift in philosophy from material causes towards an inclusion of formal causes. For Aristotle, the *eidos* or the specific form in combination with matter makes something what it is. For example, a tree is composed both of wood and its form or "treeness" without which its matter would remain unintelligible. Through sense observation, physical science analyzes this form into its constituent parts, such as its bark, leaves, etc., but this science is only part of the structure of reality.[5] In Aristotle's philosophy the soul (psyche) or life principle was the form of the body and, analogically, this life principle informed all organic matter. As well as material and formal causes, Aristotle also considered final causes, or ends, and the efficient causes which initiate change. In accordance with his materialist philosophy, Epicurus would claim that both body and mind were mortal; Aristotle maintained that human reason shared in the divine immortality of pure spirit as demonstrated on those occasions when the mind was not directly dependent on sense.

From a starting-point that assumed an intelligibly coherent world, Aristotle probed intellectually every aspect of life: the divine, the physical world, and the specifically human. Rather than suppress religion as the Epicureans would do, he embraced it. In divine philosophy, in place of the licentious Greek deities who in the wider Mediterranean world were local only to Greece, Aristotle turned his

---

5   Cf. Martin Ostwald's notes, *Nicomachean Ethics* (Indianapolis and New York: Bobbs-Merrill, 1962) 305.

attention to the new astral religion. This religion of the stars whose authority applied to all was grounded in a previously undreamed order of the heavens where a complex explanation had been found even for the apparently irregular movement of the planets (Greek: vagabonds). In the geometric model of the universe imagined by the Greeks, an advance even greater than that made by Copernicus, the heavens were admired not only for their majesty but were invested with a new, rich, intellectual and emotional content that assumed an intimacy between the deities and the work of their hands. The intelligible universe was given the name of cosmos which in its analogical everyday sense signified order, regularity, decency, comeliness.

Aristotle also had the clear observant eye of the biologist. In his study of natural philosophy on the island of Lesbos, Aristotle was surrounded by the divine spectacle of nature in the marvels of earth and sea. Here, especially in the island's lagoon, he undertook pioneering investigations of plant and animal life through the empirical inductive method of sense observation. Of the five hundred biological species eventually recorded, Aristotle himself is said to have dissected fifty. His multiple classifications included material causality, such as creatures that are bloodless or that have blood, and functions, such as the liver as found in various species. In his biological study Aristotle did not limit himself to inquiry through observation but also considered what modern science would later reject as irrelevant; that is, purposive direction in "nature at her constructive task,"[6] such as the end of the acorn in becoming an oak. In these ends or final causes of things in nature Arisotle found the equivalent of beauty in art.

Aristotle's work on natural philosophy was collected into the *Physics* by a later editor; a dozen other treatises collected similarly were given the title of *Metaphysics* (Greek: *meta*, after) to indicate that they were to be read after the *Physics*. The *Metaphysics* stand in an important relationship to the *Physics*. Aristotle recognized both the efficacy and the proper limitations of the method of physical observation and of materialist philosophy which would limit understanding to a single method of inquiry. Limiting all reason to its method as the atomists had done reduces metaphysics to physics and eliminates metaphysic's own function which, for Aristotle, meant discerning form in its

---

6   Cited by Benjamin Farrington, *Aristotle: Founder of the Scientific Philoso-phy* (New York: Praeger P., 1969) 38.

relation to matter: from nearly formless matter at one end to pure form or the Unmoved Mover which energizes the whole of existence and the process of change as each thing struggles to attain its complete or perfect form. In his departure from Plato's contention that forms or ideas exist in another world apart from material things, he maintained that form is within material things and it is in the union of form and matter that reality is found.

In another dimension to his work, in the *Organon* or *Instrument* Aristotle discusses what came to be called logic or discourse, the verbal paths that reason follows in knowing. The titles of the treatises on this subject indicate the range of the reasoning that he analyzes. For example, in the *Analytica posteriora* and *Analytica priora* we find analyses of the *a priori* and *a posteriori* reasoning that according to Mark Pattison ruled in turn, each to the exclusion of the other, in the nineteenth-century battle of methods at Oxford. In *Sophistici elenchi* (*Sophistical Refutations*), he exposes fallacious reasoning such as circular arguments, and in the *Topica*, he gives suggestions useful in debates that will establish or refute a given thesis, elucidating general logical laws or rules.

Finally, a fourth group of Aristotle's treatises deal with practical philosophy and literature. That is, in addition to empirical and philosophical scientific reasoning, Aristotle's corpus also deals with the genus of reasoning in those matters regarding practice and conduct whose orientation towards the particular resides outside science's narrow exactness. His writings on this kind of reasoning include ethics and politics, rhetoric's deliberations on the fray of life, and literature's reflections of this fray.

Only fragments cited by later authors now remain of Aristotle's own literary work where his personal voice was originally heard in dialogues, letters, and poetry. However, its excellence is suggested in Cicero's reference to Aristotle's style as a river of gold. In spite of the loss of his work, Aristotle's esteem for poetry is nonetheless amply evident. As court tutor to the adolescent Alexander who was destined for epic conquests, Aristotle gave a prominent place to poetry in the Greek tradition of schooling youth in Homer. The deeds and character of Achilles in the *Iliad* inspired Alexander as he set forth on his conquests in the Oriental wars. Aristotle's research included not only an assemblage of the various types of constitutions, not only a compilation of the victors at the great national games, but also a collection of the official records of the plays produced at the annual dramatic competitions at the Athenian spring festival of Dionysius. When Aristotle returned to Athens to establish the Lyceum, he gave classes not only in philosophy for his more able students but also in Letters. The extent of his own knowledge of the plays is indicated internally in the *Poetics* which treats especially of poetic tragedy.

Like in our modern era when the humanities have had to defend their legitimacy in response to philosophic concepts of mind that have rejected the reasoning of literature, Aristotle countered in the *Poetics* Plato's mistrust of poetry and of the relation in poetry between the reason and the passions. In the eighteenth century, Rousseau considered that through obedience to the necessary law of things the faculties were rightly ordered, the superfluous imagination suppressed, and selfish desires controlled. In a similar fear of the passions as selfish, Plato maintained that in the right ordering of our faculties reason must be the master of passion. In his *Republic*, the danger of selfish passion in the individual was to be eliminated in the small class of Guardians who controlled his ideal City by putting their wives, children, and property in common. Plato's objection to the plays performed for the general populace of Athens was based on a similar distrust of the emotions both for the individual and for the *polis*. The poets unleashed emotions like lust and anger and the performance of dramas for the undisciplined crowds was a threat to the rule of law.

Plato provides an early example of how habituation to one mode of reasoning in great men diminishes their appreciation or their capacity for other modes of reasoning. Unlike Socrates who believed that the scientific knowledge of virtues like piety and justice would lead to right conduct, or that to know what was right was to do what was right, Plato saw that while we may know what is good, we do what is wrong; when confronted with actual, concrete situations, the mind's theoretical knowledge risks being overwhelmed by the passions. However, rather than acknowledging that practical conduct as modelled in the dramas involves a different habit of mind than the impersonal deductions and abstractions of philosophy, Plato would banish poetry as a threatening, corrupting influence.

Aristotle's defence of poetry in the *Poetics* proceeds in part from his analysis of the different relation between the emotions and reason in those areas that lie outside of science's exactness. He maintained that in these areas feelings work integrally with reason. In our ethical formation, from childhood emotions were to be directed to the right objects. Through this habituation of the feelings to the right objects, the feelings become a guide to virtue as reason makes its judgements and decisions. As desiderative deliberation, ethics, rhetoric, and poetry all required a balance of desire and thought. Like music which habituates the listener to feel emotions in the right way towards the right object (*Politics*, viii; 1340a), the drama directs the feelings of the audience. Aristotle argued that the emotions aroused by the great public performances of the tragedies were not to be feared, as Plato claimed, because tragedy's affective function was to chasten the audience through exciting pity and terror.

Again, in answer to the objections of his teacher, Aristotle also argued that the poetic drama, like philosophy, offered an education in universals or ideas. Plato maintained that ideas or universals (*katholou*) had a substantive eternal existence, a reality separate from their imperfect imitation in particular perishable things. In poetry's imitation of life, which in turn was an imperfect imitation of ideas, poetry was an imitation of an imitation twice removed from the true reality of the world of ideas. Aristotle recognized that ideas do not exist independently from the world of nature but are aspects abstracted from the sensible things which they inform. In the drama, universals are embodied in the plots which are the soul or life force of plays. Philosophy is not alone in teaching universals; poetry not only teaches universals but makes them accessible to the general populace. As an imitation of life, poetry is not to be regarded as twice removed from the truly real. Rather, poetry's imitation of life is simply natural; from childhood imitation is the way we learn.

In the *Poetics*, there is no trace of this parrying with opinion, of Aristotle's confrontation with difficulties and formulation of preliminary opinions, or his assessments of the views of his predecessors like Plato. Like most of his extant works, the *Poetics* are lecture notes from his teaching and research at the Lyceum, the school he established next to a wrestling school on a plot of ground consecrated to the service of the god Apollo Lyceus. Instead of socratic conversation, in the clipped, sometimes fragmentary form of these notes we find a meeting of poetry and science as Aristotle subjects the plays to scientific analysis and lays bare the nature of tragedy.

As he proceeds, he will describe tragedy as a rational construct as legitimate in its own right as the scientific reasoning of philosophy in conveying the perennial truths about our humanity; unlike philosophy, these truths are embedded in a concrete imitation of life rather than expressed abstractly. Because it has been natural to us since childhood to learn through imitation, tragedy not only teaches us but also delights us. Like other species of the practical intellect, tragedy affords a way of knowing life in the concrete through grasping things as an organic whole, including the tensile unity of opposites and the mutability of unfolding reversals in fortune. The very language of tragedy reflects literature's rationality in the personal voice of characters where in the mutual movement of feeling and thought decisions are made and responses registered. Similarly, the audience is exercised in this literary rationality as they respond with heart and mind to the human truths recognized as the play unfolds before them. The great arbiter of method and master of those who know begins his lucid analysis of literary rationality in the clear language of the scientist examining underlying structures as he announces his purpose to investigate the nature of poetry:

> Let us discuss the art of poetry in general and its species -- the effect which each species of poetry has and the correct way to construct plots ..., as well as the number and nature of its component parts, and any other questions that arise within the same field of enquiry. We should begin, as is natural, by taking first principles first.[7]

In his brief history of the development of the genre of poetic tragedy, Aristotle writes in the manner of the biologist as he describes the life-cycle of tragedy from its origin in improvisation through "many transformations" to its completion when "tragedy came to rest, because it had attained its natural state" (*Poetics*, 3.3; 49a). But when the scientist turns his attention to the study of the tragedies to see what is common to them all, his subject-matter is very different from the fixed objects of natural science; the subject-matter of tragedy belongs to the realm of literature which Isocrates (436-338 BCE) claimed to be the best means of education because of its connection to complex, contingent realities in the ordinary, shifting situations of life. In the century following the first performances of the great tragedies, Aristotle lists in order of importance the headings under which he

---

7   *Aristotle Poetics*, trans. and intro., Malcolm Heath (London: Penguin, 1996) 3 (1; 47a). All subsequent citations from the *Poetics* are from this edition.

will examine them: plot (*mythos*), character, the character's reasoning, diction, melody, and spectacle. However, underlying the first three important divisions which Aristotle examines at greatest length is the idea of the *logos*, a Greek word signifying both reason and word as inseparably one. Aristotle's analysis of poetry encourages poetry to be considered, first, as a legitimate exercise of reasoning and, secondly, as the verbal expression of this thought.

The complex human subject-matter of the tragedies can be evoked only through the literary mode of thought rather than through scientific reasoning. The authors of the tragedies, as we have seen, portrayed the fray of life where, as in the Greek myths, contradictory life-forces were engaged in conflict. In turning to the analysis of tragedy, Aristotle directed his attention to the world of human lives caught in irreconcilable claims: duty to close family ties in conflict with duty to the city-state or with duty to the gods. In Aeschylus' *Agamemnon*, a father agrees to the sacrifice of his own daughter, Iphigenia, for the sake of the state as the Greek ships wait for winds to sail for Troy. In Sophocles' *Antigone* (441 BCE), King Creon single-mindedly supports the civic law which denies the rite of burial to Antigone's brother because he is a traitor. Creon maintains that the gods support civic virtue. Antigone, daughter of Oedipus, insists on the primacy of family ties and the ultimate importance of religious rites although their fulfillment violates the highest law of the state. In *The Bacchae* (405 BCE) of Euripides, King Pentheus gives reasons to resist the claims of the god, Dionysius, the antithesis of his own kind of rationality and god not only of the vineyard but also god of the theatre and of change; Pentheus' single-minded resistance recoils upon him as he is torn apart by the female followers of the god whose numbers include his own mother. This complex, various, multi-leveled world of Greek tragedy enacts before our eyes a living mode of thought, the mode of probability and literary reasoning which encompasses the complexities of life where choices are made and the unforeseeable looms in the background.

In his analysis of poetic tragedy, Aristotle makes clear from the beginning that poetry is a legitimate mode of knowing. Poetry offers a personal way of knowing that both delights and teaches audiences through its concrete models of life. He says that tragedy imitates life and that our recognition of what is imitated teaches us and engages our feelings. Although the tragedies represent extremes, Aristotle states at the outset of the *Poetics* that, like other arts, tragedy is by nature mimetic (3.1; 48b) and what tragedy imitates (*mimesis*, i.e. imitation) is life. Tragedy provides a concrete model of human action. Aristotle tells us variously that tragedy is an imitation of "actions and of life" (4.3; 50a); that tragedy "is an imitation of an action that is admirable ..." (4.1; 49b); that tragedy imitates people who are better than our contemporaries (2.2; 48a). He makes clear that poetry provides a way of knowing through imitation which affords pleasure; the *mimesis* of life in poetry delights us because of the way it teaches us.

In this first, penetrating criticism of poetry, Aristotle lays the groundwork for his many humanist successors who, like Cicero, understood poetry as teaching, delighting, and moving (*docere, delectare, movere*). Significantly, the great arbiter of method uses the same argument for his defence of poetry's reasoning as for his defence of speculative thought in the *Nicomachean Ethics*; both modes of understanding are justified because both are natural to us and, because they are natural to us both are enjoyable. Aristotle observes that "the universal pleasure in imitation" is as natural to us as learning our earliest lessons from childhood through imitation. Although both speculative reasoning and poetry fulfil our human need to understand, unlike the difficult abstractions of philosophy poetry is a concrete vehicle for understanding through imitation that is accessible not just to intellectuals, but to all. Aristotle also makes clear that the delight of the audience in the poetic drama is not the pleasure of distracting entertainment but a pleasure comparable to that of the philosopher's understanding of perennial truths about our humanity. In a comparison of poetry to the visual arts, he refers to the delight we take in the most accurate possible images of objects which would in themselves cause distress if we actually saw them. He writes:

> understanding is extremely pleasant, not just for philosophers but for others too in the same way, despite their limited capacity for it. This is the reason why people take delight in seeing images; what happens is that as they view them they come to understand and work out what each thing is (e.g. 'This is so-and-so') (3.1; 48b).

Poetry, then, affords an engaging literary kind of knowing through concrete models that is more generally accessible than the knowledge of life expressed in philosophy.

In the poetic drama, Aristotle maintains that the rationality of literature lies especially in the poet's intelligible connections of the plot. As he continues his analysis of the nature of poetry through an examination of the component parts of tragedy, he emphasizes how a drama which is concrete is yet made into an intelligible, literary way of knowing for the audience through the dramatist's art of plot construction. He tells us that tragic dramatists are "serious-minded people" (3.2; 48b) who in their *mimesis* of human action do not record actual, particular events of life, like historians; instead, they selectively shape or structure the facts of their material, even in their use of traditional stories where some characters already have names. Aristotle accorded primary importance to this structuring of events in the plot (*mythos*) as the form or soul of tragedy because the sequential, causally-connected organization of the whole gives intelligibility to the multilayered complex of actions and events.

Tragedy is about human action, but it is the function of the dramatist to structure the action in such a way that it becomes an experience of the universal for the audience. The intelligible coherence of particulars which makes poetry "more philosophical and more serious than history" (5.5),[8] is based on the only two possible modes of making connections in reasoning; that is, through "probability or necessity," the broad divisions of reality demarcated by Aristotle in Book vi of the *Nicomachean Ethics*. This principle of connection in plots through probability or necessity makes a play consistent and plausible to an audience through the two primary ways we know: either through a sequence of events that is unchangable or necessary, that is, of events

---

8   Aristotle states: "Poetry tends to express universals, and history particulars." (5.5; 51b). However, in the period of Sophocles, Euripides, and Socrates, Thucydides and Herodotus were establishing history as a discipline. As observed in *Cunning Intelligence in Greek Culture and Society*, for Thucydides history was not simply a collective memory of past actions but aims at a fuller understanding of the present and foresight concerning the future. Marcel Detienne and Jean-Pierre Vernant, *Cunning Intelligence in Greek Culture and Society* (Paris: Flammarion, 1974) 315.

Stephen Halliwell refers to Aristotle's view of the capacity of poetry to provide a structure of meaning which directed "the mind from particulars to objects of higher significance." Poetry through *mimesis* embodies its material and through character, action, and vividness of detail signifies universals. *Aristotle's Poetics* (London: Duckworth, 1986) 136-7.

which do not admit of being other than they are; or through a sequence of events that are probable and which do admit of being other than they are. The poet's structure of meaning in plot engages both the scientific and non-scientific or probable way of knowing

In his argument that literature, like philosophy, is a pathway to perennial truths, Aristotle suggests how reason is embedded in the concrete as the drama unfolds. He insists again and again that in plot, "the first and most important part of tragedy" (5; 50b), actions should occur in accordance with probability or necessity. The length or magnitude of a play is determined by the "series of events occurring sequentially in accordance with probability or necessity ..." (5.2; 51a). The dramatist's selection of a single action which gives unity to a play is exemplified in Homer's exclusion of events in the *Odyssey* because one event "did not make the occurrence of the other necessary or probable" (5.3; 51a). When Aristotle contrasts history's expression of particulars with poetry's "tendency to express universals," he explains that the poet does not say what *"has* happened," but "the kind of thing that *would* happen, i.e. what is possible in accordance with probability or necessity" (5.5; 51a). "The *universal,*" he tells us, "is the kind of speech or action which is consonant with a person of a given kind in accordance with probability or necessity" (5.5; 51b). Again, in his discussion of the species and components of plot, he suggests the importance of intelligible connection. He observes that the feeling of fear and pity experienced by the audience will be more astonishing when there is a sense of causal sequence and purposive action:

> even chance events are found most astonishing when they appear to have happened as if for a purpose -- as, for example, the statue of Mitys in Argos killed the man who was responsible for Mitys' death by falling on top of him as he was looking at it. Things like that are not thought to occur at random. So inevitably plots of this kind will be better (6.1; 52a).

And he claims that tragic reversal and recognition involved in the change of fortune in complex plots "must arise from the actual structure of the plot, so that they come about as a result of what has happened before, out of necessity or in accordance with probability" (6.2; 52c).[9]

---

9   In "The Psychology of Aristotelian Tragedy," Amélie Oksenberg Rorty
     suggests three ways in which "a plot connects the incidents that compose

In his observations on literary rationality in the connections of plot, Aristotle finds common ground with his analysis of organic life as a biologist. Like in his part-whole analysis of animals in *De Partibus animalium*, the various parts of the plot must be taken in as a whole. In the mode of reasoning typical of literature, connections converge from various quarters towards a universal understood through the relation of the various parts to the whole. In other words, Aristotle emphasizes a fact important to all literary interpretation which sees a work integrally as a whole rather than selectively seeking out a point to prove. He writes that the causal connections in tragedy where one thing comes about as a result of what happened before make the drama an indivisible, complex unity.

Aristotle begins his discussion of the basic concepts of the plot with reference to tragedy's completeness; tragedy is an "imitation of a complete, i.e. whole, action of a certain magnitude." He states: "Well-constructed plots should therefore not begin or end at any arbitrary point."[10] Similarly, in his comments on magnitude, Aristotle indicates the importance of an audience being able to take in the various parts of the play as a whole. He writes that plots "should have a certain length, and this should be such as can readily be held in memory."

---

it." The plot may be connected causally with one event happening because of another. It may be connected thematically through the texture of repetition or through ironic reversal. For example, "Antigone lived to bury her dead: her punishment was to be buried alive. But since she deliberately did what she knew to be punishable by death, she took her own life in the tomb where Creon had condemned her." Similarly, Oedipus was blind to his real identity, but blinded himself when he discovered who he was. The third way a plot connects incidents is "by exhibiting the connections between the protagonist's character, his thought and his actions." Thus Oedipus "revealed himself kingly in all that he did, in all his actions: in the images of his bold speech, in the large scope of his thoughts ...." *Essays on Aristotle's Poetics*, ed. Amélie Oksenberg Rorty (Oxford: Princeton U.P., 1992) 8-9.

10   In Aristotle's well-known passage on the connected structure of a tragedy, he writes that as a whole, a tragedy has a beginning, a middle, and an end. The beginning does not follow necessarily from anything else, but some second thing naturally exists or occurs after it. Conversely, an *end* is that which does itself naturally follow from something else, either necessarily or in general, but there is nothing else after it. A *middle* is that which itself comes after something else, and some other thing comes after it (5.1; 50b).

Again the biologist is evident as he observes that a play that is too short is like a living organism that is excessively small and confuses observation. A play that is too long is like an organism that is too large to take in because "the observation is then not simultaneous, and the observers find that the sense of unity and wholeness is lost from their observation, (e.g. if there were an animal a thousand miles long)" (5.2; 51a).

It is especially in the relation of its particular, concrete parts to the whole that the mode of understanding particular to tragedy and to all literature differs from abstract philosophic reasoning. Tragedy is not philosophic in the same way as a scientific abstraction from particulars that can exist in its own right. Rather, it is a concrete unity understood through the relation of its several, particular parts. As Cicero observed of rhetorical reasoning, in this concrete unity of the poetic tragedy no part is dispensable. The fine-tuned relation of various parts does not allow for the exclusion of any part without damaging the whole or for the transposition of any part without damaging the intelligible, causal sequence. Aristotle observes that tragedy is like a "living organism or any other entity composed of parts" possessed in proper order and the right magnitude (5.2; 50b). He objects to defective, episodic plots in which "the sequence of episodes is neither necessary nor probable" and to poets who showcase actors "for competitive display" by drawing out "the plot beyond its potential, and are often forced to distort the sequence" (5.6; 51b). But most importantly, he remarks that plot imitates "a single, unified action -- and one that is also a whole:" its "structure of the various sections of the events must be such that the transposition or removal of any one section dislocates and changes the whole. If the presence or absence of something has no discernible effect, it is not a part of the whole" (5.4; 51a).

This importance to the whole of every part indicated by Aristotle underscores a second important distinction between literary reasoning and scientific rationality which depends on single abstractions; that is, in literature's essential inclusion of the unique and of particular differences. Because scientific rationality demonstrates the sameness of things according to a single aspect, it can use an indeterminate number of particulars as proof of the soundness of a principle. Tragedy, on the other hand, is constructed around differences where particular parts cannot be removed from the whole because their differences are constitutive of the whole. Plot is ranked first in importance because in the tragic dimension of life enacted in the drama, we do not act merely by implementing scientific or universal principles with the certainty of expected results but are affected by other people with different aims, by unexpected events both for better or for worse, and by revelations of divine significance. Tragedy deals not with the scientifically controllable and static but with the immediate, the complex, the conflicting, and the changing where all particulars must be heeded. The arc of the plot holds in tensile unity a world of differences and multiple facets which are subject to change: irreconcilable, conflicting claims; accountable human action and undeserved human suffering; time-bound human plodding seen finally in the light of divine knowledge; good fortune in the process of its transformation into its opposite.

Indeed, radical change is intrinsic to the complication of the plot described by Aristotle as "everything from the beginning up to and including the section which immediately precedes the change to good fortune or bad fortune" (8.5; 55b). After the reversal in fortune, which involves "a change to the opposite in the actions being performed" (6.3; 52a), the various strands become unraveled (*lusis*) in the resolution. Two plays are taken as examples of the tragic change to opposite fortune through the disclosure of unexpected aspects and unanticipated events:

> in the *Oedipus* someone came to give Oedipus good news and free him from his fear with regard to his mother, but by disclosing Oedipus' identity he brought about the opposite result; and in the *Lynceus*, Lynceus himself was being led off to be killed, with Danaus following to kill him, but it came about as a consequence of preceding events that the latter was killed and Lynceus was saved" (6.3; 52a).

The multiple facets and nuances characteristic of probable reasoning and ethical choice are conveyed in tragedy not only through the plot but also through its characters. Aristotle ranks the component of character and the character's reasoning as second and third in importance after the connected outline of the action in the plot. The characters and their reasoning are like prisms for the action giving colour in varying shades and hues to the intelligible connections of the outline. Aristotle explains:

> So the plot is the source and (as it were) the soul of tragedy; character is second. (It is much the same in the case of painting: if someone were to apply exquisitely beautiful colours at random he would give

less pleasure than if he had outlined an image in black and white) (4.4; 50b).

Although Aristotle considered plot primary because in the imitation of tragic lives characters "achieve well-being or its opposite on the basis of how they fare" (4.3; 50a), or through action, nonetheless action is inextricably linked with character and reasoning. He observes that tragedy "is an imitation of an action, and on account above all of the action it is an imitation of agents" (4.4;50b). Action and character reinforce each other. Aristotle understood both reasoning and action to be the result of a person's disposition towards virtue or vice acquired through habitually directing the appetite in the choosing of good or ill and acting according to the choice. The developed character (*ethos*) is the source of the ethical quality that colours both the deliberative choice and the action. Aristotle describes this connection of character, reasoning, and action in various ways: "It is on the basis of people's character and reasoning that we say that their actions are of a certain kind" and "character is included along with and on account of the actions" (4.3; 50a). Or again: "Character is the kind of thing which discloses the nature of a choice; for this reason speeches in which there is nothing at all which the speaker chooses or avoids do not possess character" (4.4; 50b). And later he remarks that "speech or action will possess character if it discloses the nature of a deliberate choice (*prohairesis*); the character is good if the choice is good" (8.1; 54a).

Heraclitus' image of the spider web is an emblem of this typically literary mode of thought in tragedy with the web of connections of the plot and the complex relations of the characters held in unity. The spider in the centre of the web feels and responds to any tug in any part of the complicated structure[11] just as the whole of the play is affected by the personal stance of a character and by the transposition or removal of any section of the plot.

Plot and character, then, are parts of the causal connections that constitute the literary rationality of the tragedies. However, in the literary *logos* language is inseparable from this reasoning and mirrors its complexity. In its reflection of the deliberative activity of the intellect, the interior world of feelings, and the experience of the soul, language in its literary use is antithetical to the scientific use of language. Science

---

11   Martha C. Nussbaum *The Fragility of Goodness* (New York: Cambridge U.P., 1986) 69.

requires clear definitions, standard usages, literal univocal language; the reasoning of science must bar equivocal or ambiguous words with multiple simultaneous meanings and the play of words. Unlike the drama, in science's impersonal mode words that express passions and personal moral qualities are to be eschewed.

The model of the literary use of language and its reflection of feeling-thought in the poetic tragedies analyzed by Aristotle shows the measure of difference between scientific and non-scientific reasoning. This reasoning is not based on abstract aspects, single definitions, or generalizations. It is the reasoning of those engaged with concrete situations, such as the personal plight of particular women bereft in the wake of their city's defeat in the Trojan war. The moral quality of characters is connected to the right measure of feeling for such loss, and thought functions in tandem with feeling. Language and thought are not separable but fused. The whole rich range of the lexicon required to register such feeling-thought makes science's literal, univocal language drearily inadequate to the task. Words are not standard but bear the weight of emotionally-charged meanings. The various views of the characters, their congruent reasoning drawing the past and the future into the present, mean that single words are fraught with multiple meanings; equivocal and ambiguous words reflect the inner world of motives, the collective in conjunction with the individual, and the interconnected planes of the human and divine. In the context of such expression, the analogical reasoning implicit in metaphor is considered by Aristotle as poetry's finest feature, an unteachable gift to the poet. For the audience, the affective function of tragedy is dependent on the poet's skill in finding the apt word for the occasion.

This language of the human drama where thought and word are inseparable is registered in the personal voice of characters or what Aristotle calls the character's reasoning. The reasoning of the characters belongs to the same persuasive literary mode of thought as rhetoric; it colours the plot by heightening or diminishing the importance of events or by observing them through the filter of emotion. Aristotle tell us that reasoning "is the ability to say what is implicit in a situation and appropriate to it." (4.4; 50b). He describes the general function of the character's reasoning as dealing with "those effects which must be produced by language; these include proof and refutation, the production of emotions (e.g. pity, fear, anger, etc.) and also establishing importance or unimportance" (9.1; 56a). He remarks that the same principles clearly apply to the events of the plot "when it is necessary to make something seem pitiable or terrible, important or probable" (9.1; 56b). The similarity Aristotle finds between reasoning in the drama and its prose counterpart in the "arts of statesmanship and rhetoric" indicates the largely deliberative nature of reasoning in tragedy where judgments and choices are made.

With the advent of the self in the modern era, what Aristotle calls the character's reasoning has fascinated the sensibilities of modern commentators more than the plot itself. Their critical attention is drawn by the power of language and the characters' account of events which colours the plot; multiple perspectives and various points of view, each constitutive of the whole, cast light on each other. In his comments on Aristotle's *Poetics*, Kenneth McLeish remarks on the layers in Greek tragedy which he finds to be less an enactment of physical deeds than "accounts of deeds and feelings." He observes that characters themselves in a single deft phrase frame a particular emotional and intellectual attitude.[12] McLeish writes that when physical deeds such as suicides, take place on stage, they are prepared and hedged about in such a way that the deed itself seems "a focusing of several points of view." We watch not only someone speaking but the reaction of someone listening or may be aware of wider significances than that appreciated by the characters on stage. In some plays like Sophocles' *Antigone*, the characters form "a cat's cradle of relationships, in which characters are impinged on by others, by the state and laws they live by, and by the authorities, mortal and fallible or divine and infallible, who moderate those laws."[13]

The Chorus with its propensity for general comment on the action functions, too, like a character as part of the many-faceted whole. In the *Poetics*, Aristotle says that the Chorus should be like "one of the actors: it should be part of the whole and contribute to the performance" (*Poetics*, 8.9; 56a). McLeish observes similarly that in a forwards and backwards movement the Chorus may comment on the preceding actions, casting them in a new light and giving to the words a new density and resonance.[14] He says that in Aeschylus' larger

---

12   Kenneth McLeish, *Aristotle's Poetics*, (London: Phoenix, 1998) 17-18.

13   Ibid., 25.

14   In Martha Nussbaum's discussion of the density and compression of *Antigone*'s choral scenes, she notes a striking comparison between their

use of the Chorus, he presents "a kind of wider panorama of relevance and meaning, and then narrows the focus on to specific characters and specific emblematic scenes. The general is constantly refracted through the particular, and vice versa …."[15] In this focus on character, McLeish points out that, although not suggested by Aristotle's schematic reasoning, even the characterization of the gods in the plays fits with "the nuancing and insinuation so characteristic of dramatic method." Aeschylus shows us a Titan (Prometheus) who snarls and rails at Zeus; and "Euripides' gallery of gods includes a sun-princess tormented because she chooses to take on mortal feelings (*Medea*)."[16]

Similarly, in an article on Aristotle's *Poetics* in the nineteenth century John Henry Newman finds that what is more important poetically than the plot in Greek tragedy is the characters and their mental feeling or emotional thought; that is, their sentiments.[17] Newman's comments on the characters' thought draw attention to the convergent pattern of reasoning in literature. In *The Bacchae* of Euripides, the connected, multiple facets of the play are reflected through the different, emotionally-charged attitudes of the various characters experienced around a single event. Newman describes "the mad fire of the Chorus, the imbecile mirth of old Cadmus and Tiresias, and the infatuation of Pentheus."[18] He observes that these various elements "are made to harmonize with the terrible catastrophe" in the violent death of Pentheus. Rather than a sequential pattern of events, what is important in *The Bacchae* is a clustering of the emotionally-charged attitudes of various characters around a single centre.

---

lyric intensity and the "compressed, dense, and riddling style of the major ethical thinker of the half-century preceding this play, that is, to the style of Heraclitus." *The Fragility of Goodness*, 68-9.

15   Kenneth McLeish, 46.

16   Ibid., 25-6.

17   *The Oxford Universal Dictionary* includes the following in its definition of "sentiment": "A mental feeling, an emotion. Now chiefly applied to those feelings which involve an intellectual element or are concerned with ideal objects; ….A thought coloured by or proceeding from emotion … an emotional thought expressed in literature or art."

18   Newman, "Poetry, with Reference to Aristotle's Poetics," *Essays and Sketches*, vol. 1, ed. Charles Frederick Harrold (New York: Longmans, Green and Co., 1948) 62.

Similarly, in Aeschylus' *Agamemnon*, he finds the essence of the drama in the filter of emotional thought through which characters perceive an event, anticipated "in the resolves of destiny" and "long meditated in the bosom of the human agents." The mental feelings or sentiments of the characters colour the impending action. Early in the play, the Chorus, as "the prophetic organ … employed by heaven, to proclaim the impending horrors," seems "oppressed with forebodings of woe and crime which they can neither justify nor analyze. The expression of their anxiety forms the stream in which the plot flows-- everything, even news of joy, takes a colouring from the depth of their gloom." Later, the prophetess, Cassandra, speaking "first in figure, then in plain terms," intimates the death of Agamemnon which is at last accomplished. Using a musical analogy, Newman maintains that throughout the play there is not a progressive thickening of incidents in a plot, but one and the same note "growing in volume and intensity … a working up of one musical ground, by figure and imitation, into the richness of combined harmony."[19] The plot is not scientifically or linearly sequential in its progression but develops a single idea through another pattern of rationality that is both dense and moving.

Aristotle's analysis of the character's reasoning is followed by his comments on diction, ranked fourth in importance after plot. The affective function of the poet's choice of words in arousing the pity and terror in the audience characteristic of tragedy is such that even reading the plays should elicit this response. Although Aristotle does not underestimate the effect of music and spectacle, in a comparison of epic and tragedy he emphasizes the importance of language, stating that "tragedy has vividness in reading as well as in performance" (12.2; 62a). Elsewhere he writes: "The plot should be constructed in such a way that, even without seeing it, anyone who hears the events which occur shudders and feels pity at what happens; this is how someone would react on hearing the plot of the *Oedipus*" (7.3; 53b).

The poet's subtle use of language in the drama to reflect human complexity and affective thought stands in contrast to the standardized univocal language of science. In his analysis of diction, Aristotle includes practical comments on phonetics important, for example, where the differences between syllables affect verse-forms, and on grammar as essential to an accurate understanding of a text. As for the

---

19   Ibid., 60-1.

poet's use of language itself, only the full range of the lexicon can convey ever freshly the emotionally-charged plight of individuals within their own particular contexts that is at the same time the perennial experience of humankind in all ages. For its purposes, the language of poetry is at the opposite pole from the general, standardized, clear language of scientific reasoning. Aristotle says that the poet must use some standard words for the sake of clarity, but he also uses "non-standard words, metaphor, lengthening, and anything contrary to current usage" (9.4; 58a). He then provides examples of the nuance achieved through poetic language, comparing the phrase, 'a little, weak, ugly man,' with the poetic rendering: 'a scant and strengthless and unseemly man.' He observes differences between two dramatists where "the change of a single word - a non-standard word in place of a current one - made one line seem excellent, and the other trivial by comparison: Aeschylus wrote, in his *Philoctetes*, 'the canker that eats up my foot's flesh'; Euripides substituted 'feasts on' for 'eats up'" (9.4; 58b).

In his further observations on poetic language, the metaphor is given highest praise by Aristotle. There is much to commend metaphor for the purposes of poetry. In its analogical openness to the whole cosmic terrain of the divine, human, and physical spheres and in its conjunction of what may be unexpectedly alike, the metaphor has it own pleasure; like the riddle, it engages the audience in its recognitions. With its thought compressed in a concrete comparison rather than in an abstract notion, and in its multilevelled, unitive simultaneity, the metaphor is quintessentially literary. Like the plot itself, metaphor embodies truths that impress the imagination and engage the affections.

In his analysis of diction, Aristotle maintains that among the qualities of poetic style "the most important thing is to be good at using metaphor" (9.4); he defines metaphor as "the application of a noun which properly applies to something else" (9.3; 57b). One kind of metaphor is a transfer by analogy where one thing stands in a similar relation to something else. He notes that "Sometimes the thing to which the noun replaced stands in relation is expressed." For example, as one may say that "old age is to life as evening is to the day; so one may speak of evening as the old age of the day (as Empedocles does), and of old age as the evening of life, or life's twilight" (9.3; 57b). Because metaphors involve personally perceived analogies rather than real extrinsic analogies, Aristotle remarks that metaphor "is the one thing that cannot be learnt from someone else, and is a sign of natural talent; for the successful use of metaphor is a matter or perceiving similarities" (9.4; 59a)

The typically literary use of language as thought and word together also emerges in Aristotle's final observations in the *Poetics* on "problems and solutions." Here he deals with the difficulties of textual interpretation proceeding from what is peculiarly literary. By its very nature, poetry requires interpretation with its various interwoven strands, the different stances of the characters, and its expansive, versatile use of language. Aristotle suggests that difficulties arise primarily for two reasons: first, because the poet does not make a literal transcription of actuality but a *mimesis* with its own intelligible end; and, secondly, the diction of poetry "includes non-standard words, metaphors, and many modifications of diction" (11.1; 60b). The fullest interpretation of a play depends in part on how well the audience enters into the mind of the poet in his mimesis of life. Because poetry is not a literal transcription of actuality, Aristotle gives advice on the need to understand an author's intention: he may be imitating people as they should be, as it is said of Sophocles; or he may be imitating people as they are, as is said of Euripides; or he may be imitating "the kind of thing that is said or thought to be the case" (11.1; 60b) or "is what people say; e.g. stories about the gods" (11.2; 60b); or he may include details of the way things used to be in another time (11.2; 61a).

The problems for interpretation posed by diction result from the subtle, unusual, or nuanced use in literature of language which is multivalent, non-standard, and always determined by the context. A twentieth-century classical scholar, Jean-Pierre Vernant, gives examples from *Antigone* of the multivalent function of language in the tragedies where conflicting claims of characters are held in unity. He points to the multiple senses of single words in the Greek language, such as authority (*nomos*), which includes religious, legal, political, and everyday registers. Characters like Antigone and Creon using the same word in different ways are locked into impermeable, one-sided views that will collide, recoil, and bring on themselves "bitter experience of the meaning" each "was determined not to recognise."[20] He notes the many simultaneous meanings suggested by the ambiguity of words within

---

20   Jean-Pierre Vernant, *Tragedy and Myth in Ancient Greece*, 87-8.

Clytemnestra's speech as, with murderous intent at the threshold of the palace, she greets Agamemnon, her husband, returning from the Trojan war. Her words fall on the ears of Agamemnon with

> the pleasant ring of a pledge of love and conjugal fidelity; for the cho-
> rus it is already equivocal and they sense some threat within it, while
> the spectator can see its full sinister quality because he can decode
> in it the death plot that she has hatched against her husband ….It is
> a duplicity of almost demoniacal proportions. The same speech, the
> very words that draw Agamemnon into the trap, disguising the danger
> from him, at the same time announce the crime about to be perpe-
> trated to the world in general. And because the queen, in her hatred
> for her husband, becomes in the course of the drama the instrument
> of divine justice, the secret speech concealed within her words of wel-
> come takes on an oracular significance. By pronouncing the death of
> the king she makes it inevitable, like a prophet.[21]

The audience's reception of such literary language that may appear contradictory complicates and layers its interpretation. Aristotle cautions against the practice of some people who impose a meaning on the text from "unreasonable prior assumptions" … and if anything contradicts their own ideas they criticize the poet as if *he* had expressed *their* opinion" (11.2; 61b). Because words in their literary use are not simply literal or univocal but change their hue according to their setting, he emphasizes the need to "consider the number of meanings a word "could bear in the context" (11.2; 61a). Aristotle suggest that other problems in interpretation may be solved by considering such features as punctuation; linguistic usage and ambiguity of language; and subtle differences in pronunciation resulting, for example, in an imperative voice rather than an indicative tense. Objections to impossibilities may "be referred to poetic effect, or idealization of the truth, or opinion ….Irrationalities should be referred to what people say ….Contradictory utterances should be subjected to the same scrutiny as refutations in arguments" (11.3). Finally, the subtle, multifaceted nature of poetry shaped particularly by the way character colours what is said is taken into account. Aristotle articulates the sweeping criterion perennially true both for poetry and for rhetoric that

---

21   Ibid., 88-9.

[i]n evaluating any utterance or action, one must take into account not just the moral qualities of what is actually done or said, but also the identity of the agent or speaker, the addressee, the occasion, the means, and the motive" (11.2; 60b).

Aristotle's observations include not only *poesis* in this word's sense of a thing made but also in its sense of the poet or maker. His brief direct comments on the poet's approach to writing tragedies are also important because they indicate two essential literary characteristics that are distinct from scientific reasoning: first, as a reflection of life, literature is concrete, and, secondly, emotion is integral to it. In his suggestions for maintaining plausible connections in the concrete details of the plot, Aristotle advises visualizing things vividly "as if one were actually present at the events themselves" to find what is appropriate and to avoid inconsistencies. As a way of assuring authenticity in the imitation of emotional expression, he sets out the apparently well-established view on using gestures when writing a play because it brings the dramatist closer to actually experiencing the emotions of the character.[22] Aristotle writes:

> One should also, as far as possible, work plots out using gestures. Given the same natural talent, those who are actually experiencing the emotions are the most convincing; someone who is distressed or angry acts out distress and irritation most authentically. (This is why the art of poetry belongs to people who are naturally gifted or mad; of these, the former are adaptable, and the latter are not in their right mind) (8.3; 55a).

Both author and audience operate through the same converging mode of thought common to ethical action and literature which sees life organically. Since there is no science of the particular, Aristotle had remarked in Book vi of the *Nicomachean Ethics* that ethical action is best understood by observing those who practise it (1140a 25). For the audience, tragedy provides just this kind of occasion for observation through its imitation of people engaged in the activity of making ethical choices in shifting terrain impeded by ambiguities, by wrong desire, by an absence of knowledge of future events, by single-minded stances, by impossibly clashing values. And it provides a model of the

---

22   In his notes on his translation of the *Poetics*, Malcolm Heath refers to the fun Aristophanes has in his play, *Thesmophoriazusae*, with this method of work of an author. 56.

consequences in the connected web of life when choices are wrong; failure to make choices that are both emotionally and intellectually right wreaks havoc not only in the individual who has made them but also in all those around them.

Kenneth McLeish suggests the personal frame of reference essential to this kind of thought that apprehends opposites held in unity and simultaneous levels of meaning. McLeish writes: "No Greek tragedy is simply about what its events depict. Each carries an enormous weight of assertion, nuance, implication and suggestion, both intellectual and emotional, drawing strength equally from the predispositions of author and spectator."[23] Religious belief, for example, will alter an audience's response or recent experience of war will colour the audience's understanding of it in a tragedy.

Jean-Pierre Vernant illustrates this personal nature of the audience's reception of tragedy through a scholarly impression of the sensibilities and assumptions of the original audiences who gathered annually to watch and judge the dramatic competitions some 2,500 years ago when tragedy became a regular part of the Athenian spring festival of Dionysius in 534 BCE. He suggests the simultaneous tensions characteristic in the period between the levels of the collective and the individual, between the human and the divine, and he illustrates these tensions through the example of Oedipus. In a manner alien to modern western audiences, clashing claims of family, civic, and religious life were enacted before audiences who understood that "[c]ut off from his family, civic and religious roots the individual was nothing; he did not find himself alone, he ceased to exist." [24] According to the most ancient ideas about misdeeds like the tragic error (*hamartia*, or missing the target) which sets off the dramatic sequence of events, errors or misdeeds were at once individual, collective, and connected to a daemonic force. Thus, Oedipus is not humanly guilty but his actions of incest and patricide are criminal and pollute the collective Thebean community.

The criminal action of Oedipus is both an act of blindness and a daemonic power of defilement attached beyond the individual to "his whole lineage," rebounding from one generation to the next. "It may

---

23   Kenneth McLeish, *Aristotle's Poetics* (London: Phoenix, 1998) 43.

24   Jean-Pierre Vernant, *Tragedy and Myth in Ancient Greece*, 58.

affect an entire town, pollute a whole territory."[25] Oedipus as king is an individual responsible for the collective well-being of the city; if he goes astray, the entire town pays for the fault of this one individual through famine, sterility, and pestilence. Oedipus, king, responsible for the collective welfare of Thebes, becomes at the end Oedipus, the scapegoat (*pharmakos*) who will rid Thebes of the defilement brought on it by him.

At the same time, Vernant locates a new quality in the historic moment of the great tragedies through emerging individual responsibility represented in the legal categories established after the advent of the city-state; clear categories for individual responsibility for a crime included premeditation, absence of criminal intention, or unforeseeable accident, such as a death at the Olympic games. The action of tragedy is played out simultaneously along the two poles of mythical divine order and responsible, individual human action as complementary aspects "of a single ambiguous reality." The audience watches probabilities develop, sending tremors through the whole. Then, at the reversal or "culminating point of the tragedy, where all the threads are tied together, the time of the gods invades the state and becomes manifest within the time of man."[26]

The Greek plays continue to exercise an abiding effect on modern audiences who within their own personal frame of reference are taken into this complex, multileveled world, a world of oracles and gods, of human initiative and human error driven both by necessity and by a seemingly inevitable combination of probabilities. Although the sensibilities of a modern audience are different, the mode of thought that attends on tragedy as part of our human constitution does not change. The plays cultivate the literary rationality of the audience as the concrete enactment of action draws on our imagination and engages our emotions as constituents of our understanding. This mode of thought capable of apprehending the tragedies draws on the whole person: not only on the intellect, the imagination, and the emotions, but also on personal experience.

Indeed, the spectators' fullest understanding of a tragedy depends on a comparison of the concrete action of the play with their own concrete experiences. If the audience is to be taken into the full reality

---

25   Ibid., 39.

26   Ibid., 23.

of the life tragedy imitates, then the individuals in the audience must themselves be experienced in life sufficiently to compare their own experiences with those dramatized in the tragedy. Although the young and inexperienced may take delight in aspects of the poetry of a play, they will become increasingly aware of the dimensions of life that it imitates only with growth in knowledge and experience. In a comparison of poetry with painting, Aristotle comments on the kind of pleasure possible to the inexperienced in viewing a picture: "If one happens not to have seen the thing before, it will not give pleasure as an imitation, but because of its execution or colour, or for some other reason" (3.1; 48b).[27]

For the audience, equal in importance to the play's portrayal of universals in human experience is the medium of feeling-knowing literary thought through which they are expressed. This personal mode of thought is inextricable from the plot, the characters, and the audience's manner of apprehending the play. The integration of feeling and intellect essential to the well-being of the characters and experienced by members of the audience as a way of knowing is similar to Aristotle's concept of ethical action as deliberative desire or desiderative deliberation. In this mode, the well-formed character habituated through good action will first desire the good end and then deliberate on the means to effect it.

Martha Nussbaum comments on the tragic element of disjuncture in the characters between feeling and intellect through conflicting claims of family and religion. In her interpretation of the tragedy of family in Sophocles' *Antigone*, she speaks of the rationality of both feeling and imagination in connection to thought in those decisions or choices which require a complex reaction to a dilemma. Deliberation and reasoning not only prepare feelings, but passions also lead thought towards human understanding and help constitute this understanding. She contrasts Sophocles' Antigone and Creon with Abraham in the

---

27   Etienne Gilson comments that the audience's response to art cannot be universalized because of the individual reaction to particular objects perceived by sense. Because art is cumulative, the individual may respond to one aspect or another rather than to the impetus of the whole. For example, in a painting by Canaletto, a person may respond to the cityscape, to a particular building like the Doge's Palace, or to the colours used by Canaletto. *The Arts of the Beautiful* (New York: Charles Scribner's Sons, 1965) 46-48.

Old Testament who would follow God's command to sacrifice his son but nonetheless never loses his feelings as father. Antigone's single-minded cause and Creon's collapsing of distinct values into a single civic virtue make both of them become bloodless as they see others only as a function of their single cause. The contrast with Abraham applies, too, as we watch Agamemnon monstrously sacrifice his daughter, Iphigenia, through desire spurred by his own passion to open up the way before his army for victory, a different reason from the gods. Clytemnestra's subsequent murder of her husband, Agamemnon, is just retribution but is also spurred by wrong desire in her ambition, hatred, and resentment of Agamemnon's sacrifice of their daughter.[28]

The right balance of feeling and thought where both reinforce the other is essential not only to the characters but also to the spectators. Through the poet's skilful arrangement of plot, sympathetic spectators of the tragedies will desire the good end and will feel in right measure emotions appropriate to specific situations. In the process, they will engage in a literary mode of thought inextricable from the play and will cultivate the habit of the intellect common to literature, ethical reasoning, and religious reflection. For Aristotle, the emotions evoked in the audience are not only a defining feature of tragedy but are beneficial to the audience. In his comments on the preferability of plot to spectacle in engaging the audience, he observes first that the characteristic pleasure of tragedy is fear and pity and "the poet should produce the pleasure which comes from pity and fear" (7.3; 53b). He tells us that the experience of pity and fear which at best is integral to the plot effects the "purification" [katharsis] of such emotions" (4.1; 49b). Thus, we feel chastened by the drama as we hear Oedipus, for example, exclaim to Creon at the end "let me perish, the patricide, the unholy one, that I am."[29] Like the balance of desire and thought

---

28   Martha Nussbaum, *The Fragility of Goodness*, 26-82.

29   Aeschylus, "Oedipus Rex," *7 Famous Greek Plays*, ed., introd. by Whitney J. Oates and Eugene O'Neill Jr. (New York: Vintage Books, 1950) 178.

In "What I Owe to the Ancients" in *Twilight of the Idols*, Friedrich Nietzsche claims that Aristotle misunderstood the idea of tragic feeling. He maintains that Aristotle understood this concept as a getting "rid of pity and terror ... to purify oneself of a dangerous emotion." He writes: "Affirmation of life even in its strangest and sternest problems, the will to life rejoicing in its own inexhaustibility through the *sacrifice* of its highest types--that is what I call Dionysian, *that* is what I recognized as the bridge to the psychology of

in desiderative deliberation, the unity of feeling and thought in the spectator viewing the action is in itself healing, a right "hitting of the mark" in our mental constitution.

Tragedy, like literature, enacts within us a feeling way of knowing as we are engaged by events and by the suffering[30] they cause to the characters. We respond to tragedy's *mimesis* of suffering in the same way we respond to news of tragedy in life. We pity those who suffer and experience a sense of terror as we recognize the same might happen to us in the future. Aristotle analyzes how the poets who are our teachers have constructed their tragedies to engage thus our feelings. Our pity, Aristotle tells us, is evinced by the reversal in good fortune of someone who "is suffering undeservedly." Our fear has to do "with someone who is like ourselves." Characters such as Oedipus are like ourselves because external status and ethical character are two distinct things.[31] On the one hand, the protagonist "is one of those people who are held in great esteem and enjoy great good fortune, like Oedipus ... and distinguished men from that kind of family." On the other hand, the person who excites fear is like us: "not outstanding in moral excellence or justice" whose "change to bad fortune" ... is not due to any moral defect or depravity," but to a serious error of some kind (7.2; 53a). Of such error and of such fall from good fortune we are all, by our common humanity, capable.

Our feeling-knowledge is also engaged because the tragedies are enacted on ground common to us all. Aristotle observes that the best tragedies take place in families; here members are irreplaceable and tragic events irreparable. The plots "are constructed around a few households ... whose lot it has been to experience something terrible -- or to perform some terrible action" (7.2; 53a). The poets naturally turned to households in traditional stories "in which sufferings arise within close relationships, e.g. brother kills brother, son father, mother son, or son mother -- or is on the verge of killing them ..." (7.4; 53b). The emotions and the intellect of the audience are engaged especially in the scenes of recognition (*anagorensis*) in a family. This recognition

---

the *tragic* poet." Friedrich Nietzsche, *Twilight of the Idols / The Anti-Christ* (London: Penguin, 1990).

30 Aristotle includes suffering as a component of plot that "involves destruction or pain." *Poetics* (6.5; 52b).

31 Stephen Halliwell, *Aristotle's Poetics,* 159-60.

of "some person or persons" discloses either "a close relationship or enmity" (6.4; 52a). Aristotle describes the three possibilities for such disclosure. Like Medea avenging Jason's infidelity to her by arranging the killing of their children, characters may act "in full knowledge and awareness." Or, like Sophocles' Oedipus, characters may "do the terrible deed in ignorance and only then ... recognize the close connection" (7.4; 53b). Or, most movingly, someone may be "on the verge of performing some irreparable deed through ignorance, and for the recognition to pre-empt the act" as when "a mother may be on the verge of killing her son but does not do it, but instead recognizes him" (7.4; 54a).

The recognitions which best engage the literary mode of thought in a feeling way of knowing for both characters and audience are those internal to the web of events in the plot. Aristotle says in his assertion of the primacy of plot: "the most important devices by which tragedy sways emotion are parts of the plot, i.e. reversals and recognitions" (4.3; 50a). Rather than contrived scenes with tokens or necklaces revealing identity, recognition may occur through "memory, when someone grasps the significance of something that he sees" as when in Homer's epic poem, "Odysseus listens to the lyre-player, is reminded of his past and weeps"; it may occur through inference on the part of a character or "from a false inference on the part of the audience" whose expectations of the manner of recognition are not met. Best of all, recognition may arise "out of the actual course of events, where the emotional impact is achieved through events that are probable, as in Sophocles' *Oedipus* ..." (8.2; 55a).

Finally, not only do our sensibilities help constitute the way we understand a particular drama through pity and fear, but, as Aristotle observes in his *Rhetoric*, pity and fear reaffirm the beliefs in a view of life on which these feelings rest. In our feeling of fear, we recognize that it is not always possible to prevent pain or harm. The audience's fear which is integral to tragedy asserts the role played by externals like good or bad fortune which lie beyond the control of scientific reasoning. Our sense of this is reinforced when reversals in fortune evince astonishment as "when someone who is clever but bad (like Sisyphus) is deceived, or someone who is courageous but unjust is defeated" (8.8; 56a).

In general, Greek tragedy and Aristotle's analysis of it in the *Poetics* affirm an organic view of life where the individual and the collective, the divine and the human are an interconnected whole. Tragedy also affirms the mode of thought through which this organic view of life is apprehended. As a mimesis of life, tragedy provides for the audience an occasion for exercising the literary mode of thought of concrete understanding which draws on our imagination, engages us both emotionally and intellectually, and moves the whole person. In the audience's exercise of this mode of thought, tragedy puts to the proof Isocrates' claim that a literary education develops in us a sense of complex intuition and a perception of the imponderables which give a just estimate of things in the circumstances of daily life.[32] From the perspective of this literary reasoning which shares common ground with the deliberation of rhetoric and of ethics, we can understand why Aristotle compares prudential or practical reasoning to the sailor tacking in the wind.

At the same time, we find affirmed an organic view of life as we watch characters in their particular extremes and we appreciate the demands of the thought characteristic of literature: an awareness of separateness, of differences, of the need for flexibility to adapt to what is unique in the immediate. We learn with Oedipus through a feeling way of knowing of the potential for dire consequences in our lives limited by partial knowledge and an unknowable future, that in life generalities may deceive, that the most telling truth is in the experience of particulars, and that the apparently clear and plausible may represent a shallow or incomplete understanding. As we "work out what each thing is" in the intelligible construct of a poet's plot, we may learn of the fragility of our position, of the limits of rational control when buffeted by the unexpected or forces greater than the human. We are exposed to intractability in human relations and to the human prostrate before the divine. We see the cost in suffering through a false step such as any one of us might take .

Through the contrivance of the poet, we have apprehended all this through the literary mode of thought. As Martha Nussbaum observes, this mode of knowing in the plays "advances its understanding of life and of itself ... by hovering in thought and imagination around the enigmatic complexities of the seen particular (as we, if we are good

32   Henri-Irène Marrou, *Histoire de l'Education dans l'Antiquité* (Paris: Editions du Seuil, 1950). Marrou writes: "Isocrates cherche à développer chez son disciple l'esprit de décision, le sens de l'intuition complexe, la perception de ces impondérables qui guident 'l'opinion' et la rendent juste" (134).

readers of this style, hover around the details of the text), seated in the middle of its web of connections, responsive to the pull of each separate thread."[33] Tragedy is expressed through a mode of thought that does not offer solutions to the irreconcilable, incommensurable claims of different characters but holds differences in tension, offering to the audience "healing without cure" in the "tension of distinct and separate beauties."[34]

33 Nussbaum, *The Fragility of Goodness*, 69.

34 Ibid., 82.

3

THE GENUS AND SPECIES OF
LITERARY RATIONALITY

JOHN HENRY NEWMAN, THOMAS HOBBES,
AND THE GREEK CHURCH FATHERS

The specific nature of literature is expressed in the Greek word, *logos*, signifying reason and speech as inseparably one. However, as a species of reasoning, literary rationality and its criterion of judgment belong to a genus that is as broad and varied as human deliberation itself as it considers particular problems. In "The Blue Cross," G.K. Chesterton's French detective bent on the task of solving his case deliberates in a way that is also characteristic of literary reasoning. In "a naked state of nescience" when clear first principles and plodding logic are not possible for solving a mystery, he must follow another path where he becomes attentive to oddities, the unforeseen, and the unreasonable.[1] A similar approach is followed in developing a new hypothesis in the physical sciences when the number of variables is too large and there are as yet no accepted scientific principles to guide further hypotheses and experimental testing. A scientist who was awarded the Nobel prize for his research into the senses recommends instead what he calls the mosaic approach which moves outside the particular field under consideration. In this approach, Georg von Bekesy suggests, a researcher proceeds through other related comparisons, "takes each problem for itself with little reference to the field in which it lies, and

---

1   G.K.Chesterton, *Great Tales of Action and Adventure*, ed. George Bennet (New York: Dell, 1959) 53-4.

seeks to discover relations and principles that hold within the circum-scribed area."[2] He also says that for his extensive art collection he fol-lowed the same principle as in his scientific research: that is, by con-stantly making comparisons.

In their different particular pursuits, the French detective and the Hungarian-born scientist were both alert in the same receptive way to connections proceeding from several diverse quarters. As literary rationality engages with the particular questions of life in the concrete, it, too, proceeds in this way; it draws on the unforeseen and the unreasonable, on unexpected connections and on juxtapositions that shed reciprocal light both through what is unlike in opposites and through what is alike in parallel situations. As literature mirrors the human drama, it reflects the multifaceted interconnections in the life of individuals, families, and of the *polis*. This human relational world involves mutuality, deliberation and choices, and the repercussions of these choices on both the protagonists and on those around them. It speaks through the connection between actions and the inner ethical world of judgments, motives, and moral responses like guilt and remorse. Unlike the static, abstract categories of science, literature reflects movement and change, subtle shifts, and the unexpected arrival of good and bad fortune. And in all of this, parts are understood as belonging to a larger whole where both good and evil reside, where past and present and future possibility meet, where irreconcilable opposites are held in tensile unity. Finally, literature's perennial truths

---

2   Marshall McLuhan cites from Georg von Bekesy's *Experiments in Hear-ing*. Von Bekesy writes: "It is possible to distinguish two forms of approach to a problem. One, which may be called the theoretical approach, is to for-mulate the problem in relation to what is already known, to make addi-tions or extensions on the basis of accepted principles, and then to proceed to test these hypotheses experimentally. Another, which may be called the mosaic approach, takes each problem for itself with little reference to the field in which it lies, and seeks to discover relations and principles that hold within the circumscribed area ....When in the field of science a great deal of progress has been made and most of the pertinent variables are known, a new problem may most readily be handled by trying to fit it into the existing framework. When, however, the framework is uncertain and the number of variables is large the mosaic approach is much the easier." Marshall McLuhan *The Gutenberg Galaxy* (New York: *The New American Library*, 1969) 55-6.

about the human condition are embedded in the concrete in such a way that particular contexts and enduring truths are connected inseparably from one other.

The sleuth, the physical scientist investigating uncharted terrain, and the literary author, then, all reason through the convergence of diverse connections. Each also reasons through a frame of reference that is uniquely personal. Like the French detective and the twentieth-century scientist, both Cicero defending a public cause and Erasmus in his meditations on maxims follow a course of reasoning through connections perceived by them personally and depending on a personal criterion of judgment; that is, their grasp of objective fact is through collateral references and associations that are unique to them and through a criterion of judgment based on these references and associations. Through this kind of rationality, life in the concrete is understood not through a prior knowledge of principles but by drawing on everything that can be connected to the matter at hand: on considered hunches, tacit comparisons, recollected conversations, fleeting impressions, on a well-furnished mind, and on the whole experience of life itself in the thinking-feeling person. Heart and intellect, imagination and memory work in tandem to grasp the truths embedded in the concrete through a converging pattern of reasoning that knows through analogies, through opposites, juxtapositions, resemblances, and contradictions.

Advocates of the humanities which cultivate this converging pattern of reasoning through literature have long understood the connection between literary rationality and those several other areas where the same kind of personal reasoning is exercised. The habit of mind cultivated through literature is applicable to the whole genus of reasoning to which literature belongs; all the species of deliberation belonging to this genus of reasoning require the same subtlety, a similar awareness of unstated connections and of what is implicit in a matter, a perception of principles embedded in particular contexts, and the relation of parts to a whole. For example, the twentieth-century political philosopher and historian of ideas, Isaiah Berlin, describes the usefulness of a liberal education in terms of the kind of reasoning exercised by the skilful statesman. In *The Sense of Reality*, he states that we rightly admire those statesmen who, without pretending to detect laws, are able to do more than others to accomplish their plans, because of a superior sense of the contours of ... unknown and half known factors, and of their effect on this or that actual situation. They are the persons who estimate what effects this or that deliberate human act is likely to have on the particular texture which the situation presents to them ... without the benefit of laws or theories; for the factors in question are below the level of clear scientific vision, are precisely those which are too complex, too numerous, too minute to be distilled into an elegant deductive structure of natural laws susceptible to mathematical treatment ....[3]

Similarly, at the well-springs of liberal education in ancient Greece more than two and a half millennia earlier, Isocrates (436-338 B.C.E.) considered the rationality cultivated through the study of literature to have important practical benefits. The "Father of humanism" believed that the truly cultivated person could find the best solution to a difficult situation under the circumstances where knowledge of theory was insufficient to the moment. For Isocrates, the specific efficacy of literature as a training of the intellect lay in its connection of thought to language; that is, in the *logos*, that indissoluble unity of thought and word characteristic of literary rationality.[4] He believed that the effort to express the right thought through the right word in literary education required the kind of subtlety needed to refine the sense of judgment in the domain of practical human affairs.[5] Training in this literary mode of thought was intended for the average Athenian whom Isocrates hoped would thus be able to recognize demagoguery were it to threaten the cultural heart of Athens.

Even here at the well-springs of liberal learning, an uneasy relation existed between the literary mode of reasoning taught by Isocrates,

---

3   Isaiah Berlin, *The Sense of Reality: Studies in Ideas and their History* (London: Pimlico, 1996) 38.

4   Isocrates placed a hymn to the *logos* in two of his books, *Nococles* and *Antidosis*, where he praises the *logos* as distinguishing the human from the animal and as the condition of all progress whether in law, the arts, or mechanical inventions. Henri-Irénée Marrou, *Histoire de l'Education dans l'Antiquité* (Paris: Seuil, 1950)124.

5   Ibid., 135. Marrou cites Isocrates: "La parole convenable est le signe le plus sûr de la pensée juste." (The apt word is the most sure sign of accurate thought).

Plato's contemporary, and the scientific reasoning of philosophy at Plato's Academy. Isocrates' school taught a literary rationality directed towards concrete particular matters; Plato's school which taught reasoning through abstract principles regarded its rival with disdain.[6] Plato's pupil, Aristotle, the great arbiter between methods, analyzed lucidly and dispassionately the broad distinction between these two rival modes of reasoning and indicated their different tasks.

In this luminous Greek era, Aristotle differentiated between the domain of scientific reasoning and the domain of thought characteristic of the whole genus to which literary rationality belongs. He recognized distinct ways through which we know two broad areas of reality: on the one hand, the unchangeable realities expressed in clear statements of valid premises with which scientific reasoning begins; and, on the other hand, all those other realities without initial premises and requiring deliberation or interpretation which are known through what he calls calculative reasoning. In the *Nicomachean Ethics*, Aristotle opens his discussion of the several virtues of the intellect and the ways that we know by distinguishing first between these two broad areas of truth and the two different parts of the mind or soul through which we know them. He says:

> Let it be supposed that there are two rational elements: with one of these we apprehend the realities whose fundamental principles do not admit of being other than they are, and with the other we apprehend things which do admit of being other. For if we grant that knowledge presupposes a certain likeness and kinship of subject and object, there will be a generically different part of the soul naturally corresponding to each of two different kinds of object. Let us call one the scientific and the other the calculative element (*Nicomachean Ethics*, vi, 1139a).[7]

If Aristotle mediated an ancient quarrel between science and calculative reasoning, between philosophy in Plato's academy, for example, and rhetoric in the school of Isocrates, mediation is no less impor-

---

6   In *Histoire de l'Education dans l'Antiquité*, Marrou expresses the difference in spirit between Isocrates and Plato as the difference described by Pascal between a subtle mind, or "esprit de finesse," and a mathematical deductive mind, or "esprit géométrique." He also remarks that Pascal dismissed Descartes as "inutile et incertain" or as useless and uncertain (130).

7   Aristotle, *Nicomachean Ethics*, trans. and ed., Martin Ostwald (Indianapolis: Bobbs-Merrill, 1962) 147.

tant in the modern period in the difficult relations between empirical induction and verbal theoretical science. In our own period, science in its modern sense has become so dominant that it has obliterated Aristotle's meaning of this word that prevailed for well over a thousand years. By scientific reasoning, Aristotle did not mean formulating general laws about the physical world from our sense observations in accordance with the inductive science promoted by Francis Bacon at the beginning of our own era. By science, Aristotle meant deductive reasoning regarding the human realm that took as its starting-point premises that were true. This verbal process of reasoning provided scientific demonstration because its conclusions followed necessarily from its premises. For example, in the classic Aristotelian syllogism that begins with the premise that all men are mortal, the unerring conclusion can be drawn that since Socrates is a man he is mortal.

As an arbiter of method, Aristotle considered the proper task of each kind of reason and its strengths and limitations. Verbal scientific reason led necessarily to true deductions providing its premises were true. For the premises that are the starting-points of its reasoning, deduction depended on induction which Aristotle placed in the calculative domain. Because there are no sure existing scientific principles for its guidance, he did not consider the process of arriving at general abstract laws through induction to be scientific. As with empirical induction in modern science, its starting-point in particulars means that its generalizations or conclusions are always provisional, pending the addition of other particulars that might be an exception to these general laws. As well, the truths arrived at by induction are only as good and certain as our own perceptions.

As for calculative reason exercised, for example, in the concrete matters of rhetoric, Aristotle maintained that this kind of reason was as capable of certitude as verbal science. Scientific reason and calculative thought were adapted to knowing different objects: one through the logic of clear premises that led to inevitable or necessary conclusions; and the other through probabilities that taken all together also led to certitude. As they followed their respective paths, where scientific reasoning was capable of leading to certitude when its premises were true, so, too, reasoning through the convergence of probabilities was no less capable of arriving at certitude. Aristotle's confidence in calculative thought is expressed, for example, in the final chapter of the *Posterior Analytics* where amid a philosophical account of our human capacity to "have pieces of knowledge more certain than demonstration" (B 99b), he uses an image to describe "another type of understanding" not subject to scientific demonstration; that is, not coming "about from already existing knowledge" (A 71b and 71a). He compares this non-scientific reason to a rout in battle where "one man makes a stand another does and then another, until a position of strength is reached. And the mind is such as to be capable of undergoing this" (B100a).[8]

In the nineteenth century, two thousand five hundred years after Aristotle's reflections on method, induction was rapidly taking the field in the battle among methods. Science now meant inductive reasoning and, increasingly, to reason at all meant drawing abstract general conclusions from sense observation and personal experience. The deductive reasoning that Aristotle considered to be scientific was dismissed as beginning with pre-judgments, the préjugés or prejudices castigated by the enlightenment's empirical philosophers. In short, *a priori* deductive reasoning was not considered scientific simply because it did not conform to the criterion or principle of judgment of the dominant science by beginning at the opposite pole with particulars. The kind of literary reasoning taught by Isocrates where thought and word are one fared no better. As exclusive habituation to induction made the literary mode of reasoning unrecognizable, its verbal expression of thought appeared to be tinselled ornament, lacking in the plain substance of things and the facts of science.

This increasing ascendancy of the inductive method in the nineteenth century can be remarked in the books then written on the subject. William Whewell (1794-1866), Professor of mineralogy when Charles Darwin was at Cambridge, wrote two books on induction: *The History of the Inductive Sciences* and *The Philosophy of the Inductive Sciences*. The work on inductive logic by the utilitarian philosopher, John Stuart Mill, which followed Whewell's, exercised a broad, continued influence. In mid-century, the complete edition of the works of Francis Bacon, the great prophet of the inductive method, was begun by R.L. Ellis and James Spedding. And champions of the inductive method like the scientist, T.H. Huxley, extended its application beyond the physical sciences to make it a universal method applied to all

---

8 Aristotle, *Aristotle's Posterior Analytics*, trans. and notes by Jonathan Barnes (Oxford: Clarendon P., 1975). Cf. Joseph Dunne, *Back to the Rough Ground* (Notre Dame: Notre Dame P., 1993) 291-304.

areas including morality and religion. In opposition to the arbiters of method, he maintained that the subject matter of reasoning does not change the process of reasoning and objected to the claim that "reason and morality have two weights and two measures."[9]

In this period that demonstrated an avid interest in method, there were fewer defenders of the mode of reasoning of literature or of its way of knowing through the imagination. One of these was Samuel Taylor Coleridge (1772-1834) who earlier in the century delved into method and spoke of the faculties of mind from the perspective of a literary temperament. He studied the history of logic in various Greek schools and sought to effect a harmony between the philosophy of Bacon and Plato; he explored the power of the poetic imagination. He also instigated an encyclopedia project, the *Encyclopedia Metropolitana*, that was to show the interconnectedness and organic unity of the many separate branches of learning necessarily divided by science.

In the nineteenth century, John Henry Newman (1801-1889) was also an arbiter of method who sought to withstand the assault on the less-privileged modes of reason. In his own day, Newman was celebrated for his influence as a preacher, especially during the religious controversies at Oxford in the 1830's and 1840's. His reflections on education in *The Idea of a University*, written while rector of the Catholic University of Ireland in the 1850's, are still cited today by those who defend the value of the liberal arts. Throughout his life, in sermons and books Newman meditated on the genus of reasoning to which both literature and religious belief belong; in these sermons, in his poetry, and in his novels he also exemplified literary rationality.

Newman recognized the need to defend this mode of reasoning both because of his own sensibility, like Coleridge, and through formative influences like his education at Oxford. There he read Aristotle's *Poetics* and his *Rhetoric*, two works on literary rationality, and the *Nicomachean Ethics* where Aristotle's observations on the various ways we reason or know were far more inclusive than the assumptions made by modern empirical philosophers on the nature of the mind or by scientists like T.H. Huxley who had become habituated to evidence from a single mode of reasoning. For example, Aristotle wrote of *theoria*, or theoretical deductive reasoning from ideas and principles; *phronesis*,

---

9   T.H. Huxley, *The Essence of T.H. Huxley*, compiler Cyril Bibby (London: Macmillan, 1967) 113.

or the way the mind works in making practical ethical decisions; *nous,* the light of the mind that knows rather than reasons and is translated variously as intelligence, insight, intuition, and contemplative knowledge. Because he recognized the looming modern crisis in the intellect itself proceeding especially from the increasing hegemony of empirical reason, Newman spent his life meditating and writing on the other equally important modes of thought: in sermons at Oxford between 1826 and 1843; in lectures in Dublin while Rector at the Catholic University of Ireland; in his final book, *An Essay in Aid of a Grammar of Assent* (1870).

As he perceived the tendency in contemporary intellectual currents to limit all reason to scientific reasoning, to claim that acceptable evidence was limited either to impersonal conclusions drawn from the sensate or to clear logical explanation severed from the concrete, Newman was acutely aware that the whole domain of concrete reality known through the calculative reasoning of converging probabilities was under siege: the universals known in the concrete in literature through its various converging strands; or knowledge of concrete matters known through congruent thought in rhetoric's reasoning which by Newman's time was becoming a pejorative term; or knowledge of God in an individual's religious belief. Both as Rector of the Catholic University of Ireland where he defended the liberal arts for their cultivation of theoretical and literary reasoning, and as priest and pastor of souls, he saw clearly that the aggressions of the empirical method of the physical sciences in particular and its usurpation of the other kinds of reason meant the marginalization or eclipse of both literature and the invisible spiritual world of religious belief. Sense observation and inductive judgment are the instruments of a scientific knowledge of the physical world but are inadequate both to knowledge of the concrete human world conveyed in literature and to knowledge of God mediated through the concrete in religious belief.

In defence of what was outside the reach of science, Newman argued that scientific reason was not the whole of reason. As he pleaded the cause of the way we know both in our experience of the particular or concrete and in our subsequent explicit reflection on this experience, his description of the mind's activity applies not only to religious belief, the primary focus of his analysis, but to the whole domain of knowledge in concrete matters. The pathway of the mind in this concrete way of knowing operative in both literature and in the individual's personal relation with God engages the mind in another way than the methods followed in inductive and deductive science. Newman wrote that although the objects of poetry and religion are different, they make use of the same faculties: both move the affections through the function of the imagination.[10] Just as in poetry we are moved through feelings connected to the imagination, so Newman writes that in religion

> The heart is commonly reached, not through the reason, but through the imagination, by means of direct impressions, by the testimony of facts and events, by history, by description. Persons influence us, voices melt us, looks subdue us, deeds inflame us.[11]

He speaks of the largely concrete character of Scripture that makes it accessible to the human imagination; similarly, in the Athanasian Creed the luminous intelligence of concrete words accessible to all reveals by analogy a Personal God: words like Father, Son, One, and Three.

However, unlike contemporaries who would suggest that both literature and religion involve only the imagination in its connection to the feelings, Newman also makes clear that neither literature nor religion are deficient in reason. While in both we are indeed moved through the concrete registered in the imagination rather than through theoretical reason or rational argument, in religious belief as in our immediate experience of literature the imagination functions jointly with an unarticulated kind of reason.

---

10   In "The Mission of St. Benedict," Newman describes the Benedictine monastic life as the most poetic of religious disciplines because both poetry and the contemplation of God move the affections through the function of the imagination. *Historical Sketches*, vol. 11 (London: Longmans, Green, 1888-).

In an appendix to "Poetry, with Reference to Aristotle's Poetics" when it was republished in *Essays and Sketches* (1871), Newman corrected an imbalance he perceived in the much earlier article by distinguishing between the formal object of poetry in beauty and its function in moving the affections through the imagination. Cf. *Essays and Sketches*, vol. 1, ed., Charles Frederick Harrold (New York: Longmans, Green and Co., 1948) v.

11   "The Tamworth Reading Room," *Essays and Sketches*, vol.ii, ed. Charles Frederick Harrold (New York: Longmans, Green, 1948) 89.

In the *Grammar of Assent,* in his exposition of this union of the imagination and the mind in our apprehension of the concrete, Newman deliberately chose to avoid the word "imagination." In its place, he spoke of the "real" (Latin *res:* thing), a word that emphasizes instead the particular or concrete object apprehended by the mind. In this final book, Newman himself compares the way the mind works in its apprehension of concrete matters to Aristotle's description of *phronesis*, the practical intelligence operative in ethical conduct which is best understood by observing those who practise it.

In our apprehension of the real in our experience of the particular or concrete, Newman maintains that reason operates tacitly with the impressions registered in the imagination. In religion, through this implicit reason the soul in its direct relation with God can take in what is essential in the imagination's impressions without explicit analysis. For example, in the experience of conscience the Thought implicit in the soul's Image of the Unseen can remain unarticulated. Newman speaks, first, of how we can apprehend an Image of the Invisible Being of God through the vivid experience of emotions elicited by the sanctions of right and wrong dictated by our conscience. If we recognize the cause as coming from One higher than ourselves and our own desires, the imagination is impressed with an Image of God as an Invisible Personal Power. At the same time, we may not be able to articulate the attributes implicit in this Image: such as omniscience, justice, power, or God as retributive, heart-reading, ever-accessible, loving.

Implicit knowledge in the immediate experience of literature is similar. The spectator at Euripides' *Medea* who has sufficient real experience of life can also recognize without complex, explicit analysis the perennial truth that lies within the concrete representation of the play as Medea takes appalling, brutal revenge for her rejection by Jason. In this kind of apprehension, both in literature and in religion the imagination is a vessel laden with thought.

In the mutuality of reason and imagination engaged in concrete matters, Newman asserts that the imagination itself has no reasoning power. Like in the physical sciences where the imagination is simply the register of sense impressions, so, too, in both religion and literature the function of the imagination is to register impressions, including the images of mental impressions; in doing so it has fulfilled its purpose. As we take in the unfolding events of a drama or absorb the gradual impressions made over time by the concrete accounts of Scripture and the experience of prayer, the imagination itself neither makes comparisons nor draws conclusions. Such activity is the function of reason.

The unarticulated, implicit reason that is so closely connected to the concrete differs from inductive and deductive science both in the personal nature of its judgments and in the free-ranging, idiosyncratic scope of associations and connections that lead to a subjective grasp of objective truth. Rather than operating through impersonal, clear, and logical connections, it is through idiosyncratic, jumbled references and associations that the spectator of *Medea* recognizes the nature of the passion of revenge or that the individual knows the Person of God in religious belief. To bring home the character of implicit reason's invisible activity operative in our insights into the concrete, Newman uses an analogy from the physical plane: the practical activity of a rock-climber. Of this inward, unarticulated kind of reasoning that we all commonly use, Newman writes:

> The mind ranges to and fro, and spreads out, and advances forward with a quickness which has become a proverb, and a subtely and versatility which baffle investigation. It passes on from point to point, gaining one by some indication, another on a probability; then availing itself of an association; then falling back on some received law; next seizing on testimony; then committing itself to some popular impression, or some inward instinct, or some obscure memory; and thus it makes progress not unlike a clamberer on a steep cliff, who, by quick eye, prompt hand, and firm foot, ascends how he knows not himself, by personal endowments and by practice, rather than by rule, leaving no track behind him, and unable to teach another. [12]

This tacit, unarticulated reason acting in conjunction with the concrete elucidates Aristotle's claim that the Greek drama provides a way for recognizing universals available to the Greek populace rather than just to philosophers, or that poetry which is concrete is also philosophical. It also resonates with Isaiah Berlin's description of the statesman's practical subtleness of mind aware of what is implicit in a

---

12   Newman, *Fifteen Sermons Preached before the University of Oxford between A.D.. 1826 and 1843* (Notre Dame, Ind.: University of Notre Dame Press, 1997) 256-57.

matter, of unstated connections embedded in particular contexts, of unknown and half known factors grasped within their contours. Indeed, this tacit reason lies beneath the surface in our understanding of all concrete matters: when seeking to understand what is contingent or unique in experience, when differences prevent a rule from obtaining, where variables defy abstract logic, where uncharted territory has no obvious law, in the arena of life where deliberation is required and choices must be made, and in literature that mirrors this life.

When in a further development we follow our natural desire to be conscious of our reasons, this implicit reasoning rooted in the particular and the concrete, acting jointly with the imagination, is the source and point of reference of our conscious reflections. Newman describes this explicit reason as it emerges from what is at first implicit, entangled in the particular and concrete in the imagination, and unable to give an account of itself. He says that explicit reason simply investigates prior tacit thought, which is complete in itself, to put order into it, to analyze, to detect and apply principles, to supply deficiencies, to trace out connections of facts. Through its attendance on what was apprehended first implicitly and jointly with the imagination, explicit reason illuminates, deepens, and anchors our understanding. As interpreters of Shakespeare, Scriptural exegetes, or individuals reflecting on their religious belief make explicit to themselves what was first implicit, reason remains close to its home in the concrete. In contrast to the general principles extracted in the scientific reasoning of theology or the theoretical principles and ideas applied in the arguments of literary criticism, the purpose of a "reading" of literature, of the interpretation of Scripture, or an individual's reflection on religious belief is to understand in the concrete: in the relation of parts with other parts and their place in a larger organic whole. This kind of explicit reason meant to illuminate the concrete follows the pattern provided by protagonists in tragedies: when Lear gradually comes to recognize his folly as a father or Oedipus understands finally that he has married his mother and killed his father, their moment of recognition is connected to all that has preceded it.

Our explicit apprehension of concrete matters belongs to the larger domain or genus of non-scientific thought that Aristotle called calculative reasoning. This calculative reasoning can also become the source of theoretical scientific reasoning in religion, literature, mathematics, and in the uncharted areas of the physical sciences as it yields principles and premises through the convergence of diverse probabilities. In the *Grammar of Assent*, Newman gives examples of this explicit reason through probabilities converging from various quarters as operative in the diverse spheres of mathematics, religion, and astronomy; it is through a convergence of probabilities in all these areas that experienced minds are persuaded of truth that has not been scientifically demonstrated. He cites testimony from a treatise on astronomy regarding the earth's rotation where the scientist maintained that when various probabilities "all upon different principles, are considered, they amount to a proof of the earth's rotation about its axis, which is as satisfactory to the mind as the most direct demonstration could be."[13] Or again, he points out that Newton began his *Principia* with an unproved proposition on the grounds that to consider the opposite proposition to be true was against likelihood.

In a scientific age that held suasory reason suspect, Newman argued that science's own foundations lay in this other large domain of calculative reasoning. The common ground in probable thought of the physical sciences, religion, and literature is apparent in Newman's description of how we are persuaded of truth in all probable areas, a description that is equally applicable to the literary reasoning of Cicero's rhetoric as to the explorations of modern science. Newman writes that in all probable matters we are persuaded of truth "by the strength, variety, or multiplicity of premises which are only probable … by objections overcome, by adverse theories neutralized, by difficulties gradually clearing up, by exceptions proving the rule, by unlooked-for correlations found with received truths." (*Grammar*, 254).

In other words, suasory reasoning through probabilities in physical science as it seeks premises, the persuasion that lies both at the heart of the reasoning of rhetoric and to our assents in religious belief, and the reason that makes literature cohere all belong to the same domain. In education in antiquity while theoretical scientific reasoning from abstract premises had been fostered through philosophy, calculative reasoning through probabilities had been cultivated through the literary reasoning of rhetoric as it considered particular concrete matters. In the nineteenth century when Newman became Rector of a new

---

13   Newman, *An Essay in Aid of a Grammar of Assent* (Notre Dame, Ind.: University of Notre Dame Press, 1979) 252. All further citations are from this edition.

university in Dublin, he defended passionately the value of the liberal arts because they cultivate both of these equally important and mutually connected modes of reason. In *The Idea of a University* (1852), he championed especially the fundamental importance of theoretical reason. A few years later in a lecture entitled "Literature" that he delivered to the Faculty of Philosophy and Letters, Newman pleaded specifically the cause of literature or of Letters. In antiquity, Aristotle had defended literature by countering Plato's accusation that the drama was twice removed from reason's source in Ideas and that in the drama passions dominated dangerously over reason. In a new scientific age, Newman again defended literature against its assailants. He resisted the claims of an intellectual community that increasingly would limit the imagination to the literal sensate register of physical science; that would dismiss the imagination as it functions in literature as fantasy and fancy, as effeminate and unreal; that would claim that literature lacked entirely the intellectual vigour of science.

When Newman undertook his defence of literature, he recognized that the study of literature at the university was considered useless both by those who would make professional training the sole focus of education and by advocates of the applied sciences. In the estimation of the proponents of the useful sciences who privileged inductive reasoning from sense observation and facts, literature was not reasoning. Unlike Aristotle who recognized that poetry was philosophical, the nineteenth-century advocates of empirical science maintained that literature in the classics cultivated the feelings, the imagination, and the aesthetic sense but did not cultivate the reason at all. In the volleys exchanged in the debates on education in the period, a literary education was dismissed as a training in elegant imbecility. Newman knew that this dismissal of the classics by promoters of the applied sciences was in fact an assault on all literature. As in Aristotle's period in the fifth century BCE, again in the nineteenth century the rationality of literature had to be defended before the tribunal of scientific reason.

In his lecture on literature as a specific kind of reasoning, Newman examined how language as used in literature reveals the character of literary thought where, unlike in science, objective truth is subjectively grasped. Like Isocrates, Newman identifies literature with the Greek word for reason: that is, *logos*. The word *logos*, or reason, is itself deeply layered with multiple meanings referring especially to the intelligible embedded in the concrete. In the *logos* of literature thought begets words that resonate with a writer's interiority and bear cumulative levels of meaning. However, in its broadest philosophic sense, the Greek *logos* means "the form which is the cause of all becoming" that makes things what they are, as in Aristotle's understanding of form in matter. This rich and complex word also refers to the intelligible principles informing intellectual and moral life. The *logos* as intellectual goodness pertains to clarity about rational principles as a sense of right proportions. It has a similar connotation of right proportion in moral judgments. In kinship with the feeling-knowledge of literature, moral goodness involves judgment according to the right degree of generosity, for example, or of anger proper to a given situation.[14] The *logos* also refers to the rational account we give of our decisions and actions. Aristotle maintains that the fully human level is attained when a person knows the moral and intellectual grounds of his activities, the universal implicit in his experiences, and can give an account of them.

In his lecture on "Literature" where Newman locates the specific character of literature in the idea of reason expressed in *logos,* he states that this single Greek word represents a unity comprised of two parts "distinct, but inseparable from each other" which English can only translate by using two words: in English *logos* is both thought and word together.[15] Literature is characterized by a particular type of rationality so intimately connected to its expression in words that thought and word are one. Thought begets words in accordance with the classical maxim: *"rem tene, verba sequentur"* (Seize the matter, the words will follow).[16] In this two-fold *logos* of literature, language reflects an author's idiosyncratic, personal exercise of reason. This personal voice of the author is a defining feature of literature which includes broadly the work of historians, letter-writers, essayists, and orators as well as poets, dramatists, and novelists.

---

14   Cf. John Burnet, introd., *Ethics of Aristotle* (London: Methuen, 1904).

15   Newman, "Literature," *The Idea of a University* (Notre Dame: Notre Dame University P., 1982) 219. All further citations are from this edition.

16   In his preface to David Whalen's *Consolation of Rhetoric: John Henry Newman and the Realism of Personalist Thought* (San Francisco - London: Catholic Scholar's P., 1994), Dennis Quinn writes of the rhetorical tradition in which there was a connection between learning and eloquence: "the truth is itself generative of eloquence," or as the "Roman Cato put the matter bluntly: *Rem tene, verba sequentur"* (Seize the thing, the words will follow) ix.

Like the larger genus to which it belongs, then, the rationality of literature involves a personal engagement between the writers and the matter expressed. The apt, exact expression of personal reasoning in literature requires a receptive attentiveness to the inner world of thought which generates the words reflecting it. Newman speaks of orators, historians, poets, and essayists who "were working by a model which was before the eyes of their intellect, and ... were labouring to say what they had to say, in such a way as would most exactly and suitably express it" ("Literature," 214). In this intimate connection between thinker and thought, the tone of a work resonates with the personal relation between writer and the matter at hand. Newman says of the writer:

> He writes passionately, because he feels keenly; forcibly, because he conceives vividly; ... he can analyze his subject, and therefore he is rich; ... he has a firm hold of it, and therefore he is luminous. When his imagination wells up, it overflows in ornament; when his heart is touched, it thrills along his verse ("Literature," 220).

Even the phrasing and the aural echoes in a work reflect the personal connection between the work and the writer. Particularly in poetry, "not only the words alone, but even the rhythm, the metre, the verse, will be the contemporaneous offspring of the emotion or imagination which possess" the poet ("Literature," 210).

Literature partakes of the large genus not only in this personal engagement but in its convergent mode of thought. Newman, whose own reasoning is typically literary, describes eloquently this personal process of converging thought in literature and its exact reflection in the writer's language:

> The throng and succession of ideas, thoughts, feelings, imaginations, aspirations which pass within him, the abstractions, the juxtapositions, the comparisons, the discriminations, the conceptions, which are so original in him, his views of external things, his judgments upon life, manners and history, the exercises of his wit, of his humour, of his depth, of his sagacity, all these innumerable and incessant creations, the very pulsation and throbbing of his intellect, does he image forth, to all does he give utterance, in a corresponding language, which is as multiform as this inward mental action itself and analogous to it, the faithful expression of his intense personality, attending on his own inward world of thought as its very shadow: so that we might as well say that one man's shadow is another's as that the style of a really gifted

mind can belong to any but himself. It follows him about as a shadow. His thought and feeling are personal, and so his language is personal ("Literature," 207-8).

The unique personal resonance of reasoning in the *logos* means that language instrumental to this mode of reasoning is not ready-made or capable of a kind of mechanical application. It is the work neither of committees and groups nor of computer programs. Newman writes: "It is not some production or result, attained by the partnership of several persons, or by machinery, or by any natural process, but in its very idea it proceeds, and must proceed, from some one given individual" ("Literature," 205). Because a writer's "thought and feeling are personal … so his language is personal," expressing not only the author's great thoughts, but the author's great self ("Literature," 208). Person, thought connected to the matter under consideration, and its verbal expression are as inseparable as the convex and the concave of a curve.

Because like its larger genus literature's personal mode of reasoning locates principles and universal truths within the concrete and particular, it is accessible to all and serves the common good of humanity in its two-fold mode of thought and word. Contrary to the accusation of inutility levelled by advocates of the applied or useful sciences, an author's articulation of perennial truths embedded in the concrete fulfills two important and useful communal functions: first, in giving concrete shape to what many feel but few can express and, secondly, in forging for a native language a legacy of words and phrases that express these thoughts. Newman writes that the function of the poet is to grasp and name the unseen by locating it in the sensible and the concrete, making great prototypal ideas accessible to our contemplation. He cites from *A Midsummer's Night's Dream* where Shakespeare says that the poet's eye ranges from heaven to earth and from earth to heaven, and

> … as imagination bodies forth
> The forms of things unknown, the poet's pen
> Turns them to shapes, and gives to airy nothing
> A local habitation and a name ("Literature," 213).

The enduring authors of the classics of literature are important because they reflect through their literary sensibility types which we recognize as "common to the whole race of man." As Newman eloquently observes, these authors are "spokesmen and prophets of the human family" through whom "the secrets of the heart are brought to light, pain of the soul is relieved, hidden grief is carried off, sympathy conveyed, counsel imparted, experience recorded, and wisdom perpetuated ... the past and the future, the East and the West are brought into communication with each other" ("Literature," 220-1).

Because the language of authors who are spokespersons for the human condition bears a personal stamp, they also fulfil an important function as wordsmiths. Language evolves and is enriched through the individual author who "takes his native language, masters it, partly throws himself into it, partly moulds and adapts it, and pours out his multitude of ideas through the variously ramified and delicately minute channels of expression which he has found or framed" ("Literature," 215-16). The authors' personal use of language passes then into proverbs among their people; a great writer's phrases become "household words and idioms of their daily speech, which is tesselated with the rich fragments of his language" ("Literature," 220).

Both literature's path towards understanding and the language that is its instrument are more akin to music and to art than to science: in the beauty of craftsmanship and the unmistakable touch of the artist; in personal resonances and layers of meaning; in the arrangement or in the repetitions and variations which converge towards one effect. For musicians, painters, and the writer of genius the same principle of intelligible unity applies that is central to converging reason and inherent in the rationality of the drama described by Aristotle. In the best painting and music nothing is superfluous; in good literature no word is extraneous to the filaments of thought; no word is inexact or misplaced.

The contrast in the distinction between the literary use of words and their scientific use is a further way of defining the nature of literature. Unlike science's univocal language, in literature's way of knowing words are not literal but polyvalent. They do not stand for sensate things only as in empirical induction but through analogy slip easily up and down between the human, divine, and physical realms in images, similes, and metaphors. The sensate may conjure up terror or pity; a storm may externalize inner disarray; eating an apple may alter a relation with God. As well, because in literature intelligible principles are immersed in the concrete, contexts define words; different characters interpret the same words differently and an audience, too, brings its own associations to a work. Finally, words reverberate with all the possibilities of both their specialized and popular usages along with the cumulative weight of their use by authors in previous particular contexts.

In the *Grammar of Assent*, Newman contrasts this rich and resonant use of language in literature with the controlled and narrow use of language by science. Because scientific reasoning does not seek the particulars or the differences that constitute what is individual in matters but abstracts one single aspect common to many things, scientific language is characterized by clarity of definition, by the univocal use of words in propositions, and by their systematic development within a single field. Newman's description of the difference between the use of language in literature and science applies equally to the received premisses of deductive science and to the general laws reached through empirical induction in the modern sciences. He writes:

> Words, which denote things, have innumerable implications; but in inferential exercises it is the very triumph of that clearness and hardness of head, which is the characteristic talent for the art, to have stripped them of all these connatural senses, to have drained them of that depth and breadth of associations which constitute their poetry, their rhetoric, and their historical life, to have starved each term down till it has become the ghost of itself, and everywhere one and the same ghost ... so that it may stand for just one unreal aspect of the concrete thing to which it properly belongs, for a relation, a generalization, or other abstraction, for a notion neatly turned out of the laboratory of the mind, and then sufficiently tame and subdued, because existing only in a definition (*Grammar*, 214-5).

Much grief and grave misunderstanding, especially in Scriptural interpretation, has been caused by the failure to recognize the difference between literature's rationality and use of language and science's use of language which reflects the demarcations of its own reasoning. When literary language is read as though it were science, as for Robinson Crusoe who saw only what was useful to him on his island, nine tenths of what is in a text will appear unmeaning or irrelevant. In a literal or scientific reading of literature that seeks out facts and things, much of what is most important to literature's way of knowing will be dismissed as ornaments of style; style will appear as separate from substance and the two-fold *logos* where words resonate with interiority will be split in two. Newman says of such readers: "Thought and word are, in their conception, two things, and thus there is a division of labour" ("Literature," 209). For those unaccustomed to the literary mode of reasoning and the resonance of its language, style will be "a sort of ornament super-induced, or a luxury indulged in, by those who have time and inclination for such vanities" ("Literature," 208). Or again, the "narrow critic" will see the richness of literary style as "verbiage when really it is a sort of fulness of heart" ("Literature," 211).

Newman illustrates this problem of seeing literature's thought and language through the lens of science through the example of Laurence Sterne, eighteenth-century clergyman and author of the novel, *Tristram Shandy* (1759). The diminishment suffered by both poetry and Scripture is disclosed in one of Sterne's published sermons where he discusses the vacuousness of imagery and language in poetry's higher aesthetics, such as Homer's *Iliad* and *Odyssey*, on the one hand, and, on the other hand, of the literal simplicity of language in Scripture which, he says, stands for things as in science.

Because literal translation of words that refer to things is straightforward, for Sterne facility of translation was a test of the substance and worth of a text, both in poetry and Scripture. From his literal perspective, in Homer's poetry fear embedded in a storm or awe conveyed in the action of a god is simply verbiage that dissolves in its translation from Greek into Latin. That is, proof of poetry's lack of substance is found in this exercise of translating into Latin its cumulative emotion-laden images. Sterne wrote that Homer's "famed representation of Jupiter--his cried-up description of a tempest, his relation of Neptune's shaking the earth and opening it to its centre, his description of Pallas's horses, with numbers of other long-since admired passages, flag, and almost vanish away, in the vulgar Latin translation."

With the lack of substance in Homer's poetry exposed through translation, he pronounces that such classical literature "consists chiefly in laboured and polished periods, an over-curious and artificial arrangement of figures, tinseled over with a gaudy embellishment of words, which glitter, but convey little or no light to the understanding. This kind of writing is for the most part much affected and admired by the people of weak judgment and vicious taste" ("Literature," 203). However, when Sterne applies the same test of literal translation to Scripture, he finds that it passes the test because Scripture is about things, ideas, and conceptions which are easily translated and "shine through the most simple and literal translations." The sacred writings, he says, "consist more in the greatness of the things themselves than in the words and expressions" ("Literature," 204).

As an arbiter between methods, Newman simply points out that while parts of Scripture are indeed scientific and easy to translate, as Sterne suggests, others are literary and difficult both to understand and to translate. In the scientific portions of Scripture, words are impersonal symbols of universal truths that convey clear ideas like the premises in Aristotle's syllogisms. For example, the Prologue to John's Gospel speaks in the scientific terminology of the Word or *Logos*, Aristotle's form that was the cause of all becoming, used in its Christian sense of divine Person. In John's Prologue, the Word as both transcendent and immanent is described as "with God in the beginning," as the One through whom "all things came into being," in whom was the "life that was the light of man." Newman agrees that such parts of Scripture, like the clear statements of the Creed, "have the grandeur, the majesty, the calm, unimpassioned beauty of Science; they are in no sense Literature, they are in no sense personal; and therefore they are easy to apprehend, and easy to translate ("Literature," 218).

On the other hand, other portions of Scripture are literature in the same manner as the Greek oratory of Demosthenes, or Greek tragedies like the plays of Euripides. For example, the personal voice of St. Paul in his pastoral letters to ancient communities in Ephesus or Corinth are "literature in a real and true sense, *as* personal, *as* rich in reflection and emotion, as Demosthenes or Euripides; and, without ceasing to be revelations of objective truth ... are expressions of the subjective notwithstanding" ("Literature," 217-8). In the Book of Job, the poignant drama of innocent suffering, of conflicting advice, and of God's ultimate claims make it a sacred drama "as artistic, as perfect as any Greek tragedy." Similarly, in the beauty of their images, rhythms, studied cadences and phrasings the Psalms are divine poetry.

Contrary to Sterne's claims, the difference between the literary use of language and its literal use means that translation of the literary portions of Scripture is not easy. Their translation into the idiom of another language requires the same sensibility as that described by Aristotle for the interpretation of the tragedies. Where an author's thought and word are one, where language is not standardized, where particular contexts must be understood in relation to others and to a literary whole, where the intention of the author must be sought out, words must be considered carefully if a personal presence or literary resonance is to be translated from one language into another language. The whole procedure is further complicated by the differences in languages shaped by their own traditions through the genius of their native authors.[17]

The gravity of the consequence of denying to literature its own use of language reflecting its specific mode of reasoning is evident in this juncture of science and literature on the field of religion in Scripture. The denial of the literary nature of much of Scripture and the insistence on a literal reading meant a rejection of the realities that can be apprehended only through the literary function of the imagination and literature's converging mode of thought. The two different ways of reading Scripture's language divided the readers of a book set apart from all others, a book that oriented people's lives through its revelation of the relation of humankind to God.

This division represented by Sterne indicated a rupture with a long tradition in exegesis that used the same tools for interpretation of the sacred books of Scripture as those used by the Greek interpreters of Homer's poetry. In Newman's own area of scholarship in the Greek Church Fathers of the second, third, and fourth centuries, exegetes had assumed that the only way to understand much of Scripture was not simply through a literal reading but through other analogical levels in a spiritual reading that followed the same principles for interpretation as poetry.

The study of literature provided the foundation for the Scriptural interpretation of the Church Fathers and for those who succeeded them in the following centuries. Newman wrote of the transmission of the work of the Church Fathers and of classical literature in the

---

17 A medieval translator of Aristotle describes this problem. Robert Grosseteste warns his reader: "' It must also be acknowledged that the Greeks use many compound words for which the Latin has no corresponding compounds. Thus, it is necessary for translators ... to put a number of Latin words in place of one of these compounds. Such Latin words, however, cannot express in all fullness of meaning the mind of the author in the same way that a single Greek term can .... It must also be realized that in Latin translation, especially in a literal one, there necessarily are many expressions which are very ambiguous and amenable to multiple meanings, which in Greek are unambiguous.'" Cited by Candice Taylor Quinn in "Robert Grosseteste and the Corpus Dionysiacum: Accessing Spiritual Realities through the Word," *Editing Robert Grosseteste* (Toronto: U. of Toronto P., 2003) 90.

long monastic period that began in the fifth century.[18] In monastery scriptoriums throughout the middle ages, monks transcribed both the rich commentaries on Scripture by the Church Fathers and the manuscripts of classical literature which served to train them for their work in Scripture. These monks were educated through the classical authors: through Latin poets like Ovid and Virgil; the playwright, Terrence; and Cicero, the admired master of rhetorical prose. In the eleventh century when speculative theologians began to synthesize the long legacy of commentaries on Scripture, they were also similarly trained in classical literature.

In opposition to this long tradition, in the eighteenth-century Sterne's hostility to the rationality of poetry along with his claim that Scripture is susceptible to literal translation because it refers to things has its roots in seventeenth-century Baconian empirical science and in the materialist philosophy that rose along with it. The abyss between literature's idea of language and reason and the idea of language and reason in this philosophy again illustrates by contrast the nature of the literary *logos* with its textured layers of meaning.

Thomas Hobbes provides an instance of the materialist philosophy which accords with Sterne's assumption that language should be univocal or literal because it stands for things. For Hobbes, reliable words were equated either with sensate things or with the abstract aspects of things in words like "white" where thought is separated from things. For him, imagination registered only sensate impressions and reason began only with impersonal clearly-defined words. His mistrust of the passions meant the exclusion from reason of personal feeling conjoined with thought that is at the heart of literary rationality and integral to practical ethical judgment. In this model of reasoning, both the rationality of literature and the Church Fathers' view of the world as opening on to what is incommensurable were simply unreal.

Thomas Hobbes (1568-1679) was both a neo-epicurean philosopher and a classical scholar. He knew Bacon, the great advocate of inductive empirical philosophy, and occasionally acted as his amanuensis. On the continent he met Gassendi, the reviver of epicurean philosophy and a fellow mathematical reasoner, as well as Galileo.

---

18   Newman, "The Mission of St. Benedict," *The Rise and Progress of Universities and Benedictine Essays*, Mary Katherine Tillman, ed. (Notre Dame: University of Notre Dame Press, 2001).

Hobbes is considered the father of utilitarianism and of nineteenth-century liberalism. His philosophy is the pattern for twentieth-century logical positivist philosophy, such as the school of Wittgenstein, which is grounded in grammatical analysis and linguistic theory. Many of the tenets of his political philosophy are readily recognized in the assumptions of politics and economics in our own day.

Although Hobbes did not recognize the rationality of literature, his early work as a classical scholar influenced his philosophy; his political theory was shaped in part through translating Thucydides' history of the Peloponesian wars in the fifth century BCE. As well, after a lifetime spent writing on philosophy and the science of politics, at the age of eighty-seven Hobbes returned to the classics again to translate Homer's *Iliad* and *Odyssey*. Nonetheless, in his concept of the human understanding expressed in *Leviathan* (1651), his work on political science, he excluded literature from reason. His neo-epicurean philosophy was rooted in atomist physics that turned its back both on the literary ethos of the Renaissance and the speculative deductive reasoning long associated with liberal learning. Although unlike most neo-epicurean philosophers for Hobbes reason meant deduction from clearly-defined terms, nonetheless his sensate idea of knowing restricted the range of reason and excluded the kind of studies connected to the university since its beginnings in the twelfth century.

In the *Leviathan*, we find a pattern for Sterne's scientific view of language in Hobbes' materialist epistemology. For this sensate philosopher, sensation is matter in motion pressed on our organs; imagination is described as faded or decaying sense; memory and imagination are one and both are connected only to direct sense experience. As for reasoning itself and its expression in language, Hobbes limits words to what is sensate by explicitly rejecting from the outset the concept of reason and language expressed in the *logos* where thought and word are one; that is, he rejected what the Greeks had considered most characteristically human.

Instead, Hobbes defines reason through the Latin word, "ratio." In his interpretation of this word, reasoning involves a relation between words that name things and their abstract aspects; for example, "hot" or "living" are aspects which give an account of matter, or again, nouns like "heat" and "life" are abstract because severed from an account of matter. Hobbes then traces the origin of *ratio* to *rationes*, or accounts of money, in their connection to *nomina* or names as the heading for items listed in ledgers and on bills. In his mathematical model of logic, reasoning is like the reckoning of accounts of money; it is an adding and subtracting of the consequences of clearly defined general names where the connection of two things or names makes an affirmation.[19] For Hobbes, only mathematics and the exercise of this kind of logic yield what Aristotle called necessary truth.

In Hobbes' concept of mind, his philosophy of the passions restricts further the range of words considered reliable in reasoning. For him, happiness lies not in tranquility, as Epicurus maintained, but in the continual progress of the desire from one object to another. In a ruthlessly competitive and rawly self-referential world, individuals are driven by the passion for power such as the power of continued wealth, or of reputation, or of office. This desire for power by individuals is what defines virtue and vice.[20] In keeping with this relativization of the virtues and vices, conscience is not considered a divine sanction but merely a consensus regarding facts when two or more men know of the same fact.[21] Fear of being despoiled by others and fear of violence or death at their hands are countered by fear of an accepted common political power and through the contractual agreement or covenant of laws which alone forbid man's natural desires.

In contrast to the rationality of literature where feeling is integral to thought, Hobbes' theory of the passions and its relativization of words that refer to the virtues and vices makes these words unreliable in his idea of reasoning through clearly defined terms. Hobbes explains that the meaning of such words varies according to "the nature, disposition, and interest of the speaker .... For one man calleth *Wisdome*, what another calleth *feare*; and one *cruelty*, what another *justice*." Because of their shifting relative meanings in a world where conscience is merely what two people agree upon, Hobbes concludes that "such names can

---

19   Hobbes, *Leviathan* (New York: Penguin, 1968)106-7.

20   In the spirit of a reverse decalogue or as a list of secular beatitudes, Hobbes writes of natural man that "Covetousnesse of great Riches, and ambition of great Honours, are Honourable ; as signes of power to obtain them. Covetousnesse, and ambition, of little gaines, or preferements, is Dishonourable." Nor does it matter whether a great and difficult action is just or unjust as "Honour consisteth onely in the opinion of Power." (*Leviathan*, 156) Good is identified with the Latin "*pulchrum*" or beautiful.

21   Ibid., 188, 132.

never be true grounds of any ratiocination" (*Leviathan*, 109). In this philosophy of reason where reliable words give an account of matter only, neither the Greek philosophy of the *logos*, nor the scriptural theology of the *Logos*, nor the literary *logos* along with its genus of convergent reasoning have any place. The closely-related reasoning of ethics is also radically altered. Where Aristotle considered ethical reasoning (*phronesis*) to be one of the virtues of the intellect, like his modern philosophical counterparts Hobbes considered ethics to be either statements of fact or expressions of emotional states with very little rational content.

Within his circumscribed definition of reason, then, there is no place for the literary *logos* as a legitimate mode of reasoning or as a serious vehicle for philosophic truth. For Hobbes, rhetorical figures, tropes of speech, and metaphors are inconstant figures which openly profess deceit and can have no place in reasoning. He would allow only in private and for personal amusement words that are equivocal or the play of sounds in words that comprise the hidden music of poetry. In public places, he writes, "there is no Gingling of words that will not be accounted folly" (*Leviathan*, 137). Finally, he concludes a discussion of the science of reason with a Baconian vision for the material betterment of humankind which at the same time dismisses literary language and any other use of words that does not conform to his sensate epistemology and the requirement of clearly defined univocal language. He writes:

> The Light of humane minds is Perspicuous Words, but by exact definitions first snuffed, and purged from ambiguity; *Reason* is the *pace*; Encrease of *Science*, the *way*; and the Benefit of man-kind, the *end*. And on the contrary Metaphors, and senslesse and ambiguous words, are like *ignes fatui* [will o'the wisps]; and reasoning upon them, is wandering amongst innumerable absurdities ... (*Leviathan*, 116-7).

Like Rousseau in the following century, Hobbes took aim not only at Letters or the arts but also at philosophy; that is, the verbal speculative thought which together with letters was still considered by Newman in the nineteenth century to be central to university education. The seventeenth-century confrontation between the old learning with the new represented by Hobbes involved antithetical starting-points: on the one hand, the speculative reasoning in scholastic philosophy and theology rooted in the cosmic view of the *logos* where the intel-

ligible informs matter; and on the other hand, Hobbes'materialist philosophy that refers to the material plane alone. After explaining the
epicurean theory of sense perception as the motion of matter pressed
on our organs, Hobbes objects that "the Philosophy-schooles, through
all the Universities of Christendome, grounded upon certain Texts of
Aristotle, teach another doctrine."[22]

Hobbes' complaints about the "frequency of insignificant Speech" in
the learning of the universities is directed specifically against speculative reasoning grounded in the theology of the *Logos*. From the perspective of his materialist criterion of truth, the schoolmen wrote of
mad stuff, on incomprehensible matters that correspond to nothing in
the mind. Hobbes repeatedly decries the non-sense, or their absurd
and insignificant use of language. He inveighs against their words and
phrases based not on his materialistic view of the world and concept
of mind but on a cosmology that included Spirit as transcendent and
immanent. He objects to words referring to the influence of the Holy
Spirit, such as "In-powrd vertue" and "In-blown vertue," or to the final union of the soul with God in the "beatific vision." Such words,
Hobbes maintains, are used by those who don't understand "what we
call causes"; or by those who from not knowing "what imagination
and sense are" receive matters not from their own meditation but "by
the authority of an *Aristotle*, a *Cicero*, or a *Thomas* ...".[23] Finally, for
Hobbes, as for Sterne, the process of translation validates his theory
of language. He finds that the mystery of the latinate French word,
"Verbe" (Latin: *Verbum*; Greek: *Logos*), signifying the Word of God is
exposed as insubstantial when it is rendered into ordinary French as
"parole."[24]

---

22   Hobbes explains the Aristotelian doctrine of cognition: "For the cause
of *Vision*, that the thing seen, sendeth forth on every side a *visible species*
(in English) a *visible shew, apparition*, or *aspect*, or *a being seen*; the receiving
wherof into the Eye, is a *Seeing* .... Nay for the cause of *Understanding* also,
they say the thing Understood sendeth forth *intelligible species*, that is, an
intelligible being seen; which comming into the Understanding, makes us
Understand" (*Leviathan*, 86-87). Italics are Hobbes.

23   Ibid., 106

24   Ibid., 108. Hobbes claims that the non-sense of the speculative theologians is demonstrated by the difficulty of translating intelligibly into any
modern language their conversations on such topics as the Trinity, the De-
ity, the nature of Christ, transubstantiation, or free-will.

By the eighteenth century the univocal idea of language common to science and to materialist philosophers like Hobbes had become a habit of mind for Sterne in his aversion to poetry and his understanding of the language of Scripture. This levelling of language by philosophy and science eliminates the possibility of literature's densely textured levels of meaning and its polyvalent use of language. The literal view of language applied to Scripture stands in stark contrast to the luxuriant literary interpretation of Scripture by the Church Fathers where single words might have multiple references and analogical reason opened the path towards knowledge of God through layers of meaning. In the centuries following St. Paul, Greek Fathers like Clement, Origen, and Chrysostom and Latin Fathers like Ambrose, Augustine, and Jerome moved their listeners, as they have continued to move others with undiminished freshness in succeeding times: humanists like Erasmus in the Renaissance; the English divines in the seventeenth century; Newman, the champion of liberal education in the nineteenth century; and twentieth-century theologians like Hans Urs Von Balthazar and Henri de Lubac.

In an age when Alexandria in Egypt was the cultural heart of Greece, in the theocentric view of life of Greek Fathers like Origen (185-ca 254) the interior, invisible world of spirit informed all. For them, the Person of the *Logos*, or indivisible Word and Reason of God, had uttered the world into existence and the visible world was infused with the invisible. In contrast to Hobbes' sensate concept of the human understanding and his idea of reason or *ratio* as reckoning, they considered that humankind was made in the image of God through the *logos*, or the reason and language together that characterize the human species[25] and make us analogous to God as the *Logos*. Unlike the neo-epicurean, materialist idea of mind and of self-sufficiency, the Greek Fathers believed that our nature opens up towards God and that through the noetic light of the intelligence in its contemplative role we can be illuminated by divine grace.

For the Greek Fathers, reasoning through levels of analogy provided a key to what was most important; that is, to knowledge of God, if only as through a mirror darkly or in the shadowy way of knowing the

---

25   For example, Clement of Alexandria writes: "We are the rational images formed by God's Word, or Reason," who "was from the first … but … lately took a name … the Christ." Clement, *Clement of Alexandria* (London: William Heinemann, 1919) 17.

intelligible through the concrete. In their cosmology where spirit informs matter, language did not merely represent the sensate world of things; instead, words were also vehicles for a spiritual reality centred in the *Logos* and alive in the moral and spiritual lives of individuals. In Scripture's record of the drama of the religious formation of a people by God, words registered the *Logos* in its several connected meanings: for example, as transcendent divinity and as incarnate God, in the theocentric moral lives of individuals, and in their collective historical development as a religious people.

For these Greek Fathers, the interpretation of the layered levels of Scripture proceeded from similar assumptions and required the same tools as those described by Aristotle for the interpretation of poetry's mirror of life. Scripture's unfolding drama of humankind's religious development told variously through historical accounts, stories, songs, and in personal voices and testimonies is informed by the same principle of unity and internal coherence discerned by Aristotle in the unfolding development of plots in the poetry of the Greek drama. The many books of Scripture extending over a long historical period, written by different authors, and edited and ordered by still other people, form a single complex unity like the drama. From beginning to end, the whole of Scripture is also unified by a concept of humankind as not merely material but as opening towards God in the depths of each individual's being: from Genesis where human beings are shaped in God's image to John's vision in the final book of their ultimate just end and of the possibility of union with God in a heavenly city that glows with interior light. Like the unified living organism that Aristotle compares to the drama, in the books of Scripture taken as a whole nothing is extraneous, one part is understood in relation to other parts, no part can be removed or transposed without damage to the whole. As in the Greek tragedies, good and evil are held in tensile unity, later events illuminate the significance of earlier events, and the whole is understood in relation to the vaulting arc of the divine.

Like good literary criticism, the rich veins of Scripture expounded by Alexandrine exegetes are also grounded in a grasp of the universal principles embedded within the Bible which animate it as a whole. Exegetes like Origen had so fully understood the significance of the principles of Christianity derived from Scripture and stated in the Creed that it was as though they spoke from the other side of Scripture's narratives and illuminated its verbal accounts and images through the light of the divine. In the manner of Aristotle's advice to interpret the tragedies by considering the intention of the author, in the sacred books they searched out the intention of their authors in the light of the simple truths of the Creed that inform Scripture: of God or the *Logos* as Creator; of the *Logos* or God as Christ; of the Holy Spirit as God inspiring the authors of the books of Scripture as well as the continuing religious drama of humankind in spite of the heedless rejections, the mutinies, and betrayals that have characterized this drama from the very beginning.

Origen's expositions in his homilies to mixed and shifting audiences demonstrate on the field of Scripture this literary way of reasoning. As he interpreted when necessary the meaning behind the words of Scripture, his purpose was to strengthen his hearer's understanding of what is embedded in the concrete. If he pointed out the lack of logic in the story of creation where day and night precede the creation of the sun and moon or the unseemliness of God like a farmer planting trees in the garden of Eden, it was to show the need to interpret the text as a concrete way of understanding. Analogical interpretation in particular served this purpose; ordinary language in accounts of battles and marriages might contain another inner meaning.

Origen's interpretation of the Book of Numbers illustrates the concrete literary way of understanding and follows the same principles for interpretation described by Aristotle. The Book of Numbers, so named because it begins with a census of the Jewish tribes who set out from Egypt, is an historical account of their journey towards the promised land: their negotiations for travel through hostile territory, the battles they engage in, their hardships, their rebellions when faith fails, their religious ritual, and the guidance of their departures and their places of encampment through God's presence in a cloud by day and fire by night.

As Origen expounds a chapter in Numbers (Num 33) that lists the forty-two stages in the journey of the Israelites, he draws on the typical tools of literary interpretation. For example, he considers various ways of understanding a word to make more complete sense of a context; he considers one chapter in Numbers in relation not only to the rest of the Book of Numbers but also in relation to the spiritual odyssey of humankind that is the larger intention of the Bible as a whole. In keeping with the literary principle of unity and internal coherence, Origen explains that although people avoid the list of encampments in Numbers because they find it dry through a lack of understanding, nonetheless no part of Scripture, however obscure, can be neglected anymore than any favourite part can be partially understood without damaging distortions.

Unlike the univocal use of language in scientific reasoning or Hobbes' strict limitation on words as referring only to things, Origen finds a double simultaneous sense in the place names of encampments listed in Numbers. The literal level of the journey of the Israelites has also a moral and spiritual sense as in Origen's exposition the order of each stage in the journey becomes significant as a stage in the typical moral life of the individual soul. Origen finds this second analogical sense through the literal meaning of the Hebrew place names which in Scripture are often connected to events that occurred at a place or to characteristics associated with it. He observes that the Israelites start out from Ramasse, meaning in Hebrew

> "confused agitation" or "agitation of the worm." By this it is made clear that everything in this world is set in agitation and disorder, and also in corruption; for this is what the worm means. The soul should not remain in them, but should set out and come to Sochoth.

In the second stage at Sochoth or "tents" the soul learns that it is to dwell in tents like a wanderer "so that it can be, as it were, ready for battle and meet those who lie in wait for it unhindered and free."[26]

Not only through these associations made though words but also through contextual comparisons with other parts of Scripture, Origen's connections enrich and affirm the chapter's double sense. In the literary manner, part resonates with part as well as with the whole. When Origen translates the name of another encampment at Charadath into Greek as meaning "made competent," he notes that in the New Testament this is just what Paul says, 'He has made us competent to be ministers of a new covenant'" (2 Cor. 3:6).[27]

In this kind of exegesis, Origen's approach to language is in the literary tradition of Greek and Latin grammarians who considered the different levels of meaning of words. For example, the six extant books on etymology entitled *De Lingua Latina* by M. Terrentius Varro (116-27 BCE) explain the origins of words through four levels of meaning

---

26   *Origen* (New York: Paulist P., 1979) 258.

27   Ibid., 264.

derived from the speech of common folk, poets who fashioned words, philosophers who revealed the nature of words, and the difficult, often unfully fathomed words from the mysteries of the high priests. In this classical tradition, for example, a word like *logos* has not only a literary sense, but also philosophical and religious meanings.

Finally, since the authors' own words are the indispensable starting-point for interpretation, as in works of literature an uncorrupted original text is of primary importance. For the interpreters of Scripture in Greek Alexandria, the skill of Greek translators of the original Hebrew texts was crucial. In contrast to Sterne's claim that such translation was easy, Origen's careful scholarly work that made him a pioneer in textual criticism indicates the erudition required to deal with the mutations and variations from the original language in translations. With the help of stenographers and calligraphists, Origen compiled the *Hexapla* (Greek: sixfold), an edition of the Old Testament in six parallel columns which exhibited the original Hebrew text; its Greek transliteration; the Greek Septuagint, the great work of translators in Alexandria in the third century B.C.E.; and three subsequent Greek versions. In this way, all the textual evidence available was assembled for the inquirer. Discrepancies in various translations were brought into relief and controversial debate with Jews who disputed translations in the Septuagint was given clarity.

The Greek Fathers' understanding of the *Logos* and their interpretation of Scripture through the two-fold literary *logos* is antithetical to the revised concept of reason of a materialist philosopher like Hobbes and to his understanding of language as a reflection of his concept of reason. In this collision, we have the markings of the irreconcilable stances typical of Greek tragedy. We have an emblem of the predicament of our own times: of the marginalization of the humanities in the university; of philosophy deprived of the mutuality of literary reasoning; of religion and Scripture constricted by the loss of literature's reason and its rich use of language. And we have good reason to appreciate the timeliness of Newman's defense of the genus of convergent reasoning and the literary use of language that comprise such an important part of our humanity.

4

THE SEVENTEENTH CENTURY:

IMAGINATION IN POETRY, EMPIRICAL

SCIENCE, AND EDUCATIONAL REFORM

The fundamental question of what it is to be human is answered variously by philosophy, by the modern physical sciences, and by literature like poetry and the drama. In seeking answers to this large question, each order of knowledge uses in its own way the various faculties of mind as its intellectual instrument. The injunction to know ourselves, *nosce teipsum*, is answered by philosophy through assumed theoretical starting-points originating in nature and conceived by the reason; for example, through epistemologies that consider the nature of the mind in reason's relation to the senses, to the imagination, to the memory, to the passions, and to the will. Modern empirical science examines the human body as a physical organism. Aided by technical instruments, it gathers evidence for its judgments through sense observation; the responses of the brain, for example, are mapped and measured. In a way unlike the intellectual instruments of either theoretical or empirical science, literature's convergent reasoning probes the question of what it is to be human in large measure through a function of the imagination unique to literature and closely connected to the affections. Not only because of its unscientific cumulative kind of reasoning, but because in literature reason engages in its own distinct relation with the imagination distrust prevails between the theoretical and empirical sciences and literature.

A measure of this mistrust is suggested in Plato's fear of the passions unleashed in crowds who attended annual dramatic performances in

Athens. Because in Plato's philosophy reason was to dominate passion, he was wary of the emotional effects of poetic tragedy where instead reason operates in a joint venture with the affections and the
imagination. The mimetic field of the imagination as it functions in
the drama also worked against the tenets of his philosophy. For Plato,
the perishable things of this world were an imperfect imitation of eternal Ideas; drama's imitation of life was even further removed from the
true reality of the world of Ideas. The elevation of the literary imagination and its attendant affections in the drama differs from the place
and function of both the passions and the imagination in Plato's understanding of our humanity.

When in response to Plato's objections Aristotle turned to the plays
themselves to inquire into their nature, he found that the imagination
and the affections have their own proper function in relation to reason
in poetry. Through the plausible connections in its imaginative imitation of life, poetry had its own kind of rational intelligibility; the mimetic field of the imagination through which reason operates is both
natural to us and is connected to how we learn from childhood. The
passions aroused in an audience by the tragic drama's imitation of life
are not to be feared as a threat to reason. Rather, the affective function
connected to the imagination is integral to tragedy which chastens the
audience through exciting pity and terror.

In short, the great tragic dramas neither unleash passions rashly nor
corrupt spectators. They do not evoke sympathy with wrongdoing; instead they provide a moral model of human life compelling to audiences through the engagement of their imagination and their feelings. In
this engagement, without being overtly moral the virtual reality of the
dramas draws on the same parts of our mind that in our moral lives
move us to decisions and to action. In *Oedipus*, we are chastened by
witnessing the horror of a whole city where plague and incest coincide.
As the drama of Shakespeare's *King Lear* unfolds, we recoil before the
cruelty of Lear's daughters who condone the vicious blinding of their
father's faithful supporter and leave their own foolishly-generous father destitute, homeless, and on the edge of madness. Imaginative impressions move us as we watch Macbeth dismiss both the injunctions
of conscience and the foresight of moral reasoning while deliberating the murder of his king and cousin. We feel what it is to lose our
humanity as we watch Macbeth so steeped in blood after murdering
his king and butchering his own countrymen that he is unable to feel

when he hears of Lady Macbeth's suicide. Or we experience Macbeth's numb sense of waste as he recognizes that the loss of his moral integrity has deprived him of the prospect of an old age surrounded by family and friends.

In another literary genre, the simple naive story of Adam and Eve speaks to us of what it is to be human in the context of our relation to the divine. Through the language of the imagination, the story of an insinuating snake and a tempting apple tells us about our essential freedom in religious and moral choice. Like in the Greek dramas or the Shakespearean plays, the protagonists make a choice (*prohairesis*) in which they miss the mark (*hamartia*). The continuing drama of the relation between God and humankind evolves from their orginal errancy; all of humankind is implicated in the drama just as Oedipus' marriage to his mother and murder of his father pollute a whole Greek community. Without seeking to explain its own import, this simple story common to Jews, Christians, and Muslims speaks of the disturbances that are part of the human condition in its relation to the divine.

What the story signifies and the imaginative impression of the story itself are inseparable. In its religious import, God is revealed in this story as just and humanity as reponsible in its relation to God. As an image of our moral life, the tempting apple discloses the suasory function of the imagination in conjunction with our desire. Among the familiar story's many other implications, those who read its language of images find a representation not only of humankind's physical hardship in being sentenced to earn food by the sweat of the brow, but also an expression of the loss of both our intellectual and moral integrity. The forbidden apple, like Macbeth's murder of his king, leads to an interior disarray of spirit through a loss of grace. In turning away from God and from conscience, our faculties lose their coherence to become rivals acting independently of one another. Disorder reigns in the relation of reason to the senses and the imagination, to appetite and will.[1] In the loss of intellectual integrity implied in this story of a

---

1   In "For the Time Being," W.H. Auden refers to this loss of integrity in our faculties and of the potential for its restoration. The Four Faculties, Intuition, Feeling, Sensation, and Thought explain:

Over the life of Man
We watch and wait,

man, a woman, and an apple forbidden by God, we may find also an emblem of the disunity found in our own day between the rationality of literature, of philosophy, and of empirical science.

Yet another literary genre makes explicit the connection between a story's language of the imagination and the moral or conceptual formulations embedded in it. Even in the first decades of the twentieth century, schoolchildren still read with delight the fables of Aesop (sixth century BCE) where miniature tales with animal characters are followed by a moral about wise conduct. In "The Fox and the Crow," a cunning fox covetous of the cheese held in a crow's beak proceeds to flatter the crow. Persuaded by the fox that he has indeed the most beautiful voice among all the creatures of the wood, the crow opens his beak to sing, drops the cheese from his perch in a tree, and when it is caught by the expectant fox below him, the crow learns along with the readers of both tale and moral to be wary of flatterers.

In our modern age of science, like in Plato's, rivalry among the ways of knowing has led to a denial of the legitimacy of the literary imagination represented so variously on the stage, in Scripture, and children's tales. In his eighteenth-century educational philosophy, Rousseau banned fables because his young pupil was to learn only through the senses and his own experiences. Talking crows, after all, were not within Emile's experience; nor had he heard in conversation the poetic phrasing used in the fable. Since no one else was to draw conclusions for him, the moral at the end was no more acceptable than the language of the literary imagination in the first part of the fable. Morality and wisdom were to be discovered by Emile himself either through the things of the physical world or through his own experience.

Rousseau's rejection of Aesop's fables in the education of a child is a type for materialist philosophy's closing of the mind to the literary imagination. Because within the strictures of materialist philosophy

---

The Four who manage
His fallen estate:
We who are four were
Once but one,
Before his act of
Rebellion;

Modern Poetry, ed. Maynard Mack (Englewood Cliffs, N.J.: Prentice-Hall, 1964) 217.

the imagination is recognized only as a register of sense impressions, the role of the imagination in conjunction with the affections as it functions in literature is excluded. Hobbes, for example, describes imagination as decayed sense and considers the passions as a selfish drive to power. His concept of mind displaces not only the role of the affections in connection to the literary imagination but also the parallel function of the imagination and the affections in the moral life. No room is left for other colours of the affections in their relation to imaginative impressions: for magnanimity, remorse, regret, or forgiveness.

Notwithstanding the denial of the literary imagination by the materialist philosophers, its function is as much a part of our psyche or soul as its sensate literal counterpart. In Aristotle's language, it may be said that this function of the imagination fulfils part of our humanity; because it is natural to us, it is a source of pleasure. Rather than being confined to the literal register of sense, the literary imagination is free to operate on a figurative plane that opens on to the spiritual or non-physical domain; it is a vehicle for a mental landscape or interior sense which embodies the invisible workings of both the human and the divine. Through the literary imagination we pierce through images to the truth of their significance: to the heart or to the motives for our actions in the interior human realm; to God's self-revelation through the images and narratives of Scripture.

The trivialization or denial of the literary imagination by empirical reasoners in the modern period reflects the monopoly exercised by the empirical imagination. In the history of western culture, the literary imagination had long enjoyed esteem along with science. In spite of the misgivings expressed by Plato, a foundational respect inhered for the wisdom of the poets in antiquity. In the first centuries of the Christian era, the Church Fathers penetrated through the language of the literary imagination in their biblical interpretations. In the monastic period that began in the fifth century, a literary and grammatical education provided a grounding for Benedictine monks who transcribed for posterity the manuscripts of both classical literature and Scripture. In the later middle ages, speculative scientific writers like St. Thomas Aquinas (d.1274) were similarly grounded. The author of the *Summa Theologica* (Theological Synthesis) sought the resolution of questions by looking at both sides through the science of dialectics; but he was also a poet whose voice lives in enduring Latin hymns like the *Pange lingua* (Sing, my tongue) and *O Salutaris* (O, Saving Victim).

In the same part of the medieval period in which speculative science flourished, we find the culture of the imagination expressed as well in the sculptures of great gothic cathedrals such as Chartres. Like in literature, the figures wrought in stone represent simultaneously what is perceived disparately by science. In three scenes over a majestic portal the humble nativity of the divine and human child, Christ's pain in death, and His majestic resurrection are taken in at a single glance. The seasonal daily life of the vine-trimmer or of the sower represented under the signs of the zodiac are incorporated into the whole story of the human in relation to the divine. The opposite pairs of our virtues and vices or interior moral habits are figured near another portal: a miser clasps avariciously a bag of coins; or again, with the wind in his habit to show his haste, an unfaithful monk flees his monastery. Individual patriarchs and prophets, Hebrew kings and Christian martyrs are complementary parts of a single whole like the texts and two testaments of Scripture itself. In figures like the Madonna or Abraham about to sacrifice Isaac, the medieval stone-carvers knew that their sculptures were not stone idols but works of a craftsman's imagination depicting people, actions, and their interior states.

In the decline of this period when the abstractions of medieval scholastic science had ceased to be nurtured by the literary imagination and by the mode of reasoning associated with literature, erudite classical scholars like Erasmus (d.1536) sought to restore the vitality of learning and of Scriptural interpretation through the voice of literature: in the literary imagination which grasps things as a whole and through literature's convergent thought. However, even as Shakespeare's *Romeo and Juliet* and *Merchant of Venice* were being enacted for the first time on the Elizabethan stage towards the end of the sixteenth century, new forces were emerging to counter this renaissance of letters. Once more, the literary imagination and the congruent operation of literature's reason were rejected. This time they were challenged by the claims of the literal empirical imagination connected to the reasoning of the physical sciences and appropriated in religion by contemporary sects such as the Puritans.

As this counter-renaissance movement was gathering momentum, the new clash between the literary and scientific ways of knowing and their distinctive uses of the imagination was resisted by Sir Philip Sidney (1554-86) in *The Defence of Poesy*. In the final quarter of the sixteenth century this poet, diplomat, and courtier to Queen Elizabeth, undertook a defence of poetry and of the literary imagination rejected by his Puritan compatriots as impious. Sidney, who was to die at the age of thirty-two from battle wounds, was educated like Shakespeare in the traditional linguistic disciplines at a grammar school and then attended Oxford University. He had travelled widely in both Protestant and Catholic Europe where he enriched his cultural and political knowledge: in Vienna and Hungary; during studies in Padua and Venice; in France where he witnessed the religious turmoil of the St. Bartholomew's Day Massacre; and in the Netherlands.

Sidney's own literary work, all published posthumously, was completed in the short period between 1578-86. Within four years he had written not only his apology for poetry but a sonnet sequence, *Astrophel and Stella*, and a pastoral romance written for the enjoyment of his sister entitled *The Old Arcadia*. In the *The Old Arcadia* where two young princes in disguise succumb to an "amor insanus" or insane love for two princesses in Arcadia, there is much neo-platonic discussion about the extent to which reason can capitulate to the pressure of the passions. In the year before his death, Sidney also began translation of a contemporary French Protestant poet as well as a translation of the Psalms.

Sidney's *Defence of Poesy*, published in 1592, both echoes an Aristotelian renaissance tradition and responds to a particular historical context. As a poet, Sidney saw clearly that failure to understand the poetic imagination and its relation to reason was central to puritan suspicion regarding the morality of poetry. The young author of romance and sonnets undertook the task of explaining the interior role of the literary imagination to those who would reduce the imagination to its empirical role as a register of literal external sense impressions and who would install history in the place of poetry as a teacher of lessons for humankind. Through a description of the imagination as it functions in poetry, Sidney hoped poetry's capacity to exert moral influence rather than to corrupt or dissipate would be made clear.

In his defence of the morality of poetry, Sidney distinguishes between the unique role of the imagination in poetry and the empirical function of the imagination in all other contemporary disciplines. He points out that poetry is the only discipline or art bestowed on humankind that does not depend on the laws of the external world of nature: the historian, for example, describes what humankind has done; the grammarian analzyes the rules of speech; the physician ponders the nature of the body and what is helpful or hurtful to it; the astronomer observes the stars; even the abstract notions of the metaphysician build upon the depths of nature. The function of the imagination in poetry alone is such that the poet is not tied to the laws of the external world but through the free course of his own invention fashions another world: the world, for example, as it should be, or a probable world that could be. Etymologies confirm this: the Greek, *poiein*, means to make; the Latin root of fiction, *fictio*, means a shaping or a fashioning. The poet is neither bound by the particular facts of history nor restricted to philosophy's abstractions from nature. At the same time, he does not construct castles in the air. Rather, the poet "goeth hand in hand with nature, not enclosed within the narrow warrant of her gifts, but freely ranging within the zodiac of his own wit."[2]

Against the claim that poetry does not edify, Sidney argues that the freedom of the poet to range in the imagination unfettered by literal connections is a source of poetry's power for moral influence. Because this unique function of the imagination is one of poetry's defining characteristics, he excludes from his defence poetry on scientific matters: for example, Lucretius' long poem on epicurean philosophy, *De Rerum naturae*, or Virgil's *Georgics* on the subject of farming with its observations on reading the weather, on pruning vines, on herds, and bees. Since their subject-matter restricts the free-ranging poetic imagination, the status of such verse as poetry is called into question. On the other hand, in the kind of poetry held suspect by Puritans Sidney argues that the poet's shaping power can both make a bronze world golden and can attain to what is essential in people's characters in a way that is both larger than life and true. Even the integrity known by Adam before his fall can be expressed by the poet since knowledge of this perfection is possible although our "infected will keepeth us from reaching unto it" (*Defence*, 887).

Sidney argues that the key to poetry's moral influence lies in its double nature in which perennial human truths are embedded in the concrete apprehensions of the imagination. Poetry has the illuminating power of both particular concrete images and the universal (*katholou*) that is conveyed through them. Unlike mediocre talents, good poets

---

2   Sir Philip Sidney, "The Defence of Poesy," *Poetry of the English Renaissance 1509-1660*, ed. J. William Hebel and Hoyt H. Hudson (New York: Appleton-Century-Crofts,1957) 886. All further citations are from this edition.

are like good artists who do not imitate externals but convey the particular essential virtue of their subjects through outward beauty. This power through truth embedded in the concrete accords to poetry a unique capacity for moral influence which far exceeds the abstractions of scientific reason. Philosophy convinces only those who already know; the philosopher's wordish description cannot "strike, pierce, nor possess the sight of the soul" in the same manner that is yielded to the powers of the mind by an image. Sidney writes that the philosopher's dry definitions on moral, social, or political matters are the grounds of wisdom but they "lie dark before the imaginative and judging power" (*Defence*, 889). The immediacy of images, the delight we take in them, their power of moving and teaching us grant to the poetic imagination its characteristic capacity for moral influence.

In other words, following similar claims made in the fourth century BCE by Aristotle, in the first century BCE by both Horace in his *Art of Poetry* and by Cicero, Sir Philip Sidney explains that poetry teaches and delights (*docere et delectare*). In this vein, to defend the morality of the comic in the poetic drama he contrasts delight with laughter without delight. Delight, Sidney explains, has always an element in it of the *katholou*, or the permanent, in relation either to ourselves or to human nature. Unlike laughter roused by scorn for others or by what is only ridiculous, "Delight hath a joy in it either permanent or present" (*Defence*, 895). When drama is true to its own end in both teaching and delighting, even as we laugh we take delight in universals: for example, good fortune, the beautiful, the admirable. The drama engages us in delightful laughter and teaching delightfulness as we watch the very masculine Hercules dressed for love's sake in woman's garb because through this we are shown the strange power of love; or we laugh and know as we watch on the stage the "self-wise-seeming schoolmaster" unaware of his absurd mistakes and little learning.

No scientific analysis of anger by a stoic philosopher, no austere definitions of the genus and differences of our virtues and vices by a scholastic reasoner can pierce us and make us comprehend in the way that poetry does though the imagination. For example, the perennial theme of filial fidelity is incised on the imagination of both young and old by Virgil's description in the *Aeneid* of the hero with his father. In the Latin epic, we see Aeneas carrying his father on his shoulders, leading his own young son by the hand as they flee from the burning city of Troy lost, finally, after a siege of ten years. We hear Aeneas tell his old father to put his arms around his neck, assuring him that he is no great weight, instructing him to carry their household gods because his own hands are polluted with blood. Whatever happens both will face one danger, find one safety.

Similarly, the vividness of impression made by characters in Homer's Greek epic of Ulysses conveys the virtues of friendship, valor, wisdom. Or again, Greek tragedies express in the round our soon-repenting pride, self-devouring cruelty, the violence of ambition, and the sour sweetness of revenge. In this way, Sidney writes, all virtues, vices, and passions in their own natural states are so laid to the view that we seem not to hear of them but clearly see through them. When a poet is led through his imagination by poetry itself, when he shapes rightly the poetical sinews that are its reason, when his words reflect his thought, then even the hard-hearted who know no good but self-indulgence (*indulgere genio*), who despise or do not feel the inward reason of the philosophers, will in spite of themselves be delighted by the form of goodness implicit in poetry.

Sidney had no need to defend to Puritan detractors of poetry those books recognized as divine poetry in Scripture. He writes that none "that hath the Holy Ghost in due holy reverence" will speak against the Psalms, Proverbs, the Song of Songs, the Book of Job. At the same time, Sidney's references to religious poetry both in antiquity and in Scripture bolster his argument for the legitimacy of the poetic imagination: its affective power and its capacity to render through the concrete what is interior, invisible, or even entirely spiritual and divine. He writes that in Roman antiquity the poets were called *vates*, diviners or prophets, a heavenly title for heart-ravishing knowledge. Whether in Scripture or in antiquity's Orphic poetry and Homeric poems, the object of the poetic imagination is to "imitate the inconceivable excellencies of God" (*Defence*, 887). Sidney's examples make clear that like its secular counterpart religious poetry is not written in the literal, sensate register of the imagination. Instead, the imagination in religious poetry reveals through concrete images the opposite pole: the transcendentally divine, the spiritual, and the interior. For example, the Psalms telling of the beasts' joyfulness and hills' leaping make us, as it were, see God coming in his majesty; we hear in the Psalms the voice of "a passionate lover of that unspeakable and everlasting beauty to be seen by the eyes of the mind only cleared by faith" (*Defence*, 885-86); and through the Psalms' expression of God's steadfastness or

never-leaving goodness we are also brought consolation in our lapses
in integrity.

In the decade after the publication of Sidney's *Defence of Poesy,* another writer took up the subject of the function of the imagination in
relation to reason in poetry, this time from a philosopher's perspective.
In his sweeping survey of the progress of learning up to his time in
The Advancement of Learning (1605), Francis Bacon not only comments on poetry but also on this relation of the imagination to reason
as it functions both in religious poetry and in the moral suasion that
Sidney considers integral to all good poetry.

In his observations on the imagination and reason, Bacon's perceptions are derived in part from his vantage point at the juncture of the
nascent age of the modern physical sciences with the renaissance and
its classical connections. Underlying his clarity on the characteristic
differences between literature and science are two fundamental premisses that make him a great arbiter of method for the age of modern science in a manner not unlike Aristotle in a much earlier era of
scientific reasoning. First, Bacon assumed the unity of all knowledge
with distinctions between its three domains in the divine, human, and
physical spheres; secondly, he assumed the important corollary that
in these domains various methods performed different tasks. In their
several paths towards knowledge, each of these methods was defined
by its own characteristic relation between reason, sense, and imagination. Bacon knew, for example, that the development of empirical
science in the age ahead depended not only on the important distinction between the divine, human, and physical domains but also on the
recognition that sense observation with the imagination as its register
was as inseparable from empirical science as the poetic function of the
imagination from poetry.

Because Bacon's purpose in *The Advancement of Learning* was to
survey all learning up to his period, he describes the distinctive contribution of poetry and of the poetic imagination which Sidney had
defended in *The Defence of Poesy.* In his division of the principal parts
of learning according to the three parts of the human understanding,
he connects the imagination to poetry, the memory to history, and
reason to abstract scientific knowledge or philosophy. Like Sidney, he
maintains that poetry's moral value proceeds from the poet's imaginative freedom to shape events; this distinctive function of the imagination makes events in poetry larger and more rooted in retributive

justice than in life or more in accordance with revealed providence. Bacon bases this freedom of the poet's imagination to shape events on a distinction between domains: the world is inferior to the human soul which is characterized by "a more ample greatness, a more exact goodness, and a more absolute variety, than can be found in the nature of things" (*Advancement*, 82). Like Sidney, he also notes that the moral and religious function of poetry was particularly important in antiquity; then the wisdom of experience was transmitted through proverbs, aphorisms, and fables. He acknowledges that the realm of poetry is in fact superior to scientific knowledge in conveying affections, passions, and the sense of a given period and its customs. And, finally, he recognizes the indebtedness of language itself to poetry's eloquence and wit.

In *The Advancement of Learning*, Bacon's description of poetry is brief but his analysis elsewhere of the role of the imagination in suasion illuminates the connection between the poetic imagination and its suasory moral influence. He observes that the imagination is a Janus figure serving the twin sisters of truth and goodness, our judicial and executive provinces. On the one hand, in its empirical function as a messenger of sense impressions for the reason to judge, one face of the imagination is turned towards the reason. On the other hand, as a messenger influencing the affections, appetite, and will, the other face of the imagination is turned towards action. He explains: "Reason sendeth over to Imagination before the decree can be acted: for Imagination ever precedeth Voluntary Motion" (*Advancement*, 120). However, because the affections know only the present, Bacon also points out the important directive role of the reason in exercising foresight through what it sends over to the imagination. Although the office of poetry is not to move people to action, poets realize as nearly as possible Plato's remark that if virtue could be seen she would move great love and affection. Since virtue is invisible and cannot be seen by sense, the next best thing is to show virtue to the imagination.

If without being overtly didactic poetry is capable of exerting moral influence, another branch of literary reasoning was associated explicitly with moral suasion; that is, rhetoric, the now banished queen of the language disciplines. Along with the forensic and deliberative spheres, rhetoric was associated from antiquity with praise and blame or the virtues and vices. In the thirteenth century, Vincent of Beauvais (d.1262) represents the continuation of this tradition within the Christian framework of the story of the Fall. Along with relief from physical need in man's fallen condition, Beauvais pointed to two other areas where reparation of our integrity lost in the fall was required and to the means through which relief might be provided: the evil of ignorance relieved through the wisdom of scientific knowledge (Greek: *theoria*), or the knowledge of the principles of things; and the evil of our strong desires or concupiscence relieved through prudence (Greek: *phronesis*), or good judgment regarding conduct. Since both rhetoric and prudential judgment regarding conduct belong to the same genus of convergent reasoning, for Beauvais as for Cicero the eloquent reasoning of rhetoric operates on the passions of man through the imagination for moral as well as social and political good. Bacon belongs to this same tradition in representing the various instruments of the reason as working for the good of humankind. Just as empirical inductive science is an instrument for the material renewal of humankind, reason's relation to the imagination in rhetoric is also an instrument for good. Like the science of logic, rhetoric can be misused; but both instruments are meant to secure and second the reason rather than to entrap, oppress, or disturb it.

However, in moral suasion the task of the reason in relation to the imagination is complicated by the tendency of the faculties to operate separately rather than cooperatively. Bacon writes that like the reason the affections themselves bear an appetite for the good; but because they know only the present they are continuously seditious or mutinous, filling the imagination and influencing our will to do what is worse when we know what is better. Although reason perceives the future, it is often vanquished because the present fills the imagination more through its connection to the affections. Like Eve beholding the apple at the dramatic turning-point in paradise, the affections, appetite, and desire win over rational knowledge of future consequences. Bacon cites the poet, Virgil: "I see and approve better things; I follow a meaner way" ("Video meliora, proboque; Deteriora sequor" (*Advancement*, 147). In our own moral choices and in our persuasion of others, the responsibility of the reason is to make things future and remote appear as present through personal suasion and through the power of language. In this way the imagination is won from the affections' part, thus seconding reason which would otherwise become captive and servile.

In Bacon's account, then, the imagination is a *nuncius* or messenger in both judgments based on sense impression and in suasory reasoning. In moral suasion reason plays a directive role in relation to the imagination; in empirical matters reason is its judge and master. However, in the domain of the divine the imagination has a different relation to reason because knowledge of this domain proceeds from a different medium or from a medium of a different density, like the rays of refracted light.[3] In faith, as well as in the divine poetry of Scripture, the imagination has a magisterial role rather than the intermediary role of a *nuncius*. Because rational knowledge cannot provide the key in this sphere, the imagination is raised above the reason. Divine grace uses the imagination as a *locus* for illuminating the understanding,

---

3   Even in his presentation of this premiss regarding the separation of the large domains of knowledge, Bacon's choice of illustrations shows the difference between the quintessentially literary way of thinking through images and empirical science's logical use of images for explaining concepts through comparisons. He presents the distinction between the domains of knowledge both in a literary mode through reference to the inexhaustible story of creation in Genesis and in the manner of scientific explanation through a logical analogy with the reflection of light.

     In his analogy used to distinguish between the divine, human, and the physical spheres, Bacon connects the reflection of light with the beams or rays of man's knowledge: the *radius directus* with reference to physical nature; the *radius reflexus* where, as in the reflection of light, there is no difference in medium as man beholds and contemplates himself; and the *radius refractus* which is refered to God. In the ontological analogy of this last domain reason cannot report truly because knowledge passes from one medium into another medium of a different density like in the refraction of light.

     In the story of creation, in the literary manner thought is generated through the story in such a way that story and thought are one or form a complex unity. The story itself is a way of thinking and the imagination exercises a magisterial role. Subsequent commentary feels its way towards explicit interpretation of what is implicit in the concrete narrative. In his interpretation of the story of creation in the new context of empirical science, Bacon locates this domain of science in the part of the world that begins with God's blessing: "*Producant aquae, producat* terra" ("Let the waters bring forth, let the earth bring forth"). The domain of empirical science lies in knowledge of the laws of what was "extracted out of the mass of heaven and earth by the benediction of a *producat*" (94). The human domain's distinctness from the physical world through its relation to God is also observed: Bacon notes that of man only is it written that God shaped him from the soil of the ground and blew the breath of life into his nostrils.

seeking access to the mind by similitudes, types, parables, visions, and dreams. In support of this magisterial relation of the imagination to the reason, Bacon cites from Aristotle. The philosopher compared the mind's relation to the body to that of a lord over a bondman but the relation of the reason to the imagination to that of a magistrate over a free citizen who may also come to rule in his turn.

In spite of Bacon's clarity regarding the magisterial function of the imagination in religion, its freedom from immediate sensate impressions in poetry, and its role in relation to desire and appetite in moral suasion, subsequent Baconian philosophers and educational theorists were to ignore these observations. Instead, Bacon's works were heralded as prophetic of the new age of science and of its empirical method where imagination serves only in its empirical function. And, indeed, after his assessment of the strengths and weaknesses of learning up to his time in *The Advancement of Learning*, in subsequent works Bacon's whole purpose was to redirect learning towards the physical domain and to champion the intellectual instrument or method proper to it. He recognized early previous endeavours by materialist philosophers like the atomist theory of Democritus in antiquity, lamented the long subsequent night of the physical sciences, and believed that the discovery of the laws of the material world through the empirical inductive method was to open a great new era of learning. In *The Advancement of Learning*, he speaks of Greece and Rome as occupying "the *middle part* of time," and as "two exemplar states of the world for arms, learning, moral virtue, policy, and laws" (*Advancement*, 74-5). In *De Augmentis Scientiarum* (1623), the later Latin version of *The Advancement of Learning*, he writes of his own period in which learning seems to have made her third visitation to men, a period which might far surpass the Greek and Roman in learning.

What was required to effect this reorientation in learning was a great shift in rationality. Empirical investigation of the physical domain required its own *organon* with its own characteristic relation between reason and sense observation. Bacon considered that the very virtues of the intellect essential to poetry, to faith, to speculative thought, and to convergent deliberation in the probable matters of the human domain were impediments to the instrument of empirical inductive reasoning directed towards investigation of the physical world. Unlike the imagination's magisterial role and its freedom to roam in divine and human poetry, in the empirical sciences the imagination was to function strictly as a register of sense impressions and as *nuncius* to the reason.

In *The Great Instauration* and the *Novum Organum* (New Logic), Bacon presents his vision of this great new beginning of an era of empirical science and of the intellectual method that is its appointed instrument. He declares that for this modern enterprise the whole operation of the mind has to be completely restarted, that an entirely new way untried and unknown to the ancients lies open to the understanding. What is required for discoveries in the material world is a true and lasting marriage between the senses and reason, the empirical and rational faculties. In this reordering of the faculties of the mind, men are to begin with the sense observation of particulars to examine the sequence of cause and effect. In this way, they will be led to an understanding of laws or general axioms in the physical world which in turn will give control and mastery over their further application.

Our own complete familiarity with this procedure and the basis of evidence required by the empirical sciences obscures Bacon's pioneering task as a philosopher in articulating the idea of the experimental scientific method. Just as habituation to the imagination as a register of sense impressions in empirical thought can prejudice us in our own period against the imagination in its relation to reason in literature and faith, so in the first quarter of the seventeenth century Bacon had to counter the prejudice of minds habituated to deductive science and to convergent literary reasoning. We find an emblem of Bacon's mission in the woodcut on the frontispiece of *The Advancement of Learning*. Here the ship, "Discovery," with sails billowing in the wind sets out through the straits of Gibraltar, the Pillars of Hercules. Behind lies the Mediterranean classical world of learning in literature and philosophy with their characteristic modes of reasoning; ahead lies a great uncharted world waiting to be explored through the new logic, empirical science's own legitimate intellectual instrument.

In his task of public education, Bacon appeals to the imagination through suasory images. To describe the shift in rationality of the *novum organum* where the faculties are ordered in a different way than in either theoretical science or in the convergent thought of literature, he writes in aphorisms where thought is connected to images. Memorable phrases such as "we can only command Nature by obeying her" became bywards among his disciples. Or again, for the sake of a better retention of his teaching, he chose the mnemonic technique of rhetoric that locates abstract ideas in the imagination by connecting them to physical places. The idols or false appearances of the mind which impede conclusions drawn from sense observations are described variously as idols of the market-place, idols of the cave, idols of the theatre, idols of the tribe.

Bacon's depiction of the impediments to the *organon* of empirical science necessarily involves an exclusion or even an indictment of the very virtues of the intellect as they operate in both deductive and literary reasoning. In promoting empirical induction, Bacon had to contend especially with the dominance of Aristotelian speculative reasoning and of the scholastic thought prevalent in the universities. He objects that this speculative theoretical habit of mind made experiments and particulars that come under the senses beneath a man's dignity with the result that "the true path is not only untrodden, but actually shut off and barred ..." (*Advancement*, 92). In this intellectual milieu, Bacon had to plead the legitimacy of empirical reasoning's starting-point in the sense observation of particulars; that is, an antithetical starting-point to that of deductive reasoning in its received principles and premises. In a situation exactly opposite to that of our own era, *a posteriori* empirical induction asserted its legitimacy in a culture of *a priori* deductive reasoning.

Similarly, the imagination and memory as they function in the personal genus of convergent reasoning were an impediment to the cleared mind required for empirical reason's alert unbiased observation in the order of things. Bacon believed that the empirical observer discovered the laws of the physical world through the *lumen secum*, or impersonal dry light of science, both by operating within a single field and by excluding what is essential in convergent reasoning: the observer's individual personal nature, broader education, emotions, unfettered imagination, and the trove of memory. These different requirements in the two modes of reasoning are disclosed in their different uses of the word "invention." As Bacon points out, "invention" in the convergent reasoning of rhetoric had meant discovering arguments from what was already known that were pertinent to the matter under consideration. By contrast, "invention" in empirical science assumed its present popular sense of the novel, of progress, and new discoveries of the previously unknown.

The necessary exclusion of deductive speculative reasoning, of convergent reasoning, and of the imagination and the memory as they function in literature also meant that the verbal culture connected to them was irrelevant to the empirical enterprise and its *novum organon*. In the shift in rationality from thought and word towards things, language was pertinent only insomuch as it improved the commerce between the mind and things. Words representing things were to have one, clear, univocal meaning. The literary use of language was an impediment with its cumulative weight of words, simultaneous senses, and nuances reflecting the personal nature of convergent thought. Similarly, the Greek categories that guided and illuminated speculative reasoning were anathema; abstract paired opposites like "identity and diversity," or "priority and posteriority," were too general or too ambiguous for the new science. Even definitions of terms which were at least partially useful in deliberative matters and speculative thought were insufficient to the needs of applied physical science. Bacon argues that the static principles of qualities and categories lead to talk; observation of moving principles or how things happen leads to works.

In other words, the whole verbal realm of reasoning in thought and culture that had flourished up to this period was alien to the reordering of the faculties in empirical science and to its reasoning that begins not with words but with sense observation. As Bacon pleaded the cause of the new logic, he pointed to the unreliability in the very foundations of the old deductive verbal logic. Abstract premises used in logical reasoning bear the uncertainty characteristic of words. Where Aristotle considered that certitude was guaranteed through logical reasoning when the premises were accurate, Bacon points to the verbal uncertainty of premises. Although useful in deductive matters like law, theology, and morality, verbal propositions suffer from inaccuracy: "for arguments consist of propositions, and propositions of words, and words are but the current tokens or marks of popular notions of things" (*Advancement*, 126). In empirical science where judgment is related directly to sense, the experiment, and the thing itself, there is no call either for the abstract premises or the verbal middle terms of syllogistic reasoning in reasoning processes such as "All men are human; Socrates is a man; therefore Socrates is human." In fact, cogitations do not always have to be expressed in words.

Rather than the polyvalent language of literature or language's precisions in the abstract premises and definitions of verbal science, empirical science required that words serve sensate induction. In a statement that points to the verbal strictures Hobbes would impose on all reasoning, Bacon writes that in empirical science words must refer to things themselves or to characteristics abstracted from them. In the *Novum Organum* Bacon commends the well-derived species of the lowest type in words such as "chalk" or "mud" but finds less precision in the word "earth." Vague or muddled words derived from an incorrrect and unskilled abstraction impede empirical understanding; words like "moist" are considered deficient. For the purposes of the new science, language used in literature like "fortune," as in the proverb "Fortune favours the brave," refers to what does not exist and entangles the understanding.

In all these considerations, Bacon's work as a philosopher of the empirical method was pioneering, exploratory, and rudimentary. He underestimated the important role of personal judgment in establishing an hypothesis and in determining both the kind of instances needed for observation and when evidence was sufficient for a conclusion. He also believed that the rules of the new method for demonstration could be applied by anyone; through their application certitude would be reached independent of personal ability; within a few generations the laws of nature, limited in number, would all be known. In the ensuing era, science itself was to find its own way and refine its method influenced also by Descartes, by the model of Galileo's combination of mathematics with observation, and through the practical physical investigations by scientists in succeeding centuries.

However, in spite of its rudimentary nature Bacon's work on the inductive method was to exert a seminal influence in areas other than empirical science. Veins of modern philosophy and influential educational theory were to find inspiration in his philosophy of a sensate way of knowing that eliminates the literary function of the imagination, rejects the genus of convergent reasoning, and is antithetical to the abstract starting-points of reason in deductive thought. The influence of Bacon's philosophy of method as well as of the sensate method espoused by neo-epicureanism is to be found in schools of philosophy throughout the empirical enlightenment and later in the utilitarians, the positivists, the pragmatists: Locke and Hume, Bentham, Comte, Dewey.

For example, the influence of Bacon is found in the preface to the eighteenth-century *Encyclopedia* where the materialist "philosophes," Diderot and D'Alembert, assume Bacon's tripartite division of all learning as known through the imagination, the memory, and reason.

When D'Alembert locates the origin of ideas in humankind's seeking exemption from pain rather than in wonder, as Aristotle suggests, the mutual reinforcement of baconian and neo-epicurean philosophy is evident: in neo-epicureanism's materialist goal of pursuing pleasure and avoiding pain and Bacon's argument for the discovery of the laws of nature and their new applications that would provide relief for humankind's suffering and need. Even the encyclopedia's full title as the *Encyclopedia, or Reasoned Dictionary of the Sciences, the Arts, and the Trades* reveals its connection to Bacon's model for an "Encyclopedia of Nature," a collaborative collection of data including observations from the trades: from such areas as cookery, or the manufacture of glass and enamel. Like the word "invention" and words like "nature," "science," "cause," and "reason," after Bacon the word "encyclopedia" assumed its modern meaning of separate entries for the various branches of learning linked only through alphabetical sequence. As the old meaning gave way to the new, "encyclopedia" lost its root sense traditional in liberal studies as a cycle or circular education effected through an interconnected curriculum characterized by a mutuality of subject-matters and a reciprocity of methods.

Shortly after Bacon's death in 1626, the word "education" also underwent a radical change in meaning in the program of Puritan educational reformers. The criterion of practical utility alone determined what was to be taught: all learning was to begin with sense observation; the literary imagination was entirely eclipsed as the sole function of the imagination was to convey sense impressions to the reason; memory was connected to sense impressions registered in the imagination. Although the proposals of the Puritan reformers were not implemented in their own period, they exerted an important influence later: in the pedagogy of nineteenth-century England when popular education was being established; in our present-day methodology such as the communicative method for language instruction with its sensate principles and empirical assumptions.

In conjunction with their own practical divinity, these Puritan educators were impressed by Bacon's vision of useful knowledge for the sake of the common good effected by a new understanding and application of laws of the physical world; by his belief in the ensuing material benefits as a restoration of part of the natural happiness enjoyed in Eden before the Fall; by his prophecy of a great new era in the history of humankind. This prophetic mode became intertwined with

millenialist readings of Scripture that were oriented towards historical developments and exluded the analogical spiritual significance of
its grammatical interpreters: of the Church Fathers for whom words
opened out not only on to historical vistas but penetrated into the interior world of the human soul and analogically into the invisible transcendent realm of God. In contrast with the premiss of the Church
Fathers that no part of Scripture can be privileged without damaging
all the rest, the Book of Revelation and the Book of Daniel were fore-
grounded and understood as foretelling a realization on earth of the
New Jerusalem after a series of prophesized conflicts.

This belief was based on John's vision in the last book of the Bible
where an angel defeats a dragon and shuts him up in the Abyss to
make sure he would not lead the nations astray again until one thousand years had passed (Revelation 20: 1-5). In the interpretation of
this passage by millenialists (millenium:1,000 years), before the final
judgment the world would be restored to its Edenic condition for a
period of one thousand years preceding the time when Satan would be
released for one final stand at Armageddon. This reading of the passage in Revelation was coupled with prophetic works in the Old Testament. For example, in Daniel's vision of four successive world powers
and of seven vials that would be poured out, the vials were interpreted
as progressive violent struggles in the defeat of the anti-Christ; that is,
the Papacy and Roman Catholic Church identified with Revelation's
references to the Roman Empire. In their historical interpretation of
Daniel, the Reformation was understood as one of the seven vials as
the American civil war was later to be interpreted as another.

In such interpretations, the division in religion that made the Puritans a sect within the Church of England proceeds from the mind's
own divisions or its separation from itself: its exclusion of the poetic
function of the imagination and of the noetic spiritual light that illuminates this function in religion. In an admixture of millenialist
expectation and Baconian method, a measure of the intensity of the
Puritan antipathy to the poetic function of the imagination through
privileging its sensate register is evident in their condemnation of the
theatres as corrupt and their closing of them in 1642; in the suppres-
sion in 1643 of the Anglican *Book of Common Prayer* with its communal formal prayer and evocative renaissance language; in an adamant
rejection of religious symbol and of the drama in ritual; and in polem-
ics against such sacramental beliefs as the divine presence in the eu-

charistic bread.[4] Mute testimony is still borne to the clash between the sensate imagination and the imagination in its literary and religious function in mutilated torsoes and headless statues in English abbeys and churches.

In a similar disjuncture of the mind, in the Puritan platform in education a new alliance with the method of Baconian science collapsed all reasoning into the sensate mode; it denied the poetic imagination and literary rationality and repudiated both verbal liberal learning and its teaching methodology. The connection made between an exclusive cultivation of the Baconian empirical method and the realization through its instrumentality of a new era of certitude and harmony accounts for the conviction and the tone of urgency in the program of educational reformers in England like Samuel Hartlib (d. 1662),[5] John Dury, and the Czech social and educational reformer, Jan Amos

---

4   The iconoclasm and rejection of sacrament is expressed by William Perkins (1558-1602), the most widely-known theologian in the Elizabethan Church who combined reformed theology and puritan piety and who by the end of the sixteenth century in England had replaced Calvin on "the English religious best-seller list." In a polemical work entitled *A Reformed Catholic Or A Declaration Showing How Near We May Come To The Present Church Of Rome In Sundry Points Of Religion And Wherein We Must For Ever Depart From Them*, Perkins protests against Papist "idolatry manifest in what they worship God in, at, or before images, having no commandment so to do, but the contrary. They allege that they use and worship images only in a remembrance of God … their idolatry exceeds the idolatry of the heathen in that they worship a breaden god, or Christ in and under the forms of bread and wine." *The Work of William Perkins*, ed., Ian Breward (Appleford, Abingdon, Eng.: Sutton Courtenay P., 1970) xi, 574.

5   Born in Poland of an English mother, Hartlib arrived in England in 1625 to complete his studies at Cambridge, then at the height of its influence as the focal point of English Puritanism. When he returned to England in 1628, he began his life's mission of attempting to realize Bacon's utopian vision in the *New Atlantis* of a harmonious new era established through the *novum organon* or new method. For the next thirty years until the end of the commonwealth in 1659 and the restoration of the monarchy, Hartlib along with his associate, John Dury (1595-1680), wrote tracts and lobbied tirelessly for their cause: in publications like *The Reformed School* and "Some Proposalls towards the Advancement of Learning," a pamphlet echoing the title of Bacon's work and addressed to the Committee for the Advancement of Learning of the Saints' Parliament in 1653. *A Reformation of Schooles* was an English translation by Hartlib in 1642 of a work

Komenský (1592-1670), or Comenius,[6] who joined them briefly in 1641-2 and with whom they felt an identity of purpose. With messianic fervour, these educational reformers believed that truth and certitude were guaranteed by an impersonal universal method now understood for the first time; that social dissonance and the clouds of opinion connected to non-scientific probable reasoning would vanish in a spiritual enlightenment. In a new idea of intellectual integrity, the disorderliness of the faculties would be rectified by reordering them according to the sensate mode of empirical science. By cultivating the new method in the study of the Book of Nature, schools would lay the foundation for heaven on earth. Some believed that an understanding of the laws of nature would repair the image of God in humankind making the mind more like the image of God who knows all things.

In *The Reformed School* (1650), Dury sets out the new aims and the new methods of schooling for both boys and girls from four or five years of age until nineteen or twenty. The reformation in virtue and learning is to rectify "the cause of our Ignorance and Disorderliness which hath taken possession of all Schools and Universities, and hath spread itself over all matters of Humane Learning." As Dury explains: "we shall endeavour to seek out the true Method of teaching Sciences, by the Grounds and Rules which, we hope, none, that is Rationall and free from prejudice, will Contradict."[7]

The true method was to be the only method. The reformers' theory of child development, its silent exclusion of literature, of the poetic imagination, and of the literary rationality and deductive reasoning

---

of Comenius. During the ascendancy of the Parliamentarians, he was put forward as head of the Bodley Library at Oxford and of Oriel College.

6   Comenius had read the works of Francis Bacon as a student at the University of Heidelberg where he had come under the influence of Protestant Millennialists. Influenced by millenialist hopes and by Bacon's belief that a few generations would suffice for the discovery of the principal laws of things, there is an eschatological tone in Comenius' vision of pansophy: of knowledge as one, harmonious, interconnected whole perceived in the works of God blessed in creation. Like the Hartlib group, in what he called a perfect squaring of the principles of knowledge this goal was to be reached through the new method that proceeded through sense and reason along with the divine Revelation of Scripture when reason was deficient.

7   Charles Webster, *Samuel Hartlib and the Advancement of Learning* (Cambridge: Cambridge University P., 1970) 150-1.

cultivated in the liberal arts, are reflected in their three stages of learning. In the first phase, it is assumed that the only way children know is through their sense observation of things and through the impressions made on the imagination by sense. Like in Rousseau's program for the young Emile, Dury writes that up to the age of eight or nine, "while Children are not capable of the Acts of Reasoning; the method of filling their Senses and Imaginations with outward Objects should be plyed" (*Samuel Hartlib*, 154). The pupil is to be encouraged to "take notice of all Things offered to his Senses; to know their proper names, to observe their shapes; and to make circumstantiall descriptions therof by word of mouth, and painting in black and white" (*Samuel Hartlib*, 160). In this psychology of knowing, imagination and memory are both yoked exclusively to the service of empirical science. In other words, when the reformers write that at this age "the Capacity of children is none other but Sense and Imagination, with the beginnings of Memory" (*Samuel Hartlib*, 159), memory is understood only in its function of retaining the sensory impressions made by things on the imagination. By the end of the first stage of education around the age of eight, in addition to a knowledge of lines and mathematical figures, of geography, history, and the historical catechism of the Bible, a child "is able to name that which is obvious to his Sense by its proper name in his Mother-Tongue" and can speak, read, and write it. (*Samuel Hartlib*, 160).

Because scientific knowledge from antiquity was still important to the new scientific venture, in the second stage in education from eight or nine years of age to thirteen or fourteen, learned tongues are introduced as a preparation for reading Greek and Latin works in the final phase: works like Pliny's encyclopedia of the natural sciences. However, since only the inductive empirical method was recognized, humanist methodology for teaching languages prevalent since antiquity was adamantly rejected. As in teaching reading and writing in the mother tongue, other languages were to be taught only through the sense observation of things. In addition to "Learning all the Names of the Things themselves" in their own language, the students also learn their names in Latin, Greek, and Hebrew. They learn to read and write these tongues but are to interpret them only "so farre as their experience in the observation of Things doth go, and no further" (*Samuel Hartlib*, 162). For this purpose, the students were to use the English edition of Comenius' famous language textbook, the *Janua linguarum reserarta* (1631) or *Gate of Languages Unlocked*,[8] which through pictures and without grammar described useful facts about the world both in Latin and its vernacular equivalent.

The purpose of the final stage of education, from ages thirteen or fourteen to nineteen or twenty, was to exercise students in the useful arts and sciences to fit them for any employment in Church and Commonwealth. Dury writes that at this point in their language learning, they are to be taught their grammar rules more exactly and fully than formerly and brought to read authors in all the sciences, building on the foundation already obtained through the doors of sense. In a categorical rejection of the literary classics, Dury insists that without their subordination to the arts and sciences these languages "are worth nothing towards the advancement of our Happinesss" (*Samuel Hartlib*, 155-6). In keeping with Bacon's idea for an "Encyclopedia of Nature," Dury writes that students now at the age of reason will gather for themselves an Encyclopedia partly through extracts from Latin and Greek authors on subjects such as natural history and always with reference to previous experience or sense observation.[9] He ennumerates eight categories of applied science useful to the new kind of encyclopedic learning. All belong to a factual subject-matter alien to the poetic imagination described by Sidney who would exclude from poetry even Virgil's *Georgics* with its depiction of farming.

These categories for an encyclopedia include portions of Latin authors who wrote on agriculture, like Cato and Varro, to enlarge what they have already been taught concerning husbandry; selections from

---

8   Comenius' first language textbook, *Janua Linguarum Resarata* or *Gateway to Languages Unlocked* (1631), was translated into several European languages. In London in 1631 the text was exploited by John Anchoran and published as *Porta linguarum trilinguis*. In 1636 Thomas Horne, a friend of Hartlib, produced a new Latin-English edition (*Samuel Hartlib*, 22-3).

9   In this course for students, Dury does not mention the study of Hebrew because "their daily reading of the Scriptures should be in Greek and in Hebrew and their analytical exercises employed "for the most part in resolving the Rationality of the Scripture about the most Material Doctrines of Divinity." He explains that he has written only of the "Method of Humane Learning ... and no Divinity is to be taken up from the teaching of men: it is to be received from the Holy Scriptures alone" and from daily catechetical exercises and conferences in the third period of education (*Samuel Hartlib*, 163).

Pliny's compendium of natural history in connection to what they have previously seen together with the histories of meteors, minerals, etc.. In a long list, Dury enumerates other areas for the student's Encyclopedia: models and books of architecture; engineering, fortification, weapons, navigation; the doctrine of economics and of civil government; optics; the keeping of accounts; medicine, chemical operations, and the "Art of Apothecaries ... offered ... partly in books, partly in the Operations themselves by an ocular inspection thereof, and of their drugges" (*Samuel Hartlib*, 163-4).

Then, in a marginal position at the end of this extensive list we find the subjects of the language disciplines from the old *trivium*: logic, rhetoric, poetry, and "Humane Histories." History provides moral examples; poetry, logic, and rhetoric are to be analyzed for "their art of Reason and Utterance to perswade." However, the disdain for literature and its use of language is expressed elsewhere by Comenius who complains about poetry's obscure, luxuriant, harrowed words removed from the pure light of truth. In the new order where the world enters only through the doors of sense, there is no place for the poetic imagination, for perennial human wisdom sustained for children in stories about crafty foxes and gullible crows, for the convergent thought of the personal literary voice, or for learning by heart the rhythmic phrases of poetry[10] where words bear the cumulative weight of their varied course through history. Traditional exercises in the literary use of language through a *copia verborum* (abundance of words) and through circumlocutions are windiness of expression. Instead, following the new baconian science words are to be clearly defined, their true significance fully agreed upon; homonyms and ambiguous expressions are to breed no more dissension.[11]

---

10   In *The Arts of the Beautiful* (New York: Charles Scribner's Sons, 1965), Etienne Gilson speaks of the memorization of poetry. He remarks that we do not re-read information we already know. On the other hand, if we memorize poetry to have it always with us it is because poetry touches our affections and the heart can enjoy twice the pleasure of feeling the same emotion (27).

11   Similarly, the verbal sciences of logic and dialectics were brangling belonging to the quarrels of the schools. Metaphysics, whose directional role had made it the queen of the sciences, has no place because it is without application in the other sciences and dies within itself. Comenius points

The legacy of these seventeenth-century educators who would apply the method of the physical sciences to language endures in our present-day teaching of languages: in the separation of language from the deductive reasoning of grammar rules and from literature. For the reformers, grammar was no longer to serve the kind of education in literature familiar to Sydney and Shakespeare who in the first phase of the old language disciplines had studied poetry, fables, and adages. The reformers maintained that the deductive exercise of teaching through rules was not only preposterous but made children conceited and alienated their affections from plain and useful truths known through sense. And like present-day programs for teaching languages, in their bright hope for the inductive empirical method as a replacement for both literary and deductive reasoning the English educational reformers maintained that what was wearisome, tedious, and a loss of time for children in traditional education would be remedied in their true and ready way of teaching language.

Comenius' textbooks demonstrate what happens to the instruction of languages which belong to the human domain when they are taught through the method proper to the physical sciences. Language is divorced from literature, from literature's polysemous use of language, from grammatical methodology, and the practical exercise of translation. As in our own communicative methodology, in Comenius' *Orbis Sensualium Pictus* (The Visible World in Pictures), the vocabulary is limited, functional, and directed to visual observation. The woodcuts in the text represent useful objects like carts and wagons, or practical activities such as making a chair, or vendors at their stalls in a market. The rules and deductive reasoning of grammar are avoided by numbering each item or stage of an activity to connect it to a similarly numbered Latin sentence along with its translation into the pupil's mother-tongue.

If a new understanding of the world was opened through the doors and gates of sense, in these programs of education the gates of the mind were also securely barred against any other way of understanding it. The Puritan educators ignored not only Bacon's observations on poetry and the imagination but also his two fundamental premisses: the distinction between the three different domains of knowledge and

---

out that in Protestant Sweden, King Gustavus Adolphus excluded the disputations of metaphysics by edict from his kingdom.

between the various methods or paths towards knowledge within these domains. In embracing the empirical inductive method as a universal way of knowing, they left behind his observations on the imagination's unique function in poetry and religion and its role in moral suasion; his approval of spiritual allegorical readings of Scripture like those of the Church Fathers which keep close to the particulars of the text;[12] or even his own interpretations of fables and myths. Instead, among these Puritan theorists the philosopher of method was to meet the same fate that he himself had observed in Aristotle, Plato, and Hippocrates whose philosophy and science were embased by their disciples. Bacon's disciples ignored his cautions against perceiving everything through the lens of a particular philosophy or of one dominant method tainting others: his criticism of William Gilbert (1540-1603) for applying to other fields the paradigm of his brilliant investigations into magnetic attraction; his objections to the torture and press of Ramus' method which reduced verbal learning to barren, empty generalities; his disapproval of Aristotle's preoccupation with verbal expression even in experimental matters.[13]

Although the Puritans also had their own literary figures, such as John Milton, author of the great epic poem *Paradise Lost*, and John Bunyan, author of *The Pilgrim's Progress*, the rejection of literature in education by men like Hartlib and Dury was no less uncompromising. Milton's own *Tractate on Education*, which was addressed to Samuel Hartlib, resembles the utilitarian work of his fellow Puritans but is ex-

---

12   Bacon writes that God's knowledge "touching the secrets of the heart, and the successions of time" suggests moral and allegorical interpretations of Scripture that make its interpretation different from all other books. The literal sense, he says, is the main stream or river but the moral sense and sometimes the allegorical or typical sense are the most useful. He writes that the Books of Scripture have "not only totally or collectively, but distributively in clauses and words, infinite springs and streams of doctrine to water the church in every part" (*Advancement*, 217-18).

13   In spite of this clarity, in his own orientation towards knowledge useful for alleviating human needs even Bacon reduces charity to its current popular sense of benefitting others, in the good of humankind, and in the socially useful. He rejects *caritas* or charity in its sense of friendship with God exemplified in the contemplative lives of monks in the enclosures of medieval monsateries. Monkishness became a pejorative term for the contemplative life in speculative learning as well as in religion which was to be superceded by the active life in applied science and in practical divinity.

ceptional in that as a poet he also values poetry and rhetoric. Bunyan's *Pilgrim's Progress* was published in 1678 in the decades following the Hartlib circle's proposals for educational reform. The author's "Apology" that precedes his allegorical tale indicates the continuing Puritan unease with metaphor and the double sense of a literary mode that does not speak in plain unequivocal terms. Bunyan explains how in spite of himself he "Fell suddenly into an allegory" in writing his tale of the soul's earthly journey through perilous terrain peopled with characters like Mr. Worldy Wiseman, Lord Hategood, and Mrs Timorous. In this apology written in verse he feels the need to justify and explain his use of this allegorical mode, arguing that Scripture speaks in types, shadows, and metaphors; dark and cloudy words hold the truth "as cabinets inclose the gold." He writes that truth in swaddling clothes

> Informs the judgement, rectifies the mind,
> Pleases the understanding, makes the will
> Submit; the memory too it doth fill
> With what doth our imagination please;
> Likewise it tends our troubles to appease."[14]

The platform of the Puritan educational reformers that denied the poetic imagination and literary rationality sought to effect exactly what Sidney had tried to counter. He pleaded the cause of poetry as a unique delightful way of knowing moral truth and had made clear the connection of poetry to Scripture and religion. Nonetheless, the Puritans, whose name reflects their desire of a return to purity, spoke of the corruptions of literature and of the use of the reasoning faculty. As they weighed contemporary education with their utilitarian measure they deemed "scarce one tenth of all our knowledge ... to be either true or profitable" (*Samuel Hartlib*, 167-8). For them, a training of the mind through literature was unnecessary for Scriptural interpretation because words were to be understood in their plain clear sense. Literary reasoning was a detraction from habituation to the new method, from its future discoveries, and from the unclouded, harmonious era which lay brightly ahead.

Like Sir Philip Sidney in the sixteenth century, poets and novelists in the nineteenth and twentieth centuries have also attempted to counter the dismissal of the poetic imagination. In nineteenth-century

---

14 John Bunyan, *The Pilgrim's Progress* (New York: Dodd, Mead, 1968) 4-5.

England when the claims to exclusive validity by the inductive sensate method became increasingly common, Samuel Coleridge undertook the task of explaining how we enter into the imaginative world of poetry by turning from the imagination in its literal empirical register to become receptive to its other register. To enter imaginatively and emotionally into a poem, we assent to what he calls the "willing suspension of disbelief" as a kind of poetic faith. Similarly, in *Hard Times* (1854) the English novelist, Charles Dickens, satirized education in his period that prized externally observable facts but denied to the imagination its role in art and literature. In Mr Gradgrind's classroom, the little girl who performed on circus horses was entirely undercut by Bitzer, the pupil who could identify a horse as: "Quadruped. Graminivorous. Forty teeth, namely twenty-four grinders, four eye-teeth, and twelve incisive. Sheds coat in the spring; in marshy countries, sheds hoofs, too ...".[15]

And again, in the twentieth century men and women endowed with a literary sensibility continued to assert the reality of the literary imagination. Virginia Woolf, author of novels shimmering with interiority, writes in "How Should One Read a Book" of the impressions made by a poem on the imagination. The imagination takes in the world of the poem as a whole, as though in the present, and in a manner deeply connected to the affections. In this initial pre-reflective experience of poetry in which we "receive impressions with the utmost understanding," she observes that the "impact of poetry is so hard and direct that for the moment there is no other sensation except that of the poem itself. What profound depths we visit then--how sudden and complete is our immersion! ... The poet is always our contemporary. Our being for the moment is centred and constricted, as in any violent shock or personal emotion."[16]

And later in the century, the Polish poet, Czeslaw Milosz, bears testimony to the function of the imagination when its face is turned towards the transcendent. It is not through the gates of literal sense experience but through the magisterial function of the imagination described by Bacon that an eternal, universal, divine presence envelops a congregation through the drama of ritual, returning it towards the

---

15   Charles Dickens, *Hard Times* (New York: W.W. Norton, 1966) 3.

16   Virginia Wolf, *The Second Common Reader* (New York: Harcourt Brace & Co., 1986) 265-6.

grace of Eden. With reference to the English poet, William Blake, Milosz reflects on the communal experience in religious ritual that is effected in the locus of the imagination through its magisterial function:

> Not inside the four walls of one's room or in lecture halls or libraries, but through communal participation the veil is parted and for a brief moment the space of Imagination, with a capital *I*, is visible. Such moments allow us to recognize that our imagination is paltry, limited, and that the deliberations of theologians and philosophers are cut to its measure and therefore are completely inadequate for the religion of the Bible. Then complete, true imagination opens like a grand promise and the human privilege of recovery, just as William Blake prophesied.[17]

---

17 Czeslaw Milosz, *To Begin Where I Am* (New York: Farrar, Straus and Giroux, 2001) 326-7.

5

REASONING AND KNOWING IN SCIENCE AND POETRY

ERASMUS DARWIN, CHARLES DARWIN, AND

WILLIAM BLAKE

By the eighteenth and nineteenth centuries the role of the imagination in poetry that Sydney perceived to be imperilled in Puritan England was more widely diminished through the increasingly pervasive influence of modem science and its exclusive use of the sensate imagination. Erasmus Darwin, grandfather of Charles Darwin, presses poetry into the service of science; towards the end of his life, Charles Darwin laments the atrophy of the part of his mind that in earlier years had brought him delight in poetry, music, and art. In the generation between Erasmus and Charles Darwin, the poet, William Blake, is a prophetic voice decrying the loss of the imagination illuminated by the noetic faculty of mind through which we recognize spirit or being within the particular; the dominance of science's abstraction from the particular and the epistemology of materialist philosophy had exacted a heavy human toll. And yet, in spite of the obliteration of the imagination as it functions in poetry and religion, the age of science retains common ground with the genus of reasoning underlying literature, reflections on religious belief, and our practical decisions. Although Charles Darwin arrived at his theory of evolution through sense observation and the sensate role of the imagination, nonetheless the process of reasoning involved in his reflections is the same kind of reasoning through convergent probabilities that is the foundation of practical wisdom, of drama, and the rhetoric of sermons or civic deliberations.

The blurring of the distinct roles of the imagination in poetry and science in the modem period is mirrored in antiquity in the interpretations of poetry by a materialist school of philosophy. In the unsettled terrain between myth, poetry, and physical science, the Stoics in antiquity found empirical allegories in their interpretations of the poetry of Homer and Greek myths. For example, in keeping with the materialist foundation of their philosophy, gods represented the plants and the elements: Zeus represented ether; Hera, his wife, represented air; and Poseidon, god of the sea, represented water. The amours of the gods represented the continuous work of the great creative forces of nature. In this kind of interpretation, poetry was not released from the sensate as Sir Philip Sidney claimed, nor was the imagination considered the locus of revelation of the divine as Bacon maintained. In a modern counterpart to the Stoic's view of poetry, eighteenth-century reasoners attuned to empirical science and its sensate register in the imagination also found in the myths of antiquity personifications of natural science. Erasmus Darwin (1731-1802), grandfather of Charles Darwin, is representative of this outlook where myths and poetry are considered the vehicles of empirical science.

Erasmus Darwin's first name conjures up Desiderius Erasmus who vivified learning and literature in the renaissance; his family name evokes his grandson and the theory of biological evolution. In fact, Erasmus Darwin embraced both poetry and the ebullient age of eighteenth-century science. He was a highly-respected physician, a prominent participant in scientific circles, and a renowned poet in his own era. His scientific circle in Birmingham, the Lunar Society, included Joseph Priestly, the great chemist. He was instrumental in bringing together, Matthew Boulton and James Watt who were to devise the steam engines that moved the industrial revolution. Darwin's own scientific interests and inventions were far-ranging. For example, he identified the existence of warm and cold fronts and their importance for weather. His several inventions included a horizontal windmill used for many years at Josiah Wedgewood's famous pottery works, a wire-drawn river-ferry, and wind gauges. In one of his scientific treatises, *Phytologia*, he provided an important description of photosynthesis, identified correctly the chemical elements needed as food by plants, made proposals for sewage farms, the reforestation of highlands, artificial insemination, and the biological control of pests. In another work, *Zoonomia*, Darwin attempted to discover a theory of diseases through classes, orders, and genera in a manner similar to the botani-cal classifications of the great Swedish naturalist, Linneus. This valiant if unsuccessful attempt included a section that anticipated the work of Charles Darwin where with verve, but without sufficient factual evidence, he expounded the theory of biological evolution.

Like the Stoics, this eighteenth-century scientist, physician, and man of Letters found in mythology an allegory for aspects of the natu-ral world. Through a blurring of the distinction between the literary imagination and the empirical register of the imagination in physi-cal science, myths viewed through the lens of this sensate observer became explanations for empirical science. In a reversal of the tradi-tional understanding of mythology and poetry as preceding science and of the ancient poets as diviners and prophets, or *vates*, Erasmus Darwin subscribed to the belief that science was prior to mythology and to poetry which served as the vehicle of science. He suggests that the Egyptians were possessed of many discoveries in chemistry and science; that these discoveries were expressed in hieroglyphic paint-ings of men and animals; and that after the invention of the alpha-bet they were personified by the poets and became the deities, first, of Egypt and later of Greece and Rome.[1] For example, in the myth of Prosperine seized by Pluto as she gathered flowers, he approves of Francis Bacon's interpretation: that is, as signifying the combination or marriage of ethereal spirit with earthly materials. Darwin adds that the allusion is more curiously exact with the recent discovery of pure air given up from vegetables which in its unmixed state more readily combines with inflammable bodies. Or again, the allegory of Eros or Divine Love producing the world from the Egg of Night as it floated on Chaos is interpreted allegorically as representing the world itself in its infancy and its gradual progress to maturity, like the gradual evolu-tion of the young animal or plant from its egg or seed.

It is not surprising, then, that this exuberant, fertile mind should conceive of a long poem entitled *The Loves of the Plants* (1789) based on the twenty-four classes of plants, their further subdivisions into orders, families or genera, species, and the varieties which were added to species by accidents of climate or by cultivation. In the two thou-sand lines of *The Loves of the Plants*, Darwin's avowed purpose was to

1   Erasmus Darwin, "Apology" in *The Botanic Garden* (Menston, Yorkshire: Scolar P., 1973) vii-viii.

lead the reader into the delightful field of science as described in the botanical works of Linneus which had been translated into English by the Lunar Society. To do so, he reversed the usual procedure in poetry which finds similes in nature for the human and divine. Instead, in *The Loves of the Plants*, the flowers are humanized and their biological modes of reproduction represented in amusing and sometimes risqué situations. When this poem with its handsome engravings was published together with "The Economy of Vegetation" (1791) as the *The Botanic Garden*, it created a sensation and made Darwin famous in his period as a poet.

A dialogue in an interlude between cantos in the "The Loves of the Plants" includes observations on the differences between the function of the imagination in poetry and science.[2] Here Darwin makes a comparison between dreams and the train of ideas suggested to our imagination by poets. Like in our dreams, for the spectator at a production of *Hamlet* actual external objects known through sense and the empirical imagination are excluded. As well, in the immediate experience of the concrete world of poetry the voluntary use of reason which involves comparison with our previous knowledge of things is suspended. In science, by contrast, not only is the reason active but science deals in abstract language and ideas that distinguish it from the concrete language of poetry. As a result, as Darwin concludes, prose is a better medium for science than poetry.

For this reason, in the nearly four and a half thousand lines of *The Botanic Garden* Darwin achieves his declared purpose of enlisting the imagination under the banner of science by juxtaposing his verses representing concrete scenes with scientific explanations in prose footnotes which exceed the poem in length. In accordance with Darwin's marriage of the concrete language of poetry with the abstractions and reasoning of science, the four cantos of "The Economy of Vegetation" are organized under the four elements discerned in antiquity: fire, earth, water, and air. Botany becomes concrete in the form of a goddess and the elements are introduced as the Nymphs of Fire, the Gnomes of Earth, the Nymphs of Water, and the Sylphs of Air. Darwin explains that this machinery is appropriate as it accords with the doctrine of the Rosicrucians, a society that claimed secret knowledge

---

2   Erasmus Darwin, "The Loves of the Plants," in *The Botanic Garden*, 40-50.

regarding power over the elements and the transmutation of metals; for the Rosicrucians, nymphs, gnomes, and sylphs were originally the names of hieroglyphic figures representing the elements. In this yoking of poetry to the service of empirical science, he begins by claiming for the student of science both the delight and virtue that defenders of literature from Aristotle to Sidney had claimed for poetry through its capacity to teach and delight (*docere et delectare*). Then Darwin exudes in waves of iambic pentameter verse a delight both in the natural world of empirical observation and in its useful applications: in steam engines, for example, or lightning rods, or the diversion of water in canals.

In the first Canto, while Darwin enthusiastically sets the scene through the concrete images of poetry, the prose footnotes below the verse speak in the tone of empirical science's observations and abstract conclusions. In the poem, when the Goddess of Botany arrives, she descends in her blushing car through the whispering air, bright as the morn. Each circling wheel is entwined with a wreath of flowers; knots of flowers connect the crimson reins. As the Goddess bounds from her airy seat, her celestial steps press the pansied grounds. Pleased gnomes ascend from their earthy beds and play around her graceful footsteps as she treads.[3] Below the verse, the first note begins with a reference to Epicurean philosophy in connection to the disposition required for empirical science. With the appearance of the Nymphs of primal fire, another note includes observations on the fluidity or solidity of all bodies in nature as preserved through the attraction of their particles to heat, on gases produced from greater heat, and remarks on steam. The term Calorique, the fluid matter of heat necessary to vegetable and animal existence, is mentioned as the nomenclature of French Academicians; and, finally, the note concludes with the comment that modern natural philosophers have not yet been able to conclude whether light and heat are different fluids, or modifications of the same fluid, as they have many properties in common.

In this late eighteenth-century borderline world between poetry and science, the scales are weighted decidedly in favour of empirical sci-

---

3   Darwin introduces the Goddess of Botany in the lines: "She comes!--the Goddess!--through the whispering air,/ Bright as the morn, descends her blushing car;/ Each circling wheel a wreath of flowers intwines,/ And gem'd with flowers the silken harness shines." "The Economy of Vegetation," in *The Botanic Garden*, 5.

ence and the sensate imagination; both myth and poetry are secured in the service of science and the traditional symbolic power of poetry is perceived as diminishing. Darwin remarks that although certain allegoric figures such as time and death were still sufficiently habitual or familiar in his period to be meaningful, for the most part allegoric figures pertaining to the poetic imagination had become improbable and even jarring especially when mixed with natural figures as in some instances of contemporary painting or sculpture.[4] Poetry is not a serious venture. It is ornamental and meant to amuse with the exception of didactic poetry; for example, Virgil's *Georgics*, the very kind of poetry that Sidney would exclude as contrary to poetry's distinctive free-ranging imagination removed from the strictures of the actual. In Darwin's dialogue on the nature of poetry, located between cantos on the reproduction of flowers, distinctive characteristics of poetry are absent. There is no place for discussion of poetry as a mimesis of human life. Although poetry is characterized as concrete and the poet as writing principally to the eye, there is no mention of the universals or perennial truths embedded within the concrete that make it a serious art. Nor is there any allusion to the rationality of literature discerned by Aristotle in the sinews that bind together the causal sequence of narrative plot.

In Darwin's distinction between poetry and science, their mutually exclusive orientation of the imagination is best conveyed in his observations on their respective uses of analogy: that is, comparisons that include partial resemblances mixed with unlikenesses. He writes that poetry's loose analogies in metaphors and similes make prose a better medium for science because the ratiocination or mode of reasoning of science requires stricter analogies.[5] In its metaphors and similes, as suggested by Sir Philip Sidney, the poetic imagination ranges loosely up and down creation and slips easily between the three domains of the divine, the human, and the physical world. Untethered to strict sensate experience, analogies are made, for example, between old age and the evening of the day, between grace and sunlight, and in the poetry of the Psalms hills leap for joy.

On the other hand, in the physical sciences analogical observations of similarities between things are bound to the sensate world, to the

---

4   Erasmus Darwin, "Interlude" in "The Loves of the Plants," 42-45.

5   Erasmus Darwin, "Apology" in *The Botanic Garden*, vii.

empirical register of the imagination, and to an understanding of things that is neither figurative nor symbolic. For example, a similarity may be observed between the bristles and quills in some animals and human hair, or the resemblance noted between the skeletal structure of the fins of fish and the wings of birds. On the same empirical plane, in the physical sciences analogy also functions as the basis of presumptive reasoning to arrive at hypothetical conclusions that may later be verified empirically or experimentally. For example, through presumptive reasoning Sir Humphrey Davy (1778-1820), known for his revolutionary conclusions regarding the chemical agencies of electricity, concluded by analogy from his observations on the metallic base of potash that all alkalies[6] in general probably have a metallic base.[7] In contrast to such analogical reasoning in the physical sciences, when exercised in everyday thought, in moral reasoning, or in Scriptural interpretation, presumptive reasoning moves freely in its analogies through the divine, human, and physical spheres.

Apologizing in part for his own use of unverified theories in his poem, Darwin nonetheless maintains that extravagant theories are useful in those parts of science where knowledge is still imperfect. Such theories or hypotheses encourage experiments and ingenious deductions; and because of the many affinities or resemblances allying natural objects to each other, Darwin writes, every hypothesis adds to our knowledge by developing some of their analogies.[8] The devel-

---

6   In chemistry, alkali (Arabic qalay: to roast in a pan) refers to a series of bases, analogous to, and including soda, potash, and ammonia, which are highly soluble in water, combine with acids to form salts, unite with oil or fat to form soap, and which turn vegetable blues to green, and yellows to red. *Oxford Universal Dictionary* and *The New Webster Encyclopedic Dictionary*.

7   This example is taken from Joseph Angus' notes to *The Analogy of Religion to the Constitution and Course of Nature*, Joseph Butler (London: Religious Tract Society, 1881) 7. Angus adds that everyday thought, moral reasoning, and the interpretation of Scripture operate similarly through analogies that proceed through the truth of things and facts already familiar.

8   The idea of analogy is implicit in the title of Darwin's "The Economy of Vegetation" which describes the extrinsic affinities allying natural objects to each other through a regulative unity of their various parts. In its root sense, economy (Greek: law or rule of the house) referred to the regulation or government of the several parts of a household. In a similar vein, theo-

opment of an hypothesis through analogy based on the real affinities allying natural objects to each other was to fall brilliantly to Darwin's grandson, Charles Darwin (1809-1882), whose name is associated in perpetuity with the theory of biological evolution.

As for other scientists arriving at an hypothesis, the process of reasoning used by Charles Darwin in arriving at the theory of biological evolution and his marshalling of evidence to persuade others of its validity belong to the large genus of convergent thought common to reasoning in all probable matters: for example, in our everyday decisions, ethical judgments, religion, or in reflections on religious beliefs. Darwin's reasoning and judgment differ from convergent thought in these other domains only in being confined strictly to the realm of the sensate. His leap from probable evidence to judgment in his hypothesis is through *nous*, the illative sense described by Newman which simply recognizes ultimate principles in conjunction with converging probable thought. Among the various genres of literature, the process of reasoning through which he became convinced of his hypothesis most closely resembles the suasory reasoning of rhetoric as exercised, for example, in Cicero's deliberative or forensic speeches or in John Henry Newman's sermons.

---

logians speak of the economy of salvation. The economy of a poem, a play, or speech refers to an underlying unity achieved through its bare structural framework or organization. Aristotle describes the economy of a play when he compares it to the physiology of an animal; he writes that tragedy is like a living organism or any other entity composed of parts possessed in proper order and the right magnitude. Like household economy which also suggests no waste, the economy of a tragedy is such that the transposition or removal of any one section dislocates and changes the whole.

In the domain of natural science, the economy of vegetation and the animal economy refer to the regular operations of nature in the generation, nutrition, and preservation of plants and animals. In the *Advertisement* to his poem Darwin writes that in "The Economy of Vegetation" the "physiology of Plants is delivered; and the operation of the Elements, as far as they may be supposed to affect the growth of Vegetables." In his various notes on the myriad scientific interests of the period, one example shows the extrinsic connection or analogy between coolness and the health of plants and also provides an experimental analogy that affirms the connection. Darwin writes that the cold temperature that produces frost causes the water in the vessels of plants to expand and destroy them like the bursting of bottles filled with water that freezes.

Because Darwin's process of thought in arriving at the theory of evolution exhibits the characteristics common to all convergent reasoning through probabilities, it stands in contrast to the way Comenius would train students in scientific method and to Bacon's understanding of science: that is, as conducted on a single field and as operating through an impersonal inductive logic or *organon* available to all. Instead, Darwin's process of reasoning follows the pattern of the genus to which it belongs: first, it involves the exercise of personal judgment; and, secondly, the criterion for this judgment lies in the convergence of diverse collateral facts and of probabilities from several different areas, none of which alone could suffice as persuasive proof. Like G.K. Chesterton's detective, in the absence of clear first principles and plodding logic, in his scientific observations Darwin was attentive to oddities, the unforeseen, and the unreasonable. Or like the mosaic approach used by Georg von Bekesy, the Hungarian scientist awarded the Nobel prize for his work in the study of the senses, Darwin reasoned through constantly making comparisons in various related fields.

In his *Autobiography*, Charles Darwin offers his own testimony to the kind of reasoning that led to the theory of the evolution of species. The autobiography was prompted by a German editor's request for an account of the development of his mind and character, but Darwin also wrote it for his five children and their children on the grounds that he would have been interested by a similar personal insight into the mind of his grandfather, Erasmus Darwin. Where he discusses the claim that the subject of evolution was not new in scientific circles but was "in the air," Darwin makes clear how convergent thought works through the clustering of multiple probabilities around a single idea. He explains: "Innumerable well-observed facts were stored in the minds of naturalists, ready to take their proper places as soon as any theory which would receive them was sufficiently explained."[9]

In an analysis of the strengths and weaknesses of his own mind, Darwin also reveals the qualities essential for reasoning through converging probabilities in the oscillation or interplay between concrete and abstract that includes both an elasticity and patience of judgment and the kind of insight exercised by a good doctor. He writes that his mind was not disposed to the pure abstractions of mathematics

---

9   Charles Darwin, *The Autobiography of Charles Darwin* (1809-1882) (London: Collins, 1958) 124.

and metaphysics. Rather, like the wise medical judgments practised on his patients by his father, Dr. Robert Darwin, his talent lay in the connection that he made between observed facts and their underlying principles. In his remarks on his mind, he mentions careful empirical observation including what might escape the notice of others; a desire experienced since youth to understand underlying principles by grouping all facts under general laws; and a sensibility to the relation between hypothesis and facts that might require modifying or abandoning an hypothesis "as soon as facts are shown to be opposed to it" (*Autobiography*, 141). Darwin's disposition towards congruent thought is implied even in his criticism of his mind as neither quick nor witty. He says that after initial favourable impressions made on him by a book or paper, he perceived their weak points only after considerable reflection. Finally, although convergent thought in science requires a habit of concentrated attention and industry that brings all that is read and thought to bear on one's observations,[10] unlike convergent thought in Cicero's rhetoric it does not necessarily require a sharply retentive memory. Darwin's comments on his hazy memory reveal a mind that is not a storehouse of facts but knows where to look for references when an idea elicits them.

The field of physical life on which Darwin's mind was exercised was as broad and undivided in its own right as the undivided terrain of the human and divine in Cicero's field of rhetoric. Like the unified, objective, coherent cosmos assumed in Aristotle's philosophy and in Scripture, Darwin assumed similarly that the domain of physical life was coherent, unified, and objective. And like the plots of Shakespeare or of the Greek playwrights with their complex web of relationships, their drama of change, and their causal sequences, the physical world investigated by Darwin was perceived as interconnected and causally related through its sequential development and processes of change. However, Darwin's scientific domain differs from the dramas in their imitation of what is specifically human: that is, in volition, agency, and human responsibility in right and wrong choices; in deliberate actions connected to principles; in the use of language with its personal resonance; and the relation of the human and the divine.

Although confined to the strictly physical domain, Darwin's process of reasoning is in no way different from reasoning through prob-

---

10   Erasmus Darwin, *Autobiography*, 78.

abilities in the spheres of the human and the divine. The principles embedded in the broad domain of physical life taken as a multifaceted, complex, interconnected whole could only be understood in the manner described by Cicero for the recurring questions in the web of human affairs; that is, through correlatives and a combination of resemblances, differences, contradictions, causes, and consequences. In Newman's terms, Darwin would become persuaded of the theory of the transmutation of species through "the strength, variety, or multiplicity of premisses, which are only probable. ... by objections proving the rule, by unlooked-for correlations found with received truths ... by suspense and delay in the process issuing in triumphant reactions ...."[11]

In 1831 when at the age of twenty-two Darwin departed from Plymouth harbour on his voyage around the world, although he had a strong interest in natural science and had a passion for collecting since childhood, he had little formal preparation for his work in science that lay ahead.[12] For a person who was to postulate a theory covering the whole field of physical life through the convergence of multiple independent probabilities, the most important factor in his early development as a natural scientist was his friendship at Cambridge with

---

11   Newman, *Grammar of Assent*, 253-54.

12   Darwin relates how this education took place outside his program of studies at grammar school and at Cambridge, where the Greek and Roman classics predominated, and outside his studies in medicine in Edinburgh. He had abandoned medical studies at Edinburgh where even anatomy was taught through lectures rather than through dissection. Instead, in Edinburgh Darwin followed his inclination towards natural science by joining groups like the Plinian Society whose members included the assistant keeper of the Museum of Natural History. When in 1828 he began his studies at Cambridge for an alternate career in the clergy, he not only belonged to groups interested in natural science but was also an avid and serious collector of beetles. To illustrate his zeal for collecting, a passion for Darwin since childhood, he describes how he once popped a beetle into his mouth because both hands already held beetles; in the end he had to spit out the beetle after it emitted an acrid fluid and lost another one in the process. Finally, in his last year at Cambridge, his ardour for natural science was stirred by reading Sir John Herschel's *Introduction to the Study of Natural Philosophy* and Alexander von Humboldt's (1769-1859) personal narrative of his travels and scientific observations in Teneriffe, equinoctial South America, Mexico, and Cuba.

John Stevens Henslow, Professor of botany and knowledgeable in several sciences: entomology, chemistry, mineralogy, geology. Henslow saw the scientist in Darwin and recommended him as naturalist for the *Beagle's* expedition (1831-6), believing that he was qualified not through his training but through his capacity for collecting, observing, and noting anything new. While Darwin travelled, it was to Henslow that he sent back his collections. Henslow for his part encouraged Darwin, sent him scientific literature, and offered expert guidance. After receiving Darwin's first shipment of specimens in 1833, he advised him on how to pack geological items and on the importance of including roots, flowers and leaves. Later that same year, he observed that nearly all the minute insects he had sent were new, that all fossils were important.

Through such guidance and his own experience, in the course of his five year voyage Darwin soon ceased to be merely a collector as he recognized principles and made comparisons between species of animals and plants. Regarding his last large collecting effort on the Galapagos Islands, Darwin wrote to Henslow that he had collected every plant in flower that had come into view and had paid much attention to the birds which he suspected to be very curious. Darwin's dependence on Henslow evident in their correspondence and his gratitude to him is typical of his reliance on experts in the several areas of science that he continued to draw upon for cumulative supporting evidence in the years before the publication of *The Origin of Species* in 1859. Aided by a grant obtained with Henslow's support, when he returned to England his collection was analyzed by prominent experts in corallines, reptiles, conchology, entomology, ornithology, botany.

Darwin's empirical observations made during his voyage in so many different areas of science were essential to an understanding of the relation of parts to a whole, the same kind of relation that Aristotle characterizes as typical of the poetic drama and of discourses in rhetoric. Analogical reasoning figured importantly into this consideration. As in religion where analogy is necessary to bridge the enormity of the gap between the human domain and the realm of God, for Darwin, too, analogical reasoning was required to arrive at his theory because of the great gaps in empirical evidence that had to be bridged in the immense span of time of biological evolution.

One eminent scientist in particular was important to Darwin as a model for this kind of reasoning through analogy as well as for his work in the related field of geology where, like Darwin, he considered change through time. Darwin's theory of the transmutation of all living things over an unimaginable period of time would have been inconceivable without the work of the eminent geologist, Charles Lyell (1797-1875), whose first volume of the *Principles of Geology* was published in 1830, the year before Darwin's voyage.

In his work, Lyell offered a model of the way in which pioneering theories within the physical domain are reached through analogical reasoning and converging probabilities. His argument for a comprehensive theory of the laws guiding geological change was based in part on the analogy between what was observable in the present with similar processes in the past. Lyell observed that the earth was still in a state of constant flux; mountains, for example, were still being thrust up and elevations were still subsiding. By analogy, he claimed that present evidence of processes such as volcanic eruptions were an indication of similar past processes as part of slow, gradual cycles of change that extended over vast periods of time. This reasoning through analogy was required because, as Darwin wrote, geology's study of the crust of the earth dealt with enormous gaps: not like a well-filled museum but "as a poor collection made at hazard and at rare intervals."[13] Evidence through strict sense observation required by Baconian science was simply not available for either the principles of geology or the theory of biological evolution.

In his own reasoning through probabilities, Darwin was to labour under similar difficulties. Because of the lack of continuous evidence of biological transmutation, like Lyell he had to exercise personal judgment based on reasoning through analogy and congruent probabilities. Although he claimed that varieties were incipient species, change was so slow that existing transitional evidence for a continuous sequence of change was elusive. Darwin observed that the mind which cannot possibly grasp the meaning of over a million years cannot "add up and perceive the full effects of many slight variations accumulated during an almost infinite number of generations" (*Origin*, 444). While fellow scientists were sceptical of conclusions reached through analogies and probabilities, which they called an unsafe method of arguing,

---

13   Charles Darwin, *The Origin of Species by Means of Natural Selection or the Preservation of Favoured Races in the Struggle for Life* (New York: Mentor, 1958) 448. All further citations are from this edition.

like Newman Darwin defended the genus of probable reasoning as not only "a method used in judging of the common events of life," but also as the mode often used by the greatest natural philosophers (*Origin*, 442-3): for example, in arriving at the undulatory theory of light, or the belief that the earth rotated on its own axis, theories which remained probable until direct evidence was later provided.

A singular instance of Darwin's own power of reasoning through probability is found in his correct understanding of the development of coral reefs before he had seen a true coral reef. By analogy with his observations and reflections on the effects of elevation and subsidence of land on the west coast of South America along with the effect of the deposition of sediment, he recognized that coral atolls do not build on the rims of submerged volcanic craters, as in Lyell's generally assumed theory, but build up independently in shallow water near the shores of islands. Before seeing evidence for this in the coral reefs of the Pacific, he realized that as islands together with their closely connected reefs subside gradually the land might disappear entirely but the coral's polypi continue building up the reefs, gradually raising the reefs towards sea level.[14]

Although Darwin argued for the validity of the probable mode of reasoning through analogy, he also recognized that "analogy may be a deceitful guide": for instance, in advancing by analogy from his considered belief that both animals and plants are descended respectively from about four prototypes to the further conclusion that "all animals and plants are descended from some one prototype" (*Origin*, 446). In the physical sciences, if theories advance through analogies both their soundness and their capacity to persuade others require the support of concrete evidence. Before publishing *Coral Reefs* in 1842, Darwin relates that he spent twenty months of hard work reading every work on the islands of the Pacific and consulting many charts.

Along with the unstintingly generous assistance provided by scientists like Henslow and Lyell, Darwin's travels were the most important source of his formation as an empirical scientist who sought to

---

14   Darwin describes the process by which he understood coral reefs as involving deduction and the imagination (*Autobiography*, 98-9). Such perceptions and ratiocinations in physical science have common ground with the analogy of metaphor and simile in poetry. Newton compared the fall of an apple from a tree with the movement of the planets and found an analogy between them.

understand principles embedded in phenomena through converging probabilities and analogies. The multiple first-hand impressions made on him in the course of his voyage aboard the *Beagle* and the opportunity for constantly making comparisons afforded the primary matter for personal reflection that led later to his hypothesis regarding the transmutation of species. Prior to his departure, his only practical training in geology had been through a summer field trip in Wales. However, armed with Lyell's work Darwin discovered the pleasure of understanding the principles behind the puzzle of a chaos of rocks as he recorded their nature and their stratifications. He could confirm Lyell's theory concerning the continuing flux of the earth when he observed a two or three-foot upheaval of land in Chile evident after an earthquake in 1822. Because he took note of fossil bones of extinct quadrupeds in places like the Pampas of Argentina and Patagonia and found similar types of organization still present in South American mammals, he could later indicate the long development of this type of mammal in a paper to the Geological Society in 1837. He had further matter for reflection in his observations not of similarities but of differences noted in variations within the same species; for example, in the finches and tortoises in the Galapagos archipelago. As the *Beagle* continued its 40,000 mile voyage, Darwin could observe that animals in one part of the world had more in common with one another than with animals in another part.

As with the several pieces in a kaleidescope that form a pattern or like von Bekesy's mosaic approach, Darwin found that the comparisons in many different areas made in the course of his field work converged towards an underlying idea. When he returned to England in the autumn of 1836 and prepared the journals of his voyage for publication, through his own reflections he saw many facts that indicated the common descent of species. In his introduction to *The Origin of Species* published twenty three years later, he related how by 1837 he realized that the various impressions made on him during his travels in South America seemed to throw light on the mystery of the origin of species. He wrote that he then began accumulating and reflecting on all sorts of facts which could possibly have a bearing on their origin, that in 1844 he wrote a sketch of his conclusions which then seemed to him probable, and that he had steadily pursued that same object since (*Origin*, 27). In other words, by 1837 Darwin recognized the central idea of the whole complex matter of biological transmutation through what Newman calls the illative sense, or personal judgment exercised on cumulative converging probabilities. Darwin himself had become persuaded that through modification existing species were the descendants of pre-existing forms, an opinion entertained by few scientists and contrary to all common belief on the subject.[15]

However, Darwin still did not have an explanation for how this modification occurred. In the manner of convergent thought, as the idea of modification exerted pressure on what he thought and read, in 1838 he came upon a solution in an unlooked-for analogy in another field through the theory of a political economist.[16] In his *Autobiography*, he describes how he happened to be reading for amusement the *Essay on the Principles of Population as it affects the future Improvement of Society* (1798) by Robert Thomas Malthus (1765-1834). Malthus, who had taught at the East India Company's training school and was the first professor of political economy in England, pointed out the disparity between growth in population and the food supply. He suggested that population increases exponentially or at a geometric rate (2/4/8/16) while the food supply increases at a linear or arithmetic rate (1/2/3/4). Malthus maintained further that needed checks on population growth occur through the instrumentality of famine, sickness, vice, and misery. His theory was to have a practical effect on the British assumption that Ireland's potato famine was inevitable and

---

15   In "An Historical Sketch" added at the beginning of the third edition, Darwin provides a chronological outline of thirty-four naturalists who had subscribed in some measure to the idea of the modification of species. In *The Origin*, he also refers briefly to comparable evidence in the study of comparative languages. In this vein, Noah Webster, for example, had written in the Preface to his dictionary first published in 1840 of how his work came to be an "investigation of the origin and progress of our language." He compared words with the same roots in about twenty languages, noting affinities between English and many other languages and thus traced words to their source (xi). In his "Introduction," Webster notes that Sanscrit, the parent of all the dialects in India, is radically from the same language or from the same stock as Greek and Latin; that the inhabitants of India and the descendants of the Celtic and Teutonic nations are all of one family; and he draws the inference that "the white men of Europe, and the black or tawny men of India, are direct descendants from a common ancestor." *An American Dictionary of the English Language* (Springfield, Mass: George and Charles Merriam, 1856) xxv.

16   Darwin, *Autobiography*, 120.

that India's periodic famines were to keep its population in check. For Darwin, an analogous connection made with the realm of plants and animals led to a missing piece in the evolutionary puzzle and an answer to Lyell's objection that changes in the environment occurred too quickly and harshly to allow organisms to respond by developing new organs. Darwin recognized that incipient species in plants and animals could become full-blown species in a short time through their struggle for existence because those best adapted to adverse conditions would survive through natural selection.

Another piece of the puzzle regarding the sequence of change in the evolution of species also became clear through another converging probability. Around 1844, it occurred to Darwin during a carriage ride near his home that the tendency for species to modify could be explained through their adaptation to the many highly diversified places in the economy of nature. In keeping with the mnemonic role of the imagination which locates thought in places, in his autobiography Darwin says that he recollected the very spot on the road where, to his joy, the solution occurred to him.

Although Darwin himself believed that he had found explanations for transmutation, he was still faced with the daunting task of persuading others of this conviction. This task which in the field of Letters belongs specifically to the reasoning of rhetoric in science must be conducted strictly on the empirical plane. Like other empirical scientists with new theories, Darwin has to persuade his fellow scientists through the strength of cumulative evidence. Lyell's important work on the principles of geological change over an immensely long period of time, for example, had remained controversial in scientific circles in part because his own conviction reached through analogy depended on personal judgment and was deemed insufficiently supported by facts. William Whewell (1794-1866), the distinguished author of works on inductive reasoning, originator of the words "scientist" and "consilience," and Professor of mineralogy when Darwin was at Cambridge, wrote that he admired Lyell's masterful attempt to bring together "into a consistent view a large mass of singularly curious observations and details" but found his theories insufficiently supported by geological evidence.[17]

To convince others, Darwin had to use the same mode of congruent reason that had first persuaded him of his hypothesis; that is, he argued his case through the genus of converging probabilities. Like a rhetorician deliberating on public affairs or pleading in court, he had to meet objections to his claims. Not only was the radical nature of his hypothesis counter to assumptions in both science and religion, but his mode of reasoning through convergent probabilities was also deemed suspect. In *The Origin of Species*, Darwin explains that the great majority of scientists had believed that species were immutable productions separately created (*Origin*, 17). His new way of thinking about organic life evolving through laws of sequence over a vast period of time undermined a world view entrenched in western thought. The belief that species were immutable productions was reinforced by the pervasive image from Plato of phenomena as imperfect copies of universal or permanent ideas. As well, a conflation of religion with physical science in the interpretation of the story of creation in Genesis led to the similar idea of each species as a separate creation by God; similarly, phenomena such as the extinction of species were explained through Biblical stories like Noah's flood.

Rather than contending with the hybrid of science and religion in the natural theology that thrived in his period, in *The Origin of Species* Darwin remained largely silent on the subject of religion and sought to persuade others of the theory of the transmutation of species on its own grounds and through the intellectual instrument proper to it. In natural theology, religion was harnessed to natural science in a way similar to Erasmus Darwin's yoking of poetry and myth to science; that is, the imagination which in poetry and religion is released from the strictly sensate register was required to abjure its proper function and attend instead to the strictly sensate register of empirical science. Just a few years after the publication of *The Botanic Garden*, William Paley's influential work on natural theology entitled *Evidences*

---

17   William Whewell in a review of Lyell's *Principles* in *The British Critic Quarterly Theological Review*. Cited by Barry G. Gale in *Evolution Without Evidence: Charles Darwin and The Origin of Species* (Brighton: Harvester P., 1982) 39.

of Christianity (1794) had appeared. In this work, which was familiar to Charles Darwin from his exams at Cambridge, Paley's evidence for the existence of God was based on the perfection of the design of the world. Paley also approved of Malthus who found evidence for the benevolence of God in the fixed laws that rooted out population for the future improvement of society and the advantage of his creatures.

In a work on natural theology entitled *The Bridgewater Treatises* (1833-36) which was published concurrently with Darwin's voyage, natural scientists, including clergymen, were commissioned to write of God's power, wisdom, and goodness evident in creation. This project required the imagination to abandon its magisterial relation to reason in religion to serve science where instead it acts simply as a messenger between sense and reason. In this conflation of the mode of religion and the mode of physical science, contributors to the *Treatises* sought persuasive evidence of God's power, wisdom, and goodness by providing cumulative examples of accurate scientific observation, following the same kind of argument used by Darwin regarding biological evolution in *The Origin of Species*. For example, one long work by Rev. William Kirby on reptiles, fishes, birds, and mammals gives exact details based on first-hand accounts of the construction of dams and lodges by beavers: the beavers' choice of a natural basin of a certain depth, their underwater excavations, their use of the excavated earth mixed with wood to make a dome-shaped hillock four to seven feet high and ten to twelve feet long; the interior's magazine for provisions of yellow water-lily and branches of birch and black spruce. After some pages, the writer concludes with the observation that the admirable operations of the beaver through instinct and intellect, as adapted by the Creator, allow man by studying them to acknowledge the Power, Wisdom, and Goodness that forms and guides them.[18] In this mixture of the physical and divine domains, the final pious gloss placed at the end of exact empirical observations sounds as incongruous as Erasmus Darwin's poetry juxtaposed with his footnoted explanations on contemporary science.

In the seventeenth-century Bacon had recognized the incongruous, incompatible mixture of religion and science in natural theology that

---

18   William Kirby, "On the History Habits and Instincts of Animals," vol. ii, Treatise vii of *The Bridgewater Treatises on the Power Wisdom and Goodness of God as Manifested in the Creation* (London: William Pickering, 1835) 509-13.

was counter to Darwin's scientific approach in the *Origin of Species*. In *The Advancement of Learning*, Bacon acknowledged the distinct magisterial function of the imagination in its relation to reason in religion, that in Scripture images of natural science are not to be taken literally but as analogies for moral and divine matters, and that in fact little can be known about God through creation. He wrote that because the contemplation of creation reveals only knowledge of God's providence, wisdom, and power, it was unsafe to "induce any verity or persuasion concerning the points of faith" in this way. In contrast to the function of reason as it judges particulars in empirical science, Bacon observes that because the starting-point for theology is in the words and oracles of God, "we ought not attempt to draw down or submit the mysteries of God to our reason; but contrariwise to raise and advance our reason to the divine truth" (*Advancement*, 89). In Scripture natural philosophy is used only as a way of expressing moral and divine matters adapted to man's capacity; that is, through what Erasmus Darwin called the loose analogies of poetry. To seek matters pertaining to physical science in Scripture is like seeking positive confirmation of a Unicorn used for the sake of illustration in a simile (*Advancement*, 88-9). Finally, the seventeenth-century philosopher of science warned of the "extreme prejudice which both religion and philosophy have received and may receive, by being comminxed together" (*Advancement*, 89). Empirical science has its own distinct end and separate cause which cannot be entertained simultaneously with final causes either as they are understood by Aristotle or in religion.[19] Bacon writes that the final causes expressing purpose which Aristotle had included are worthy within their own province but have no place in the method of reasoning through cause and effect in empirical science. Thus, "the cause rendered, that *the hairs about the eye-lids are for the safeguard of the sight*" which concerns intention "doth not impugn

---

19   At the same time, because of the necessity of separating secondary physical causes from final causes in science, he acknowledged the potential loss of religion for those engaged in the study of science. And he suggests that education should begin with religion and morality because of the likelihood of private gain assuming ascendancy in the commerce and trade resulting from improvements in physical science.

the cause rendered, that *pilosity is incident to orifices of moisture"* which declares a consequence only (*Advancement*, 97-8).[20]

Since Darwin's strictly empirical scientific purpose and its engagement of the sensate imagination, on the one hand, and theology's roots in the magisterial imagination and its consideration of first and final causes, on the other hand, are mutually exclusive, in his arguments in *The Origin of Species* he does not mix theology with science and rightly remains silent regarding the objections of natural theology where the two are conflated. Because within its own domain the truth of science is neither theocentric nor anthropocentric, Darwin simply maintained that biological laws of sequence indicate that humankind is biologically close to animals; that random natural selection is for the good or utility of each species rather than a demonstration either of divine intelligence or of a benevolent purpose related to the good of humankind.

Darwin also met resistance to his theory of the transmutation of species from the very nature of his reasoning which depended on probabilities converging from various quarters. As he pointed out, analogy and probable reasoning were considered an unsafe way of arguing. Because the same facts can lead to different conclusions, experts in single areas resisted Darwin's argument with its corroborating evidence from several different areas. Fellow scientists like the British zoologist, Joseph Dalton Hooker, or the American botanist, Asa Gray, who gladly and generously supplied Darwin with facts within their areas of expertise, could not easily entertain multiple probabilities in the way that persuaded Darwin of his hypothesis. Conversely, others accused Darwin of being a good observer but without any power of reasoning.

Darwin could have found support for his method of reasoning through converging probabilities from a contemporary who at first glance might seem an unlikely source: that is, in John Henry Newman, the eloquent defender of the genus of convergent reasoning particularly as it pertains to religious belief. While *The Origin of Species* was passing through its various editions, in *An Essay in Aid of a Grammar of Assent* (1870) Newman applied his defense of convergent reasoning

---

20   The italics indicate Bacon's citation from Xenophon's *Memorabilia*. Cf. Michael Kiernan's annotated edition of *The Advancement of Learning* (Oxford: Clarendon P., 2000) 282.

alike to scientific hypotheses and to religious belief. Both the individual seeking explicit understanding of a particular religious belief and
the scientist developing an original hypothesis engage in an operation
of mind that draws together like a magnet multiple varied probabilities suggested by the case under consideration until the reasoner is
persuaded of their truth. In what Aristotle described as the calculative
part of the soul in contrast to the scientific part of the soul, through a
subtle, circuitous procedure the reasoner arrives at certitude in a matter that has not been demonstrated.

Even earlier while Darwin was still circling the globe aboard the
Beagle, at the University Church in Oxford Newman was already articulating in a cycle of sermons[21] the way we reason in concrete matters
through converging probabilities that was counter to the increasingly
common assumption that reasoning from evidence took precedence.
Like Darwin's argument in *The Origin of Species*, Newman's sermons
on reasoning through the convergence of analogies, examples, and pre-
sumptions are themselves a model of this genus of reasoning through
probability. With the same uncompromising eye for truth as Darwin,
he circles around the single idea of how faith understands explicitly
what it has first known through the function of the imagination and
through tacit implicit apprehension. He views his subject in many
different lights, oscillating between the abstract and the concrete in
examples, comparisons, and appeals to experience. He contrasts and
compares, states commonly-held contrary views on the nature of reason and then shows their inadequacy in getting to the heart of an individual's thought; he asks telling questions, reinforces his position, and
draws conclusions.

The arguments of both Newman in his sermons and Darwin in *The
Origin of Species* illustrate the persuasive reasoning of rhetoric as part
of the larger genus of convergent thought which has its own criterion
of judgment. In his *Autobiography*, where Darwin responds to the criticism that he was a good observer but without any power or reasoning,
he writes that in fact *The Origin of Species* "is one long argument from
the beginning to the end, and it has convinced not a few able men." He

---

21   John Henry Newman, *Fifteen Sermons Preached Before the University of
      Oxford Between A.D. 1826 and 1843*, ed. Mary Katherine Tillman (Notre
      Dame: Notre Dame UP, 1997).

also adds that he believes that he has good judgment "such as every fairly successful lawyer or doctor must have"(*Autobiography*, 140).

Darwin's long argument meant to persuade others, then, involves the same kind of reasoning used in the art of rhetoric, the art of persuasion in probable matters that was the crowning phase of the language disciplines in literary eras. Darwin's reasoning in regard to the physical domain is the same kind of reasoning that Cicero exercised on the human domain: in deliberations on public matters, in forensic reasoning, or in the evaluation of moral character. Like Cicero in his orations, after darwin himself was first persuaded of the theory of the transmutation of species he then sought to persuade others of his conviction through a similar process of reasoning but adapting his argument to his audience's frame of reference. Like Cicero in his orations and like Newman in his sermons, Darwin considered his subject from different vantage points, oscillating between particulars and one essential idea in order to grasp both idea and facts in their fullness. He considered eclectic independent probabilities in their mutual relations to make connections and resolve ambiguities. In other words, in contrast to its pejorative designation as bloated verbal style separated from reason, for the scientist, the statesman, and the preacher, the reasoning characteristic of rhetoric is a distinct and important mode of thought for locating truth through probabilities.

To appreciate the identity between Darwin's process of probable reasoning as he became persuaded of the still unproven truth of biological evolution, on the one hand, and the art of rhetoric through which we are persuaded of probable truths in the human sphere, on the other hand, we shall turn again to Aristotle. In a much earlier age of scientific reasoning, Aristotle validated the mode of persuasive reasoning which had been associated pejoratively with the sophists. In the *Rhetoric*, he defended this mode of probable thought by distinguishing it from the scientific ratiocination characteristic of the verbal syllogism. Because we do not deliberate about what is scientifically demonstrable, in contrast to this scientific reasoning rhetoric is concerned with matters that we deliberate upon without arts or systems to guide us. He also affirms the validity of this reasoning through probabilities, asserting that we can recognize truth through probabilities or "the approximately true" through the same faculty that apprehends the true;

and he maintains that "the man who makes a good guess at truth is likely to make a good guess at probabilities."[22]

Aristotle observes further that the reasoning of rhetoric in its consideration of particular practical matters is an offshoot of ethical studies, which considers right and wrong, as well as of dialectic in its consideration of the true and false. In their pursuit of truth, rhetoric and dialectic are the only kinds of reasoning that examine the truth of a question from both sides. Aristotle explains that the dual purpose of stating both sides of a question is to clarify our own thought and to allow us to see what is unfair in the thought of others. He observes that in rhetoric

> we must be able to employ persuasion ... on opposite sides of a question, not in order that we may in practice employ it in both ways (for we must not make people believe what is wrong), but in order that we may see clearly what the facts are, and that, if another man argues unfairly, we on our part may be able to confute him (Bk 1, Chapt 1, 23).[23]

Darwin follows this same kind of reasoning in *The Origin of Species*. Because his purpose was to persuade others of his own conviction regarding evolution, it is not surprising that in the introduction we find him expressing regret that a lack of space prevents him from fully stating and balancing the facts and arguments on both sides of each question, the only way of obtaining a fair result. Stating both sides of a question allowed him to meet the many objections to the theory of evolution from other scientists who, he says, could adduce facts on most single points leading to directly opposite conclusions. His use of refutative proof to meet the many objections to the theory of biological evolution accords with Aristotle's advice. As Aristotle explains, refutative proof which works out two opposing arguments makes arguments clearer to the audience by putting them side by side (Bk. 2, Chapt. 23, 155).

In *The Origin of Species* Darwin's reasoning also conforms to other aspects of rhetoric analyzed by Aristotle: rootedness in the concrete in its linking of one case to another; the multi-sidedness of its arguments through the establishment of correlative ideas; the elaboration of key

---

22   Aristotle, *Rhetoric and Poetics*, introd. Friedrich Solmsen (New York: Random House, 1954) Bk 1, Chapt 1, 22. Further citations are from this edition.

23   Ibid.

words, such as "natural selection"; the multitude of examples which, Aristotle points out, fulfil in rhetoric the purpose served by inference in induction. While examples do not in themselves prove anything, they indicate a degree of probability and the greater the number of examples, the greater the degree of probability. Finally, Darwin's intellectual integrity in *The Origin of Species*, his respect for his subject as a great problem of fact, his attentiveness to his readers, achieve what Aristotle considered the most authoritative of the various kinds of persuasion in rhetoric: that is, the ethical character of the speaker.

Like a rhetorician with a complex forensic case, Darwin spent the years between 1838 and the publication of the *The Origin of Species* in 1859 in the arduous task of accumulating supporting evidence; that is, in the phase that in rhetoric is called *inventio*, or invention, the discovery of arguments pertinent to convincing others. He prepared corroborative evidence by collecting supporting probabilities from every quarter in order to persuade the scientific community of the theory of evolution. Although Darwin was already well-respected as a geologist, following his interest in an unusual find in Chile in 1846 he turned to biology in what became an exhaustive eight-year study of cirripedes, or barnacles. He became a breeder of pigeons to investigate whether they had all evolved from one aboriginal stock in the rock pigeon. He gathered evidence for the idea that the use and disuse of parts caused change or variation by weighing the skeletons of wild and domestic ducks, ascertaining that the wings and legs of domestic ducks were lighter. As part of his investigation of the geological distribution of plants, he conducted experiments with seeds in saltwater tanks to disprove the popular belief that saltwater destroyed seeds and to prove that current geological ideas on land bridges connecting continents were not necessary for seeds to move between them. He explored the web of interdependence in nature through species like the mistletoe whose seeds must be transported by certain birds and whose flowers with separate sexes require the agency of specific insects for pollination. He made abstracts of articles in journals, noted objections that he should answer, considered his own objections to his theory, corresponded extensively with other scientists, and collected information from around the world.

When Darwin began reducing his copious prepared material for publication in relative haste because another scientist, Alfred Russel Wallace (1823-1913), had come to the same conclusion regarding the evolution of species, he undertook the phase that rhetoricians call "dispositio"; that is, the persuasive, logical arrangement of an argument. Darwin began *The Origin of Species* with evidence of variation in the breeding of domestic animals, an idea accepted by his readers, in order to proceed by analogy to convince them of evolutionary variation in nature. In the course of his long argument, the sheer weight of his examples, his presumptive analogies, his accrued testimony to his own convictions, his logic, his awareness of disagreements make his book an example of masterful rhetoric meant, as Aristotle said, to persuade.

In addition to the persuasiveness of converging empirical evidence, the authority of the work also rests in Darwin's own voice reflecting the personal criterion of judgment characteristic of probable convergent reasoning. Darwin writes, for example, of his initial doubts: "I felt fully as much difficulty in believing that since they [pigeons] had been domesticated they had all proceeded from a common parent, as any naturalist could in coming to a similar conclusion in regard to the many species of finches, or other groups of birds, in nature" (*Origin*, 46). In a section on the divergence of character in species, through rhetorical questions we begin exploring along with Darwin. As he proceeds from the example of domestic variation to variation in nature, he asks: "But how, it may be asked, can any analogous principle apply in nature?" Or again, we are drawn into his own experiments when he tells us: "I found that a piece of turf, three feet by four in size, which had been exposed for many years to exactly the same conditions, supported twenty species of plants and these belonged to eighteen genera and to eight orders, which shows how much these plants differed from each other" (*Origin*, 112-13).

Darwin argued the theory of evolutionary change with masterful persuasion in the manner Newman described as characteristic of the genus of convergent thought. He overcame objections, neutralized adverse theories, gradually cleared up difficulties, showed how exceptions proved the rule, or found unlooked-for correlations with received truths.[24] However, because of multiple difficulties such as a previously inconceivable understanding of the age of the earth, few scientists in

---

24   In the *Grammar of Assent*, Newman's description of how we reason in all probable matters mirrors exactly Darwin's mode of reasoning both in developing the theory of biological evolution and in his argument to persuade others of its validity in *The Origin of Species*. As noted in Chapter 3, Newman observed:

his own generation habituated to a point of view very different from his own could accept his theory. Darwin recognized that he had to wait for the coming generation of scientists to have the flexibility of mind to be open to both sides of the question with impartiality. In the meantime, in subsequent editions, he tried to meet new objections and to deal with a danger inherent in all convergent thought. He tried to clarify incomplete understandings as one side or another of his argument was misrepresented through omission, error, or by underestimating or overestimating its importance in relation to the whole.

In a textual change made in the fifth edition of his work, the difference between the sensate register of the imagination in empirical science and literature's free-ranging imagination released from the actual was brought home to him. In order to convey the idea of natural selection through struggle, Darwin borrowed the striking metaphor, "the survival of the fittest" from Herbert Spencer, a philosopher that Darwin found prone to sweeping unsubstantiated generalizations. In doing so, he released his work from the strict analogy of science into the looser kind of analogy typical of poetry that Erasmus Darwin had described. Unlike the simile (Latin: *similis*-like) commonly used in science to introduce new ideas through the reasoning of explicit comparisons, the metaphor is not a mode of explicit reasoning but a concrete way of knowing open to the multiple interpretations that it can conjure.

In *The Origin of Species*, problems in interpretation arose because, unlike the real extrinsic analogies foundational to Darwin's empirical work, the analogy of metaphor is not based on real affinities but on perceived relations; that is, in the metaphor a comparison is made by the mind between entirely different things independent of one another, as when we call a sly person a fox. With all the liberty of the poetic imagination, metaphors slip up and down between the realms of the divine, human, and physical worlds; stormy weather conveys

---

It is by the strength, variety, or multiplicity of premises, which are only probable ... by objections overcome, by adverse theories neutralized, by difficulties gradually clearing up, by exceptions proving the rule, by unlooked-for correlations found with received truths, by suspense and delay in the process issuing in triumphant reactions,--by all these ways, and many others, it is that the practised and experienced mind is able to make a sure divination that a conclusion is inevitable, of which his lines of reasoning do not actually put him in possession (*Grammar*, 253-4).

emotional turbulence in the human sphere without any real connection between the two things and without the image of weather being intended, as Bacon said, to have a positive existence in itself.

At the same time as conveying the idea of the struggle for existence in natural selection, the analogy of "the survival of the fittest" also implied agency and volition, qualities associated particularly with the human and divine that had no place in Darwin's study of the laws of evolutionary sequence in the physical domain. Darwin tried to make his meaning clear through examples that confined the sense of "the survival of the fittest" to the plant and animal domain: for example, of mistletoe seedlings on the same branch. As the multivalence of metaphor intruded on the univocal world of scientific language, he pleaded in vain that his use of the phrase was metaphorical. In spite of his efforts, the loose analogy of the metaphor slipped from the physical sciences up into the social domain to become a root metaphor and a pseudo-scientific law for human behaviour. Rather than being confined to the strict sense intended by Darwin, "the survival of the fittest" in different contexts became a slogan and axiomatic justification diversely for marxists, capitalists, industrial barons, individualists.

Finally, the difference between the sensate register of the imagination in empirical science and poetry's free-ranging imagination connected to the affections was also brought home personally to Darwin as he grew older. He found that his own long habituation to empirical science and its hold on his imagination diminished in him the poetic function of the imagination in its conjunction with feeling. In a personal illustration of the effect of the use and disuse of parts, a factor in the variation of species, he found that the poetry of Wordsworth and Coleridge and Milton's *Paradise Lost* no longer gave him pleasure, that Shakespeare's historical dramas which had given him intense pleasure as a school-boy had become nauseatingly dull to him. Darwin wrote that his mind seemed to have become a machine for grinding general laws out of large collections of facts and that if he had his life to live again, to prevent the atrophy of part of his brain, he would have made a rule to read some poetry and listen to some music at least once every week. He considers that the loss of a taste for poetry, music, and art is a loss of happiness, "may possibly be injurious to the intellect, and more probably to the moral character, by enfeebling the emotional part of our nature."[25]

In the previous generation, a poet and artist who had contributed two illustrations to Erasmus Darwin's *Botanic Garden*, spent his life calling for the awakening of a part of the intellect engaged by the higher aesthetics in art and by poets like Dante and Milton whose poetry reflects the cosmic unity of the human and the divine. William Blake (1757-1825) was acutely aware that the function of the imagination which opens on to the invisible life of the spirit risked atrophy in an age of experimental science and materialist philosophy. He became the great defender of the imagination as instrumental to a way of knowing in the life of the spirit in contrast to its role in the physical sciences where it is a messenger of the sensate to the reason. Blake refers to this faculty of mind through which we know spirit simply as the imagination; what is apprehended through the imagination he also sometimes calls intelligence.

In fact, both imagination and intelligence are involved in such knowledge. If the imagination is a register of images, then the perception of spirit is effected by another faculty of mind in conjunction with the imagination. That faculty is *nous*, the now nearly-forgotten noetic faculty described by Aristotle and translated variously into English as "contemplation," "intelligence," "insight," or "intuition" (*Nicomachean Ethics*, Bk vi, 6, 8). As we saw in Chapter 3, it is through *nous* that we bridge the chasm to those principles which cannot be reached by reason alone.[26] In its role in conjunction with converging probabilities, the noetic faculty illuminated Darwin's moment of insight into the principle of biological evolution; it illuminates our own insight into the universal embedded within the complexities of a drama, a poem, or a novel.

The noetic faculty is also called into play, but in conjunction with the imagination in a simpler way, when we turn our attention towards things in themselves or towards people in their singularity. The in-

---

25   Charles Darwin, *The Autobiography of Charles Darwin* (London: Collins, 1958) 138-39.

26   Cf. Jonathan Barnes trans. and notes, *Aristotle's Posterior Analytics* (Oxford: Clarendon P., 1975) 257-58.

ward luminous particularity[27] of individuals and of things in themselves is revealed through the immediate impression that they make
on our imagination illuminated by *nous*, a faculty of such importance
that Dante finds hell peopled with those who have lost the good of
this part of the intellect.[28] In its intimate relation with the imagination, *nous* appears as one with it, like a light illuminating images from
within. To give a name to this experience of the invisible inwardness
of all things, Blake coined a word that appears to be a combination of
Aramaic and Greek. He named it "Golgonooza" or "place of vision."
(Golgotha, "the place of the skull" where Jesus was crucified; and *nous*,
or "intelligence") In our actual experience of the invisible inwardness
or intelligibility of particular things, we know the ultimate universal
within them. This ultimate universal which is like the radiance of
beauty also informs the higher aesthetics that Darwin refers to in art,
music, and poetry.

   In less than two hundred years after Francis Bacon, prophet of utility and of the empirical inductive method, Blake appeared as a new
prophet crying in the wilderness recalling people to what baconian
science had shut out: that is, the inward vitality or the ontological nature (Greek *ontos*: being) inherent in some measure in all things in the
physical and human domains. In theological tradition, this ontological reality is known by us through internal or intrinsic analogy (Latin
intrinsecus: on the inside or inwardly; Greek *ana logos*: according to
the right proportion). We know not only our own human inwardness
and the interiority of other people, but through a proportionate analogy we can apprehend the inwardness in organic and animal life and
in some degree the unutterable existence of God. Because the human
mind knows the intelligible through concrete things, just as Darwin
abstracted the principle of evolution from the physical world, so this
spiritual essence of things and the subtle world of the soul are also

---

27   Timothy George speaks of the principle of luminous particularity where
     no event, no object in nature is an isolated opaque fact closed in upon itself;
     rather each is a translucent window onto a whole pattern of human exis-
     tence. "The Pattern of Christian Truth," *First Things* 154 (2005): 25.

28   In Canto iii, 16-18, of the "Inferno,"as the two poets enter the vestibule
     that leads to Hell itself Virgil explains to Dante:"We are at the place where
     earlier I said/ you could expect to see the suffering race/ of souls who lost
     the good of intellect." *The Divine Comedy*, vol. 1 (New York: Penguin,
     1984) 90.

known through the impressions of the concrete on the imagination: either through the actual or through the concrete language of symbol and image as expressed in literature and art. Even who God is can be known analogically or in some measure through concrete images like "father," or "shepherd," or "rock." In other words, it is through analogical language and the immediacy of image illuminated by spiritual light that some knowledge of God, who is entirely other, is humanly possible. In this theological tradition, such knowledge was not considered possible through natural theology.

In the generation before Charles Darwin, Blake was a seeker of this ontological or spiritual truth but he had also read works like Bacon's *Advancement of Learning* and John Locke's *Essay on Human Understanding*. On the one hand, through such reading Blake understood the foundations of the modern physical sciences and materialist philosophy. On the other hand, his poetic imagination, the locus of invisible interior truth, was nourished through his reading of the richest offerings in poetic tradition: the love of nature and sympathy for all living things in Virgil's pastoral poetry from the first century BCE; the humanity in Chaucer's tales told by pilgrims on their way to Canterbury (late fourteenth century); Spenser's sixteenth-century allegorical poems; Shakespeare's sonnets about love and its torments; and the works of the Puritan poet, John Milton (1608-74), such as his *Paradise Lost* where the rebellious angel who comes to see evil as good asserts his independence from God and is exiled into the pandemonium of hell.

Along with his interiorizing of this rich tradition in poetry, Blake's lifelong work as an illustrator also made him acutely attentive to the invisible world met in the literary imagination. His luminous paintings, watercolours, and engravings illustrate scenes from Milton's poetry and scenes from the Bible, such as God appearing to Job out of a whirlwind. As he lay dying, Blake was working on illustrations for the books of Dante's great poem: the "Inferno," where he depicts a tormented traitor in a vast lake with bodies floating around him including that of a crowned king; "Purgatory," where Blake illustrates the proud ascending steep stairs, stumbling under the weight of their loads; and "Paradise," where Dante is shown drinking of the River of Light.

Through Dante, through Milton, through books like Bunyan's *Pilgrim's Progress*, and especially through the Bible, Blake knew the language of images from the inside, illuminated with the noetic light that

conveys the world of spirit. In his own poetry, Blake dealt passionately
and urgently with the loss of our capacity to see this world and the
result of this loss in the tragic diminishment of humanity, a loss comparable to that sustained by Milton's Satan in his banishment from
heaven. Blake's great theme was the mental battle between faculties
of the mind where the abstracting power of reason, to its own peril,
banished the imagination and the noetic faculty which are essential to
its own vitality. In an inversion of *Paradise Lost*, reason had claimed its
sovereign rights and exiled the faculty that knows spirit.

In poems like "Milton" and "Jerusalem," Blake describes what only
the imagination in conjunction with *nous* can know. In the immediate, direct experience of particular things and people, unmediated by
reason's comparisons and abstractions, the imagination and the noetic
intellect know the invisible life of the spirit common in some measure
to all that exists. Blake writes that the reason accumulates particulars, murders by analyzing, and takes the aggregate for law, as in the
method of modern science ("Jerusalem," 490);[29] by contrast, the imagination knows the interiority that resides within things in themselves
and resonates with the infinite. He says that every thing has its own
vortex where we may see a vision of eternity ("Milton," 418). Within
the centre of sweet-smelling flowers eternity "expands/ Its ever during
doors" ("Milton," 436); we see a world in a grain of sand and heaven
in a wild flower. Or again, he says that honour is due to the holy in
the particular genius or spirit within each person. Because the analogy
of being within everything in creation makes all in some degree alike,
Blake writes that in eternity all are men: "Rivers, Mountains, Cities,
Villages,/All are Human" ("Jerusalem," 486).

Throughout his poetry, Blake also describes various aspects of the
experience of mental vision through which we know spirit: its connection to the singularity of particulars; the self-effacement required
by the seer; the inward resonance of our own being with the vitality
of being in things; our impression of timelessness and of the divine in
this vitality of being. In mental vision the inward eye of the imagination stands in contrast to its other function as a messenger between
the abstract analytical reason and what Blake calls the vegetable world;
for example, the biological domain that Darwin would investigate and

---

29   William Blake, *The Portable Blake* (New York: Viking P., 1963). All citations from Blake are from this edition.

that his grandfather had rendered in poetry. Blake speaks of the exercise of the "Divine Arts of Imagination, Imagination, the real & eternal World of which this Vegetable Universe is but a faint shadow" ("Jerusalem," 455). The imagination as a register of concrete impressions perceives spiritual existence in conjunction with *nous* only through the concrete or particular in what Blake refers to as minute particulars. Unlike abstractions drawn from a comparison of things, he writes: "he who wishes to see a Vision, a perfect Whole,/ Must see it in its Minute Particulars" ("Jerusalem," 489). To enter into this inward world of spirit requires a putting off of self. At the same time, since it is in the imagination and in conjunction with our own being that we apprehend spirit, what is external or without is experienced as within. Blake writes that in entering into the bosom of what is without, "tho' it appears Without, it is Within/ In your Imagination ..." ("Jerusalem," 486). Unlike the fixity of reason's abstractions, Blake says that existence apprehended through the imagination is not a state but an act of being: "the Imagination is not a State; it is the Human Existence itself" ("Milton," 438). Finally, when *nous* illuminates the imagination, this act of being is experienced as timeless, eternal, and divine. Blake writes that the human imagination is the divine vision in which "Man liveth eternally" ("Milton," 437). Indeed, because the imagination itself is spirit, in contrast to the neo-epicurean enlightenment philosophers who claimed that the mind dies with the body, Blake asserts that the imagination is eternal.

Most importantly, the imagination in conjunction with *nous* is a way of knowing; it is not a mode of reasoning or ratiocination. Reason's abstractions from particulars only divide further and further from the particular; the imagination and the noetic faculty know particulars in the concrete in an undivided way, or *per modum unius*. Blake is intensely aware that this undivided way of knowing is counter to the whole bent of the modern world under the control of scientific reason and bereft of the imagination and *nous*. For this reason, his great unremitting task was "To open the Eternal Worlds, to open the immortal Eyes/ Of Man inwards into the Worlds of Thought, into Eternity/ Ever expanding in the Bosom of God, the Human Imagination" ("Jerusalem," 459). Here, the "Imagination with a capital I" is what the Polish poet, Czeslaw Milosz, describes as the complete, true imagination opening "like a grand promise and the human privilege of recovery."

What Blake pleads for in calling for the restoration of the imagination is in keeping with the theological idea of integrity. In this theological tradition, humanity's loss in the fall included a loss of the integrity of the intellectual and moral faculties which blended together and acted as one whole. Instead, its elements were left to strive with each other. Blake was convinced that in this rupture of the faculties the key to a restoration of "paradise lost" was through the imagination. If reason paid homage to the imagination in its connection to particulars, paradise might be regained. However, reason and the visionary imagination are contraries, antithetical in their perceptions: one sees the infinite vitality in particulars, the other contracts what the senses see and by abstracting from particulars destroys their vitality. Both contraries are part of us: within each of us, behind the reason gates open to the City of Golgonooza ("The Four Zoas," 372). If this entry to the imagination is denied, man is divided, exiled from the spiritual and eternal. Blake writes: "The Visions of Eternity, by reason of narrowed perceptions,/ Are become weak Visions of Time and Space, fix'd into furrows of death/ Till deep dissimulation is the only defence an honest man has left ..." ("Jerusalem," 475).

To depict the dislocation of the faculties, as poet and artist Blake drew on the richness of all the imagery that he had interiorized and also invented further concrete expressions for it. He portrayed an epic battle caused by reason's adamant refusal to recognize the imagination and *nous*. The character of Urizen (Reason) personifies the faculty that has built up the useful arts of material civilization and the applied sciences. The sons of Urizen fix the anvil, erect the loom, form the plough and the instruments that measure and weigh: the compass, the quadrant, the rule, and the balance. They erect the furnaces which would become the dark Satanic mills of the industrial revolution powered by the steam engines devised by Matthew Boulton and James Watt, members of Erasmus Darwin's scientific circle.

Reason's material achievements are dazzling; its sensate method is reinforced by the epistemology of materialist philosophy. However, its basis in abstractions from the sensate which exclude the noetic and the imagination has meant the diminishment of humankind. Blake shows Urizen giving a "Philosophy of Five Senses" ("The Song of Los," 366) into the hands of John Locke, the neo-epicurean philosopher, and Newton (1642-1727) whose name is associated with binomial theorem and fluxional calculus in mathematics, with the law of gravity, and the measurement of planetary orbits. However, in the absence of the imagination and *nous* the senses of men are shrunk and eternity denied both in modern science and in the "Atheistical Epicurean Philosophy" with its "Atomic Origins of Existence." ("Jerusalem," 485). If Reason, or Urizen, rent from eternity, should stand before the Man of Eternity, Urizen would be seen as slumbering in cold abstractions, a "dread form of Certainty," "a stony form of death," weeping "at the threshold of Existence" ("The Four Zoas," 400-1). Urizen is a self-righteous Prince of Light like Lucifer (light-bearer) who by petrifying the human imagination forms what Blake calls a mundane shell, a concave membrane covering over the earth and closing off Golgonooza ("Jerusalem," 461).

The realization of Bacon's seventeenth-century vision of material progress for the good of humankind seems blighted when seen in the light of the imagination and of *nous* in their perception of individual singularity. Bacon believed that humankind would be restored in part to its edenic state through the relief of material want and suffering achieved through the fruits of inductive reason and useful knowledge. However, in the imagination's register of the particular, Blake perceives the grim reality in the lives of individuals who sustain the philosophy of utility: in the child who works as a chimney-sweeper, "A little black thing among the snow ("The Chimney Sweeper," 106). In the morality of the particular where compassion and misery both have a human face, he finds that London groans in pain, that oppressors in every city and village "mock at the Labourer's limbs: they mock at his starv'd Children" ("Jerusalem," 469).

This plight of the individual is only worsened by reason's abstraction of the moral law, rent from the Gospel and from the person of Jesus who preached continual forgiveness of each person's sins. ("Jerusalem," 453). In lieu of compassion for the individual, Urizen advises his kin to control the poor by speaking of moral duty while keeping their own hearts harder than a millstone. In this way, they can compel the poor to live upon a Crust of bread. When a man looks pale with labour and abstinence, they are to say that he looks healthy and happy. In keeping with the abstract economic principle of Malthus, when his children sicken they are to let them die because there are enough or too many born and "our Earth will be overrrun" ("The Four Zoas," 393).

In other words, the morality of forgiveness and compassion described by Blake is rooted in the religious imagination which functions in the same way as the literary imagination; that is, by seeing invisible truths in and through the particular and concrete. In literature the universal (*katholou*) is embedded in concrete image and narrative; in Christianity, the moral path of forgetfulness of self and compassion for others is mediated through the concrete example and pattern of Jesus. Spiritual life and moral praxis are nourished in the divine image of God giving of himself eternally and dying for humankind. Blake writes that our existence depends on this and that "every kindness to another is a little Death/ In the Divine Image, nor can Man exist but by Brotherhood" ("Jerusalem," 493). It is through the impress of the image of Jesus' compassion on the religious imagination that God resides within our bosom and that we reside in God and stretch out our hands to others. The vitality of religion and morality, like art and literature, is not in reason's arguments and abstractions but in the imagination connected to the particular: "He who would do good to another must do it in Minute Particulars:/ General Good is the plea of the scoundrel, hypocrite & flatterer" ("Jerusalem," 477).

Until his death in 1827, Blake took up unremittingly the injunction of the Greek oracle to know ourselves, the same mandate that Hobbes and the enlightenment philosophers like Voltaire, Rousseau, and Hume had followed in their materialist revisions of the human mind and their neo-epicurean regard for self. The religious imagination which is connected to compassion and creates us anew through self-abnegation is contrasted by Blake with these Deists; he refers to their religion of self-righteousness in the "Selfish Virtues of the Natural Heart" and their destruction of the wisdom of the ages. In other words, Blake rejects their self-referential dogma centred on the avoidance of pain, the pursuit of pleasure, and the protection of one's own serenity and personal security. The practice of constant forgiveness as modelled in Christ is contrasted with Rousseau's moral philosophy that assumes humankind is not fallen but good by nature. Blake retorts: "Friendship cannot exist without Forgiveness of Sins continually" ("Jerusalem," 453) as Rousseau himself found in his own life of delusion. As for the enlightenment philosophers' claim that religion is the cause of war, Blake responds that they flatter and acquit "the Alexanders & Caesars ... who alone are its causes & its actors" ("Jerusalem," 453). In contrast to the abstract cry of fraternity in the French Revolution, fraternity is forgiveness and compassion in the concrete. Blake writes that in the divine vision religion and politics are the same thing ("Jerusalem," 478). Finally, the image of forgiveness in the Saviour is contrasted with religious division and strife. Blake writes of the pretence of religion that destroys religion, of the pretence of liberty that destroys liberty, and of the pretence of art that destroys art ("Jerusalem," 473).

Blake, spokesperson for the imagination, and Charles Darwin, dedicated scientist, both knew that what we perceive depends on the intellectual instrument that we use for perception. Blake wrote: "If Perceptive Organs vary, Objects of Perception seem to vary:/ If the Perceptive Organs close, their Objects seem to close also" ("Jerusalem," 471). Because he drew on the *organon* used in physical science, Charles Darwin's grandfather, Erasmus, saw material science as the source of myth and poetry; when he wrote poetry, it was used by him as a vehicle for science. On the other hand, Blake saw myth, religion and poetry from a perspective made possible by the noetic faculty illuminating the imagination.

In the same rich tradition of poetry represented by Virgil, Dante, and by Shakespeare, through characters like Urizen and places like Golgonooza, Blake made concrete and present an invisible inner world. Through the unique function of the poetic imagination freed from the actual, he considers the large question of what it is to be human as he ranges widely to and fro, appropriating images from the poetic tradition to his own cause and building further on them. Images from the Old Testament and the New Testament, which he describes as a great code representing all the possible states of humankind, are juxtaposed with the streets of London. He interprets in a spiritual way apocalyptic imagery, like the wine-press of life and the seven-headed Satan which were associated by millenialists and fundamentalists with literal historical moments. In Blake's hands, with no less urgency, these images refer to an inner spiritual renovation: to a new age when all the faculties of the mind might work in harmony as they had in Eden.

In other words, Blake's role as poet belongs to the tradition of the *vates* who were both poets and prophets. For Blake, poetry, painting, and music had a high seriousness. He rejected poetry that was not in this high tradition as destructive of poetry: for example, the vegetative world of the landscape poet, William Wordsworth. Although in privileged moments Wordsworth experienced the ontological inwardness of landscape, as in the cosmos of Rousseau's Emile he writes of his own experience of the actual and sensate; his poetry is an "imitation of Nature's Images drawn from Remembrance" ("Milton," 443).

Blake exorts us to "be just & true to our own Imaginations" ("Milton," 412). Without the imagination that knows being, we risk becoming what the twentieth-century poet, T.S Eliot, called "the hollow men." In Blake's words, we are non-entities and negations; we are material and sensate, a mere accumulation of memories where affections belonging properly with the imagination are alienated. We "are shut in narrow doleful form! / Creeping in reptile flesh upon the bosom of the ground!" ("Jerusalem," 475). In their self-referential sensate worlds, Rousseau and Wordsworth would banish books and culture. By contrast, Blake writes: "Nations are Destroy'd or Flourish in proportion as Their Poetry, Painting and Music are Destroy'd or Flourish!" ("Jerusalem," 446).

In accordance with this criterion of Blake, in the continuous battle of methods we may take the measure of ourselves and of our times.

CONCLUSION

When Charles Darwin applied to himself the principle of atrophy through disuse, one strand in his theory of biological evolution, he observed that through decades of habituation to empirical science he had lost his aesthetic and literary sensibility. In our own time, the various gateways of the mind that lead to perceptions of different kinds of objects have suffered an eclipse similar to the atrophy experienced by Darwin in the single span of his lifetime. In a predominantly scientific culture, the exclusion of other modes of reason has led to a dimming of what can only be perceived through these other pathways of the mind. As Blake would maintain, the fulness of our humanity is imperiled by this modern narrowness of mind.

Habituation to empirical evidence essential to a scientific knowledge of the physical world has led to a suspicion of science's other mode of reason that illuminated intellectual paths especially in the human domain until the modern age; that is, the scientific reason that begins with accepted premises, principles, and universals at the opposite pole from the sense observation of things. The genus to which literature belongs has also been sidelined. Unlike both inductive and deductive science in their orientation towards abstractions, this kind of reason is oriented towards understanding life in the concrete through a convergence of various probabilities: the concrete drama of life in its everyday contingencies, the drama of life mirrored in literature, the unfolding religious drama of Scripture, rhetoric's arguments regarding concrete matters like public policy or religious belief. And in spite of the marginalization of this kind of reasoning, in the sensate sphere of modern science pioneers like Darwin also reason through the convergence of probabilities in their quest for hypotheses.

The large genus of reasoning to which literature belongs has been noticeably discredited, but the exercise of the noetic faculty that apprehends the form or life-force in particulars has so far fallen out of view that the word itself has nearly been forgotten. By contrast, in Dante's world the noetic faculty which according to Blake had been banished by science's abstracting power was of such importance that he considered its loss to be a loss of paradise or a banishment to hell.

We may trace the modern erosion of literary rationality that operates through the magisterial role of the imagination and congruent reason through a progressive example: of Desiderius Erasmus in the sixteenth century, Erasmus Darwin at the end of the eighteenth century, and his grandson, Charles Darwin in the nineteenth century. In the sixteenth century, Desiderius Erasmus took a natural delight in the emblematic interpretation of the figure of an anchor with a dolphin wound around the middle. In contrast to the literal analyses through material cause and effect of modern science, he found common ground between unlike things and truth about human life represented in the domain of concrete things. By considering the quality of things themselves, he recognized an analogy between a dolphin leaping typically out of the water and the dauntless activity of the mind; and in the anchor he saw represented the need also for slowness and delay in reasoning. The opposites are both necessary in our reasoning and both are apprehended simultaneously in a single emblematic figure.

By the latter part of the eighteenth century, this kind of emblematic understanding of truths embedded in the concrete that is characteristic of literature was already becoming alien as reason and imagination exchanged places following the demands of empirical science. The imagination in its magisterial role and reason's service to it were being replaced by the imagination in its role as messenger of the literal sensate world to imperial reason. Because of the waning of the magisterial imagination, Erasmus Darwin found that few allegorical figures remained meaningful.

The corrosion of the literary imagination and its relation to reason by the method of modern science was by then well underway. Two generations later, Charles Darwin regretted the diminishment in himself of the literary imagination in its connection to feelings and the delight that literature had offered in his youth. However, creatures like dolphins observed in connection to the world's biological evolution had for so long exercised his mind that in his old age literature repulsed him.

As the modern era began unfolding, empirical philosophers and educational theorists took up in earnest Bacon's admonition that the mind had to be entirely restarted. As both insisted that we know only through inductive reasoning based on sense observation and personal experience, all other modes of thought were suppressed. In the seventeenth century, the passionate adoption of baconian induction by Puritan educational reformers heralded the intellectual culture of our period and our present-day systems of education. Scripture was read through the lens of baconian science with its selection of objects and its univocal use of language rather than in the literary manner where concrete words can also be understood in a spiritual sense and where no part can be omitted without disturbing the whole. Moved by their compelling vision, for the Puritan reformers education was key to realizing a shining new world, a New Jerusalem that was to arrive after historical tribulations. In their scheme of reform, the literary education of the renaissance was banished and deductive reasoning from rules was replaced with baconian induction and sense observation.

Similarly, a reductive theory of mind influenced by both the baconian method and the revival of epicurean philosophy began to emerge in empirical philosophy; for example, in the seventeenth-century epistemology of Hobbes. Hobbes' philosophy of mind eliminated both the literary imagination operating in conjunction with congruent reasoning and the portal to the world of spirit. His sensate experiential starting-point reduced conscience and morality to the domain of consensual contract. The polyvalent language of literature with its congruent multiple levels of meaning and the simultaneous concrete reasoning of metaphor were declared anathema.

Again, in the eighteenth century Rousseau's philosophy as dramatized in the education of Emile collapsed all reasoning into one method. In the name of Reason, this enlightenment materialist philosopher embraced induction from sense observation and personal experience as a universal method. He banished literature, the genus of reasoning that literature cultivates, and the imagination in its conjunction with the feelings as it functions in both literature and religion. With the exclusion of the imagination and the implicit congruent reason that apprehend the real, in a further perfidy Rousseau made self-esteem a central purpose of education rather than knowledge.

The spirit of Rousseau's fictional manifesto has exerted enormous influence in education since the 1960's. His rejection of words as babbling, his orientation to the world of physical things, his reduction of the mind to the instrument that knows the material world are a deliberate rejection of the theoretical and literary instruments of reason that were cultivated in education since antiquity. The crippling chaos in our own schools where one operation of the mind is asked to do tasks where it cannot legitimately function is a testimony to the inadequacy of his philosophy of mind and his educational theory. No measure of political goodwill nor any amount of money can remedy what only a renewed respect for literary and theoretical reasoning can effect.

If the empirical enlightenment shed light on one part of the world as illuminated by one part of the mind, it darkened all the rest. It fractured the very foundations of reason by dismissing the other powers of the mind that complete it and make it whole. While preaching tolerance and freedom from prejudice, it has visited on the modern era a root intolerance that has resulted both in intellectual bigotry and quackery in education. Like other periods before us, we recognize sciences' explanations and analyses unquestionably as the fruits of reasoning. However, because the intellect makes connections in a different, often implicit way in the large genus to which literature belongs, once again in our own era literature must justify its ways before the explicit, obvious methods of science.

Empirical philosophies that mimic the method of modern science regard with suspicion and hostility the non-scientific way of knowing the particular or concrete for which there is no science. Here, unlike in science, the imagination is not a messenger-boy to abstractions but a constant point of reference that engages our feelings and registers the very goal or object of our thought. The empirical philosophies founder when confronted with this mutuality between reason, the imagination and the feelings as they in fact function outside of science: Hobbes mistrusts the passions and rejects polyvalent language as unreasonable; Rousseau suppresses the imagination as it functions in literature, bottles up passions, and avoids human relations by teaching Emile through his sense observations of things and his own experiences.

Our story is the old story of science's resistance to an antithetical way of knowing. Unlike in science, in literature and in the large genus to which it belongs we grasp truth instead through personally perceived connections and through judgments based on their congruence. We know in the only way possible those realities that are not susceptible to scientific demonstration. Through both implicit and explicit reasoning, we grasp as complex unities both the real particulars of life and the concrete model of life mirrored in literature. It is not through explanations and analyses but through multiple, diverse converging strands of probabilities refracted through the particular that we are persuaded of truth in the concrete: in convincing parallels, in opposites held in tensile unity; in illuminating contrasts; in language that reflects the role of the imagination and the affections as they work jointly with reason; in words that signify simultaneously multiple planes of reality, where "rock" can mean both "stone" and "steadfastness."

If our humanity is not to be diminished in our own period, we must know ourselves. We must reject any tyranny of method encased in a philosophy; we must reconsider methods themselves as rightful, legitimate starting-points. In an age of science deeply dependent on a single method of inquiry, we must listen to those who like Blake and Newman have pleaded for our intellectual integrity, who have resisted our disjuncture of mind in science's monopoly of reason. Literature's vitality and science's illuminations are parts of a whole. Both are important. In our contemporary dilemma of mind, the Greek dramas continue to warn us in literature's perennial manner that single-minded stances are not only bloodless but recoil upon ourselves.

BIBLIOGRAPHY

Aeschylus. "Oedipus Rex." In *7 Famous Greek Plays*, with an introduction by Whitney J. Oates and Eugene O'Neill, Jr. New York: Vintage Books, 1950.

"Alexandrie; Analogie; Charité; Exégèse; Foi; Inspiration; Verbe." In *Dictionnaire de Théologie Catholique*.

Grammar! a Conference Report. Edited by Lid King and Peter Boaks. London: Centre for Language Teaching and Research, 1994.

The Reader's Companion to World Literature. Toronto: Mentor Books, 1962.

Aristotle. *Aristotle's Politics*. Translated by Benjamin Jowett. Oxford: Clarendon Press, 1923.

———. *Aristotle's Posterior Analytics*. Edited and translated by Jonathan Barnes. Oxford: Clarendon Press, 1975.

———. *The Ethics of Aristotle*. With an introduction by John Burnet. London: Methuen, 1904.

———. *Metaphysics*. Oxford: Clarendon, 1924.

———. *Nicomachean Ethics*. Oxonii: Clarendonian, 1818.

———. *Nicomachean Ethics*. With an introduction by Martin Ostwald. New York: Bobbs-Merrill, 1962.

———. *Poetics*. With an introduction by Malcolm Heath. London: Penguin, 1996.

———. *Rhetoric and Poetics*. With an introduction by Friedrich Solmsen. New York: Random House, 1954.

Arnold, Matthew. *Poetry and Criticism of Matthew Arnold*. Edited by Dwight Culler. Boston: Houghton Mifflin, 1961.

———. *Reports on Elementary Schools 1852-1882*. London: Eyre and Spottiswoode, 1910.

Auden, W. H. "For the Time Being." In *Modern Poetry*, edited by Maynard Mack. Englewood Cliffs, N.J.: Prentice-Hall, 1964.

Bacon, Francis. *The Advancement of Learning*. New York: Dutton, 1962.

———. *Novum Organum*. Edited by Peter Urbach and John Gibson. Chicago and La Salle: Open Court, 1984.

————. *Works of Francis Bacon.* Edited by James Spedding, Robert Leslie Ellis, and Douglas Denon Heath. London: Longmans, 1858.

Bantock, G. H. *Studies in the History of Educational Theory.* London: George Allen and Unwin, 1980.

Bently, G. E. *The Stranger from Paradise: A Biography of William Blake.* New Haven: Yale University Press, 2001.

Berlin, Isaiah. *The Sense of Reality: Studies in Ideas and Their History.* London: Pimlico, 1996.

Bigg, Charles. *The Christian Platonists of Alexandria.* Oxford: Clarendon, 1913.

Blake, William. *Blake's Dante.* With an introduction by Milton Klonsky. New York: Harmony Books, 1980.

————. *The Portable Blake.* With an introduction by Alfred Kazin. New York: Viking Press, 1963.

Brett, G.S. *The Philosophy of Gassendi.* London: Macmillan, 1908.

Bunyan, John. *The Pilgrim's Progress.* New York: Dodd, Mead, 1968.

Butler, Joseph. *The Analogy of Religion to the Constitution and Course of Nature.* With an introduction by Joseph Angus. London: Religious Tract Society, 1881.

Carroll, Joseph. *On the Origin of Species by Means of Natural Selection.* Peterborough, Ont.: Broadview Press, 2003.

Chesterton, G. K. "The Blue Cross." In *Great Tales of Action and Adventure,* edited by George Bennet. New York: Dell, 1959.

Cicero, Marcus Tullius. *De Oratore.* With an introduction by H. Rackham. London: William Heinemann, 1942.

Clement. *Clement of Alexandria.* London: William Heinemann, 1919.

Coleridge, Samuel Taylor. *Samuel Taylor Coleridge's Treatise on Method.* Edited by Alice D. Snider. London: Constable, 1934.

Corbin, Henry. *Spiritual Body and Celestial Earth.* Princeton: Princeton University Press, 1977.

Coulson, John. *Religion and Imagination 'in a Grammar of Assent'.* Oxford: Clarendon Press, 1981.

Daniélou, Jean. *Origène.* Paris: La Table Ronde, 1948.

Alighieri, Dante. *Inferno.* Vol. 1 of *The Divine Comedy.* New York: Penguin, 1984.

Darwin, Charles. *The Autobiography of Charles Darwin*. London: Collins, 1958.

———. *The Origin of Species*. With an introduction by Julian Huxley. New York: Mentor, 1958.

———. *The Origin of Species*. J. W. Burrow. Harmondsworth: Penguin, 1984.

———. *The Origin of Species*. With an introduction by Gillian Beer. Oxford: Oxford University Press, 1998.

Détienne, Marcel, and Jean-Pierre Vernant. *Cunning Intelligence in Greek Culture and Society*. Paris: Flammarion, 1974.

Darwin, Ertasmus. *The Botanic Garden*. Menston, Yorkshire: Scholar Press, 1973.

Dickens, Charles. *Hard Times*. New York: W. W. Norton, 1966.

Dunne, Joseph. *Back to the Rough Ground*. Notre Dame, Ind.: University of Notre Dame Press, 1993.

Egan, Howard T. *Gassendi's View of Knowledge*. New York: University Press of America, 1984.

Erasmus, Desiderius. *The "Adages of Erasmus"*. With an introduction by Margaret Mann Phillips. Cambridge: Cambridge University Press, 1964.

Farrington, Benjamin. *Aristotle: Founder of Scientific Philosophy*. New York: Praeger Publishers, 1969.

———. *Francis Bacon: Philosopher of Industrial Science*. London: Lawrence and Wishart, 1951.

Gadamer, Hans-Georg. *Truth and Method*. New York: Seabury, 1975.

Gale, Barry G. *Evolution Without Evidence: Charles Darwin and the Origin of Species*. Brighton: Harvester Press, 1982.

Gassendi, Pierre. *The Selected Works of Pierre Gassendi*. Edited by Craig R. Bush. New York: Johnson Reprint Corp, 1972.

George, Timothy. "The Pattern of Christian Truth." *First Things*, no. 154 (June/July 2005).

Gilson, Etienne. *The Arts of the Beautiful*. New York: Charles Scribner's Sons, 1965.

Guardini, Romano. *The Death of Socrates*. Cleveland: Meridian Books, 1962.

Halliwell, Stephen. *Aristotle's Poetics*. London: Duckworth, 1986.

Hobbes, Thomas. *Leviathan*. New York: Penguin, 1968.

Houghton, Walter E. *The Art of Newman's Apologia*. New Haven: Yale University Press, 1945.

Huxley, T. H. *The Essence of T. H. Huxley.* Bibby, Cyril <compiler>. London: Macmillan, 1967.

Jost, Walter. *Rhetorical Thought in John Henry Newman.* Columbia, S.C.: University of South Carolina Press, 1989.

Kiernan, Michael, ed. *Advancement of Learning.* Oxford: Clarendon Press, 2000.

Kirby, William. "On the History Habits and Instincts of Animals." In *The Bridgewater Treatises on the Power Wisdom and Goodness of God as Manifested in the Creation,* vol. 2. London: William Pickering, 1835.

Locke, John. *Some Thoughts Concerning Education.* Oxford: Clarendon Press, 1989.

Lucretius. *De Rerum Natura.* London: William Heinemann, 1924.

Lynch, William F. *Christ and Apollo: The Dimensions of the Literary Imagination.* New York: Sheed and Ward, 1960.

Macaulay, Lord Babbington. *Lord Macaulay's Essays.* London and Glasgow: Collins, 1889.

McLeish, Kenneth. *Aristotle's Poetics.* London: Phoenix, 1998.

McLuhan, Marshall. *The Gutenberg Galaxy.* New York: The New American Library, 1969.

———. "The Place of Thomas Nashe in the Learning of His Time." Cambridge, 1943.

Mallet, Charles Edward. *A History of the University of Oxford.* New York: Barnes and Noble, 1927.

Marrou, Henri-Irène. *Histoire de l'éducation dans l'antiquité,* 1950.

Mill, John Stuart. *Autobiography.* New York: Liberal Arts Press, 1957.

Milosz, Czeslaw. *To Begin Where I Am.* New York: Farrar, Straus, Giroux, 2001.

Milton, John. *A Tractate on Education.* Oscar Browning. Cambridge: Cambridge University Press, 1883.

Newman, John Henry. *Apologia Pro Vita Sua.* New York: Doubleday, 1989.

———. *The Catholic University Gazette.* Dublin: James Duffy, 1855.

———. *An Essay in Aid of a Grammar of Assent.* Notre Dame, Ind.: University of Notre Dame Press, 1979.

———. *Fifteen Sermons Preached Before the University of Oxford Between A.D. 1826 and 1843.* With an introduction by Mary Katherine Tillman. Notre Dame, Ind.: University of Notre Dame Press, 1997.

————. *The Idea of a University*. Edited by I. T. Ker. Oxford: Clarendon Press, 1976.

————. "Literature." In *The Idea of a University*, with an introduction by Martin J. Svaglic. Notre Dame, Ind.: University of Notre Dame Press, 1982.

————. "The Mission of St. Benedict." In *The Rise and Progress of Universities and Benedictine Essays*, edited by Mary Katherine Tillman. Notre Dame, Ind.: University of Notre Dame Press, 2001.

————. *The Philosophical Notebook*. Vol. 1. With an introduction by Edward Sillem. Louvain: Nauwelaerts, 1970.

————. "Poetry, with Reference to Aristotle's Poetics." In *Essays and Sketches*, Charles Frederick Harrold. New York: Longmans, Green and Co., 1948.

Nietzsche, Friedrich. *Twilight of the Idols/the Anti-Christ*. London: Penguin, 1990.

Nussbaum, Martha C. *The Fragility of Goodness*. New York: Cambridge University Press, 1986.

Origen. *Origen*. With an introduction by Rowan A. Greer. New York: Paulist Press, 1979.

————. *Origen: Spirit and Fire*. With an introduction by Hans Urs Von Balthasar. Washington D. C.: Catholic University Press, 1984.

Pattison, Mark. *Memoirs*. London: Macmillan, 1885.

Perkins, William. *The Works of William Perkins*. Edited by Ian Breward. Appleford, Abingdon, Eng.: Sutton Courtenay Press, 1970.

Quinn, Candice Taylor. "Robert Grosseteste and the Corpus Dionysiacum: Accessing Spiritual Realities Through the Word." In *Editing Robert Grosseteste*, edited by Evelyn A. Mackie and Joseph Goering, 79-101. Toronto: University of Toronto Press, 2003.

Quintilian, Marcus Fabius. *On the Early Education of the Citizen-Orator*. Edited by James J. Murphy. New York: Bobbs-Merrill, 1965.

Raine, Kathleen. *Golgonooza City of Imagination: Last Studies in William Blake*. Ipswich: Golgonooza Press, 1991.

Rorty, Amélie. "The Psychology of Aristotelian Tragedy." In *Essays on Aristotle's Poetics*. Oxford: Princeton University Press, 1992.

Rosen, Fredrick. *Classical Utilitarianism from Hume to Mill*. London and New York: Routledge, 2003.

Rousseau, Jean-Jacques. *Discours sur les Sciences et les Arts.* With an introduction by George R. Havens. New York: Modern Language Association of America, 1946.

———. *Emile or on Education.* With an introduction by Allan Bloom. New York: Basic Books, 1979.

Scarre, Geoffrey. *Utilitarianism.* London: Routledge, 1996.

Sidney, Philip. "The Defence of Poesy." In *Poetry of the English Renaissance 1509-1660,* edited by J. William Hebel and Hoyt H. Hudson. New York: Appleton-Century-Crofts, 1957.

Thaumaturgus, Gregory. *Remerciement à Origène.* Translated by Henri Crouzel. Paris: Editions du Cerf, 1969.

Tillman, Mary Katherine. "The Personalist Epistemology of John Henry Newman." *Existential Personalism.* Washington: American Catholic Philosophical Association. (1986)

Vernant, Jean-Pierre, and Pierre Vidal-Naguet. *Tragedy and Myth in Ancient Greece.* Sussex: Harvester Press, 1981.

Vives, Juan Luis. *Vives on Education: A Translation of the De Trandendis Disciplinis.* Edited by Foster Watson. Cambridge: Cambridge University Press, 1913.

Webster, Charles. *Samuel Hartlib and the Advancement of Learning.* Cambridge: Cambridge University Press, 1970.

Whalen, David. *Consolation of Rhetoric: John Henry Newman and the Realism of Personalist Thought.* With a preface by Dennis Quinn. San Francisco - London: Catholic Scholar's Press, 1994.

Woolf, Virginia. *The Second Common Reader.* New York: Harcourt Brace, 1986.

INDEX